*In Search of Ireland's Heroes*

# In Search of Ireland's Heroes

✳

THE STORY OF THE IRISH
FROM THE ENGLISH INVASION
TO THE PRESENT DAY

## Carmel McCaffrey

Ivan R. Dee, Publisher • Chicago • 2006

www.ivanrdee.com

Library of Congress Cataloging-in-Publication Data:
McCaffrey, Carmel.
  In search of Ireland's heroes : the story of the Irish from the English invasion to the present day / Carmel McCaffrey.
    p. cm.
  Includes index.
  ISBN-13: 978-1-56663-615-5 (cloth : alk. paper)
  ISBN-10: 1-56663-615-9 (cloth : alk. paper)
    1. Ireland—History—1172– . 2. Ireland—Civilization.   I. Title.
DA910.M33 2006
941.5—dc22

                                    2006009040

*For my parents,*

*Jimmie and Vera*

# Contents

# Acknowledgments

I WISH TO THANK the many people who helped me complete this work. Thanks to the staff at the National Library of Ireland for helping me find many archival documents, and to Pat Wallace, director of the National Museum of Ireland, for suggestions and access to some wonderful artifacts that served as visual aids for me in writing the text. Thanks to Donnchadh Ó Corráin of the National University of Ireland in Cork for many helpful discussions on Irish history. I am also indebted to Raphael Siev, curator of the Irish Jewish Museum in Dublin, for suggestions on researching Irish Jews. To Nessa and Brendan Keenan much is owed for innovative tactics in gaining me access to numerous remote Irish castle sites. Thanks also to Jamie, Alicia, and Kevin Costello for acting as guides to many of Ireland's stately homes. I am grateful to Jack Kinsella for his proofreading assistance and suggestions. Jeri and Leo Eaton gave me helpful comments on textual content. I wish also to thank my publisher, Ivan Dee, and my editor, Hilary Meyer, for her guidance in preparing the manuscript. Thanks to my brother Donal for his hospitality during my time in Ireland. A special thanks goes to my son, Andrew, for comments on the manuscript and for his constant computer help without which this work would have been far more difficult to complete; and to my daughter Ciara, for her cheerful support and for accompanying me on some of my trips to Ireland.

C. M.

*Mt. Airy, Maryland*
*December 2005*

# Preface

IT IS FREQUENTLY SAID that in Ireland the past never dies but is kept perpetually alive in folklore, song, and legend. James Joyce put it more graphically: "History is a nightmare from which I am trying to awake." Irish history can be regarded as a nightmare sometimes, but the relationship between the past and the present in Ireland is one that cannot be put aside easily. Nor should it be. It is only through appreciating the rich and varied past of Ireland that an understanding of the present can begin.

Ireland has always cherished its history and its politics. Growing up in Ireland I was steeped in history without even realizing it. I learned the names of many Irish heroes in rhymes and songs long before they jumped off the pages in history books. History was all around us. Like many Dublin children, I remember my father pointing out the bullet holes in the GPO building—they are still there today—made during the 1916 Rising. I seldom walk down Thomas Street without thinking of Lord Edward FitzGerald or pass St. Patrick's Cathedral without remembering Jonathan Swift's "savage indignation."

My aim in this book is to present the history of Ireland from the first English incursions, accurately but accessibly through scholarly and original source material, with an emphasis on the personal stories of many individuals and families who passionately believed in their commitments and their country. The book attempts to present a complex history without losing the richness of these many fascinating but often tragic individual stories.

My emphasis here is on Ireland in the period before the twentieth century, and on the long struggle of the Irish before modern times. The years since 1920 are explored briefly—it would require a separate volume to deal fully with this period, and these issues are better covered elsewhere.

W. B. Yeats called the Irish "indomitable"; I hope to show that in many ways the Irish have earned this accolade.

*In Search of Ireland's Heroes*

# Ireland

**Atlantic Ocean**

Lough Swilly

Derry

O'Donnell

O'Neill

**Ulster**

Larne
Carrickfergus

Lough Neagh

Donegal

Tullaghoge
Dungannon
*Blackwater River*

Belfast

Yellow Ford

Armagh

Newry

Killala Bay

Sligo

Dundalk

O'Connor

Drogheda

Castlebar    Strokestown

**Connacht**

Trim
*Boyne River*

Pale

Irishtown

Maynooth    Howth

Tuam

**Leinster**

Dublin

Galway

Fitzgerald

*Galway Bay*

*River Shannon*

Kildare

Avondale House
(Rathdrum)

Ennis

**Butler**

Kilkenny    Ferns

Limerick

**Munster**

Wexford

Waterford

O'Sullivan    Cork

MacCarthy

Bealnablath    Kinsale

Clonakilty

*Bantry Bay*

N

0        50 mi
0        50 km

| Butler | Traditional Lands |
| **Ulster** | Region |
| – – – | Boundary of Pale (1488) |
| ········ | Northern Ireland Border (Government of Ireland Act, 1920) |

Note: All of the items on this map were not extant at the same time.

# [ 1 ]

# *The Incomplete Conquest*

AS SIGNIFICANT an event as it would turn out to be, the English invasion of Ireland went almost unnoticed by the Irish when the first incursions occurred in the mid-twelfth century. Coming as a result of a kingship dispute within Ireland and a claim by the papacy that the Irish church was corrupt, the Irish themselves took little notice of it. *The Annals of Inisfallen* simply record the moment in 1167 as: "Dermot MacMurrough returned from overseas, and Uí Chennselaig was taken by him." What lay behind this innocuous statement recorded so faithfully by an Irish annalist?

Dermot MacMurrough was king of the province of Leinster. He had sought English help with his political problems and his ambitions for the high-kingship of Ireland. In the protracted struggle among a number of regional kings, MacMurrough was deposed in 1166 from his own kingship. Undeterred, he traveled to the English Norman King Henry II for help. The Normans had conquered England a century previously in 1066 when William the Conqueror defeated the Saxon king at the Battle of Hastings. Consolidating their power in England and expanding their territory was to be a central part of their perspective and ambitions. Henry II was only too pleased to assist Dermot, but he was occupied with a dispute with the French and was initially unable to get directly involved. Instead the English king gave Dermot permission to gather a force of Norman knights and take them to Ireland to restore Dermot to his lost kingship of Leinster. Dermot arrived in Ireland in 1167 with a small

3

band of Anglo-Norman knights and quickly took control of Ferns and his home base of Uí Chennselaig.

The high king of Ireland, Rory O'Connor, immediately took steps to prevent Dermot from reclaiming the kingship of Leinster. O'Connor confined Dermot's power to Ferns, but the Anglo-Norman presence in Ireland did not end with reestablishing Dermot in his home. In fact, Dermot was only biding his time for another, larger force to arrive. It came on May 1, 1169, when three shiploads of soldiers landed at Bannow Bay in Wexford and quickly took over the town. Within a short time the soldiers marched on Dublin, the economic center of Ireland, determined to take the town. Dubliners tried to resist them and called for support from the high king, but the Normans reached and seized the city before the Irish could mobilize. The immediate effect on the capital was disastrous. Many buildings were burned and citizens killed. The Anglo-Normans soon established themselves as conquerors, and Dublin was theirs. Dermot was restored to his Leinster kingship but with a significant difference. He now owed allegiance to Henry II of England.

## HENRY II'S HIDDEN AGENDA

There was in fact a darker truth to Henry's willing response to the kingship dispute in Ireland. Dermot's problem and appeal for support gave Henry the opportunity he had long wanted: to invade Ireland and make it a part of his kingdom. It must have seemed to Henry that the stars were aligned in the heavens. Some ten years earlier the English pope Adrian IV had issued a decree known as *Laudabiliter*, permitting Henry to invade Ireland and align Irish Christianity with the emerging centralized papacy. The Irish church was an irregular organization without a European-style diocesan structure. Although known for centuries for its art, scholarship, and missionary zeal, it had nevertheless been an independent church with little adherence to outside influences. This was the golden age of Irish Christianity. Large wealthy monasteries with powerful abbots whose sons inherited their fathers' positions had formed the backbone of the Irish church. This era was about to end.

Changes were coming to Christianity in Europe as Gregorian reforms were now shaping the future of the church. Conducted over a number of decades, these reforms brought about a more

This drawing of
King Dermot
MacMurrough, in
traditional cloth
garments, is from a
margin in a twelfth-
century manuscript
by Giraldus
Cambrensis.
(*National Library of
Ireland*)

powerful papacy as the idea of a strong centralized church with
Rome at its center was gaining momentum. Independent churches
were being reined in under the influence of successive popes determined to make Rome the axis of ecclesiastic and secular power.
The Irish would now have to adhere to this transformation. Papal
support of any invasion was an important factor in medieval times
as the papacy had declared itself the legitimate arbiter of secular affairs. Although Adrian IV had died by the time of the first English

incursions into Ireland, his successor Pope Alexander III was just as anxious for the Irish to be brought under Rome's control.

Events were not as innocuous as they initially appeared either to the Irish scribes recording the events, or probably even to Dermot. Dermot MacMurrough's name would be forever linked to the English invasion and ensuing events. The English incursion ultimately resulted in the establishment of an English colony and the English monarchy's claim to lordship over Ireland. The English invasion and conquest of Ireland with its long, consequential history had begun.

## THE FEUDAL WORLD

Although only a narrow sea divided Ireland from England, the two societies may as well have been in parallel universes. Ireland's social and political structure differed greatly from the rest of Europe. Ireland had never been a part of the Roman Empire and had therefore remained outside of mainstream European political and social development. Throughout Western Europe the political and social system that evolved in medieval times was known as feudalism. Feudal society could be described in terms of a pyramid, with the lowest people at its base and the lines of authority flowing up to the peak of the structure, where the king reigned. The king had authority over everyone. All land was essentially owned by the king and given out to his lords in what was known as a grace and favor grant. Simply put, as long as the lord remained in the good grace of the king, the king granted the favor of the land. The lords oversaw the serfs, or peasants, who lived on the land as tenants, worked the soil, and paid rent to the lords. The lords' income derived from the peasants' labor. The lords paid taxes to the monarchy in exchange for the privilege of the land grant. European monarchs ruled with absolute authority. The papacy supported the monarchs by proclaiming that they were God's own anointed. This tight system left little room for dissent.

Significantly the feudal system had never been a part of the Irish experience. Family units, known as *Túatha*, were the dominant feature of Irish society. Irish kings and chieftains did not have the kind of power exercised by monarchs in the rest of Europe. There was no grace and favor system in Ireland. The land was owned and held by the common people, and the king or chieftain had little authority to impose his will. Neither was there a system of male primogeniture—the eldest son did not automatically inherit—in Ireland. Succession was based on a decision made in a discussion group, or *dáil*, after the death of a leader. Even the Irish law system, known as Brehon Law, was of different origin from other Western European medieval law, which had its roots in Roman law.

The Irish kings did not make the law, nor were they above the law. They were as subject to it as anyone else. The kings also did not have political control. There was no central political power in Ireland. The high king of Ireland, in spite of the title, did not have political jurisdiction over the entire country. Regional kings and chieftains were under no obligation to pay any respect to the high king. Those realities made for significant cultural disparity between England and Ireland. Ireland truly was a foreign country to the invaders, who represented a political system and way of life that the Irish could not easily absorb, nor did they wish to. From the beginning, the English incursion into Ireland was to have a troubled history.

## ENGLISH EXPANSION IN IRELAND

After they had assisted Dermot in regaining the kingship of Leinster, the Anglo-Norman knights proceeded to disperse throughout the country in search of new territory to conquer. Within a very short time, and with apparent ease, lands were seized and many Irish kings were ousted from their traditional homes. Native Irish soldiers were unable to defend against the invaders, primarily because they were ill prepared for the way Normans fought in battle. Until this time Irish battles did not compare in ferocity to the type of warfare conducted in Europe, so the Irish lacked vital experience. They had never engaged in the same large-scale, systematic combat that the Europeans engaged in and rarely went to war for territorial conquest. In battle the Irish wore no armor, had no knowledge of archery, and fought with knives. Irish warfare was little better than organized plundering and pillaging. The Anglo-Normans had a very different combat history. They had seized England and the English throne in the previous century. They had better war technology, were skilled archers, fought in divisions, and wore armor. These facts combined to give them victory over the Irish who had no experience in this new type of organized medieval warfare.

It did not take long for the invaders to penetrate Irish society successfully, seize large territories, and take control of major ports. The Irish must have felt that a great whirlwind had taken over the island. So successful were the invaders that Henry II grew concerned about the direction events might take. He decided to travel to Ireland to claim the submission not only of the Irish but also, perhaps more important, his own knights. The invaders conquered so easily that Henry feared they might establish a separate Norman kingdom in Ireland which could rival England. In October 1171 Henry II traveled to Ireland and appointed one of the Norman knights, Hugh De Lacy, as his representative there. Henry gave him the title of justiciar, who from this time represented the English king in Ireland. The justiciar, or lord deputy as the position later came to be called, would eventually control the military, civil, and judicial structures. He was also assisted by a council of officials. Thus began the early development of an Irish civil service under the Crown's control. Taxation was to be a large and important part of the initial administration. Money in the form of taxes from Ireland would remain an essential part of the country's relationship to the Crown.

## HENRY II AND A BROKEN TREATY

Although he managed to assert his own claim on Ireland, Henry realized that the struggle for Ireland would need to be more formalized and the Irish high king appeased. With that aim in 1175 Henry drew up the Treaty of Windsor. This treaty between the English king and the high king of Ireland, Rory O'Connor, states that O'Connor was to hold on to the lands not then taken over by the Norman English. A formal division was to be established between the Irish and English spheres of control. Henry II was to have jurisdiction over those areas held by his knights. O'Connor also agreed to yield to Henry's authority, though it is unclear whether O'Connor understood this in feudal terms. Each side's records provide a different understanding of this agreement. The Irish recorded that Henry had given to Rory O'Connor "the kingship of Ireland, both Foreigner and Gael." The Norman record states O'Connor "shall be king under [Henry II] ready to his service, as his man."

This truce was of brief duration because within a short time Henry had broken the terms of the treaty and granted new lands to his barons. This of course had the effect of shrinking the Irish-owned holdings. It was an early harsh lesson for the Irish, who learned that the "foreigners" were not to be trusted, and the signing of treaties frequently meant little more than buying some time before the next incursion. It was equally true, as the English were to find out, that the Irish may appear to submit but obtaining a lasting submission was an entirely different matter. As was traditional in Ireland, it was the poets who expressed public opinion. One of them wrote bitterly of the English (here in translation):

> Numerous will be their powerful wiles
> Their fetters and their manacles.
> Numerous their lies, and executions
> And their secure strong houses . . .

## DUBLIN—THE CAPITAL OF IRELAND

It was immediately apparent to the English invaders that Dublin was an important center of trade and commerce. They soon took control of the city. When he visited Dublin in 1171 Henry II had granted a civic charter to Dublin declaring it a royal city. Dublin was originally founded in 841 by Vikings, and became Ireland's economic center and major port. The inhabitants of Dublin were a mixture of Irish and Viking descent. The descendants of the Viking settlers still retained a distinctive ethnic ethos, and in recognition of this Henry proclaimed that they were under special royal protection as "the King's Ottsmen." Their lands were confiscated first. Henry put garrisons into Dublin to secure his claim, and did the same in Wexford and Waterford. The coastal cities of Ireland were founded by the Vikings, but the inland towns were developed as a result of the Anglo-Norman influence. Athlone, Kilkenny, Ardee, New Ross, and others were established as market towns and owe their foundation to the Normans. The English gave these new towns charters, making them independent of the Irish chieftains. The English also gave charters to the coastal towns, which thrived economically on the increased trading with overseas ports.

## IRELAND—LORDSHIP OF ENGLAND

In 1177 Henry gave his son Prince John the title Lord of Ireland and made Anglo-Norman settlers Irish lords of the king. But titles alone would not conquer the island. The struggle for control of Ireland was not easy. Because there had been no prior central administration or government over which they could seize power and thus control the entire island, the English found their power in Ireland to be less pervasive than expected. They soon discovered their claim to power continually challenged by the Irish. A people who had never known centralized administration or a king who was an overlord of the entire country found it impossible to accept a foreign overlord with such claims. To secure his lordship and display his strength, in 1185 Prince John visited Ireland. The Norman scribe Giraldus Cambrensis traveled with him.

John returned to England within six months, but Giraldus remained in Ireland for a year, traveling around the country and eventually compiling his experiences into a history and topography of Ireland. He also wrote the *Conquest of Ireland*. Most of his report served as a justification for the English invasion and continued Engish presence in the country. Yet some of his commentary is informative regarding the topography of Ireland, and his attitude to Irish life is revealing. He generally describes a well-nourished people who are "by nature's gift handsome." Giraldus expresses shock at the independent nature of the Irish and a people whose "greatest wealth is to enjoy liberty." A clash of cultures and values is also evident. He finds the Irish barbarous in habits but acknowledges their "internal cultivation of the mind."

By this time the Irish had begun to realize the gravity of the English invasion: the violence and land seizures had left their mark on Irish attitudes. They recognized that their way of life and economic survival were seriously threatened. The lack of traditional political unity meant that instead of a large-scale effort, resistance was localized. Some of Giraldus's report reflects the turbulence and difficulty the English faced within a short time of their arrival:

> Meanwhile this was the state of affairs in Ireland: everywhere there was gloom and cries of despair; all roads became impassible; no one was safe from the axes of the Irish; everyday

brought fresh reports of fresh disasters befalling our people. All this was happening outside the cities and only within their walls was there some semblance of peace.

In spite of the difficulties they encountered the Norman English did not simply give up and leave. They remained in Ireland, continuing their struggle to establish a colony. The huge attraction for the English invaders was the lucrative advantage of owning rich agricultural land. The king distributed generous grants to the settlers who used them to cultivate the land they had seized from the Irish. These economic rewards far outweighed the disadvantages of dealing with a disgruntled displaced population.

Henry II died in 1189 and was succeeded by his son Richard (the Lionhearted). In 1199 his second son John came to the throne of England. John was crowned King of England and Lord of Ireland. The pope had declined to grant the title King of Ireland. All English kings would take the title Lord of Ireland until the Tudor king Henry VIII.

## "AND THEIR SECURE STRONG HOUSES"

Many physical changes came to Ireland with the Anglo-Normans, and their remarkable building skills were among their most significant contributions to Irish life. Large stone castles burgeoned throughout the country both as a mark of the newcomers' presence and as an important symbol of their permanence in Irish society. Besides serving as comfortable homes these castles and fortifications were built as part of their occupation strategy. The English Norman knights who settled in Ireland followed a deliberate pattern, established in their earlier conquest of Wales. It seemed that everything they did was designed well. The stone castles and ramparts were placed within a planned network so that the settled invaders could assist one another in times of Irish resistance.

The most powerfully symbolic castle built by the Anglo-Normans was Dublin Castle, which is in use today by the Irish government as the center of the Irish civil service. Sited in the heart of the hustle and bustle of modern-day Dublin City, it remains a symbolic legacy of the English presence in Ireland. It was begun in 1204 when King John issued a decree that a castle should be built in

Originally built in the early thirteenth century, Dublin Castle was the center of English administration in Ireland until the early twentieth century. It was a constant target of attack by Irish rebels. (*Carmel McCaffrey*)

Dublin. Its stated purpose was to act as a fortress, with specific instructions from the king that it be built with strong walls and ditches. By then the city of Dublin had become the undisputed capital, the economic axis of Ireland, and the center of English administration. Dublin would always be the administrative and economic hub of the country. The new castle built in the center of the city was no ordinary castle. A great deal of care was taken in its initial planning and design. Much of the original blueprint was based on new technological designs imported from France and Germany. Dublin Castle initially served as a secure treasury but became for seven hundred years the center of English administration and a contentious symbol of English power in Ireland. Over the centuries, as it was expanded, it became an expressive representation of many periods in Irish architecture.

## TRIM CASTLE—SYMBOL OF A STRONG PRESENCE

Although Dublin Castle was the center of power, the largest and most magnificent castle ever built in Ireland was Trim Castle in County Meath. It is situated about thirty miles from Dublin's center. The original site was chosen because the area of Trim—the word comes from the Irish *Truimm*, meaning "elder tree"—was on an important road network leading west and north from Dublin and was situated next to the major river, the Boyne. Trim Castle's still-imposing ruins attract many tourists. Its fame was enhanced when it was used as a set for the movie *Braveheart*.

The native Irish had originally established Trim as a small monastic site. The castle was first begun in 1173 by Hugh De Lacy who had taken over an enormous amount of land in the area. At first he only built a wooden structure. After High King Rory O'Connor destroyed the castle later in the 1170s, Hugh De Lacy planned and built a stone castle. Even today, as it stands in ruin near the town of Trim, its former glory is obvious. Although much of the original structure is lost, it has recently undergone extensive conservation work, and much of the keep is still intact. In its day Trim Castle was a formidable citadel, built to intimidate and subdue the native Irish. The principal outer wall of the castle is five hundred meters (about sixteen hundred feet) long and remains mostly intact. The wall dates from around 1250 and includes eight towers and the gatehouse. The imposing remains of the wall and keep are reminders of how magnificent a structure it once was. Recent excavations suggest that the castle may have been originally painted with a whitewash, giving it a bright, dazzling appearance. The symbolic construction of this massive stone castle heralding a new era in Irish history coincided with the death of King Rory O'Connor. O'Connor died in 1198 and is buried in the ancient monastery grounds at Clonmacnoise. He was the last high king of Ireland.

When King John visited Ireland in 1210 he visited Trim Castle, which had already taken on its distinctly fortresslike appearance. On seeing this impressive bastion the English king must have believed that his knights were in a good position to maintain power. The castle also undoubtedly served as a strong message to the native Irish that the Normans were here to stay and that the lands the Normans seized were forfeited. But as with so much else that the English invaders tried, the castle was in this only partly successful. Trim would eventually mark the outer boundary of the English settlement around Dublin.

## TRANSFORMING THE IRISH CHURCH

In addition to the invasion's secular changes, Irish Christianity also experienced major alterations. Although the Irish church had been undergoing redevelopment from early in the twelfth century, the Anglo-Norman invasion accelerated real change. The process of transforming the Irish church, both structurally and functionally, was a part of the English design in Ireland. The main concern within European Christianity at the time was the new centralized papacy, with power concentrated in Rome. Now with the English invasion the Irish church would have to surrender its autonomy and become a part of this new, strictly hierarchical Christianity. The independent and informal nature of the Irish church made the task of reform a potentially formidable one. A propaganda campaign was conducted in Europe against the Irish church, which was depicted as barbarous and pagan in its practices. Much of the propaganda was not true, but the stories of barbarism became so widespread that Ireland began to be referred to as *insula barbarorum*—the island of barbarians. The clerics were charged with corruption and with being lax in their Christian teaching. The morals of ordinary people also were criticized by outside reformers who accused the Irish of numerous vices, including immorality regarding marriage and not taking the sacraments seriously. The new, more organized form of Christianity brought with it new devotional practices.

Reform within Ireland had actually started before the invasion as continental influences brought change. The Synod of Kells in 1152 had restructured the Irish church when thirty-six dioceses were established throughout Ireland. Armagh, Cashel, Tuam, and Dublin were established as archbishoprics. Previously the Irish church, unlike the rest of Europe, had no dioceses. Christianity had been an urban religion from its early days, but Ireland was not an urban society. By tradition the Irish lived rurally in large family units known as *Túatha*. Irish Christianity developed differently from its European counterpart, reflecting the native community-style living found in Ireland. Based on this indigenous model the structure of the early Irish church developed a monastic form. But instead of isolated ascetic communities, these early Irish monasteries were large and important centers of community and economic life. Family-owned monasteries had dominated Irish Christianity, with the abbots frequently passing on the monastery to one of their sons. This hereditary succession was commonplace in Ireland prior to the twelfth century. The process of transforming the Irish church away from this community model to a diocesan one was slow and difficult.

One of the reasons put forward for the invasion was the pope's command to Henry II to reform the Irish church and align it with the rest of Europe. It was not only the papacy that wanted to bring the Irish church under its control but so also did the archbishop of Canterbury in England. For despite Armagh's claim to primacy and its acceptance throughout Ireland, there is no evidence that this meant much. Individual churches and monasteries enjoyed much independence without any reference to a primary church. Because of this lack of centralized structure, the English church had ambitions of bringing the Irish church under its jurisdiction. Both forces, papal and English, working in unison brought about the joint transformations of church reform and political change in Ireland.

## THE IRISH CHURCH BROUGHT UNDER ROME

It was the Synod of Cashel in 1172 that completed the reform work already begun before the invasion. The council was convened so that Henry could fulfill his promise to bring the Irish under papal authority, as directed in the pope's invasion bull, *Laudabiliter*. The king was represented at this council, and English clerics attended. In Rome, Pope Alexander III was especially anxious that the Irish change their ways and gain respect for church property and clerics. He wrote to Henry telling him of his particular concerns and expressing his desire that the Irish adjust their ways. The Irish, the pope charged, were lax in their marriage practices and were reportedly eating meat during the season of Lent. According to Giraldus's account of the council proceedings, reforms were passed without resistance from the Irish who were present. A significant reform involved the issue of collecting tithes for the church. Under the old Irish system the wealth had stayed within the monastic families. Local chieftains and kings were forbidden from extracting hospitality and food tributes from churches, as had previously been the custom. Significantly, earlier reforms carried out by the Irish church now had the force of the king and the government behind them. Both in the political and in the clerical sense, the papacy put Ireland under the control of the English king.

## THE END OF THE NATIVE IRISH MONASTIC SYSTEM

Changes within the Irish church persisted for some time. The reforming synods of the twelfth century essentially spelled the end of the old Irish monastic system. During the twelfth and thirteenth centuries all the major European orders—Cistercians, Benedictines, Augustinians, and later Dominicans and Franciscans—established houses in Ireland. But these monasteries did not hold the power the native Irish monasteries had once enjoyed. The Irish church developed a European diocesan structure with bishops in control of large regions. The demise of family-owned monasteries was greatly regretted as they had once been known throughout Europe as centers of great learning, producing scholars who brought light to Europe in the Dark Ages.

At the heart of the matter lay the issue of economics. Monastic families had retained ownership and wealth of the monasteries for generations through the tradition of hereditary succession. The financial resources of the monasteries were based on land ownership and the patronage of smaller churches. That entire church structure would change with the introduction of dioceses. Hereditary succession in monasteries was abolished. Formerly powerful abbots and abbesses saw their status reduced. Now bishops would be in control and church officials would be appointed. Many of the newly established church officials were not even native Irish. John de Courcy, who conquered a large part of eastern Ulster, was the first to appoint a foreigner to an Irish see, in the diocese of Down. He was also the founder of many imported monastic establishments. De Courcy would earn the derision of the Irish as "the destroyer of the churches of Ireland." The annals frequently mentioned that the unique form of Irish Christianity was being destroyed. Among liturgical changes was the maxim that the sacraments were to be central to worship. The ritual of baptism, which had been long neglected, was to be universally established.

Physical changes had to be made in churches to accommodate the new emphasis on rituals. A church council held in Dublin in 1186 declared:

> Since among all the sacraments of the Christian religion, baptism is to be first in effect and in time, and to be given to all without differentiation as to age, sex or condition, it is decreed that in all baptismal churches a fixed baptistery, made of wood or stone, is to be erected in the middle of the church or in some suitable place.

The church also benefited from the building skills of the English Normans. Large cathedrals and abbeys were established at this time. In Dublin, St. Patrick's Cathedral was built in 1191, and Christ Church Cathedral, which had been a church since 1080, became a massive cathedral in 1172. Both of these cathedrals are still in use, as are many of the cathedrals built in the twelfth century. Cathedral building extended throughout the country as the diocesan model was established.

Taken as a whole, the changes had a marked effect on the Irish church as centuries-old traditions died out. Donnchadh Ó Corráin describes it this way: "The reform was a triumph for the administrators and a disaster for Irish literature and general culture. The reformers destroyed the social, economic, and cultural base of Irish learning. Nothing replaced the greater monasteries with their schools and learned cadres, which were now robbed of their resources and their status." A common refrain states plainly that "The Celtic church gave love, the Roman church gave law."

## THE DIFFICULTY OF CONQUERING IRELAND

Yet in spite of the appearance of a strong presence, no single Norman family gained control over the whole country to create a more monolithic European-like state. This is the nub of the problem that the English faced in Ireland and would face for generations. Ireland, though seemingly open to easy conquest, was in many ways unconquerable. Ultimately the twelfth-century invasion was incomplete. A major reason for this was the indigenous nature of Irish society. By tradition Ireland lacked political unity: Irish kingship did not resemble the monarchies of Europe. The *Túatha* were autonomous units. Although culturally cohesive, they were not politically related. This made centralizing government very difficult for the English. Lack of political unity in Gaelic society now is seen by many Irish historians as a crucial factor in its continued existence. Ireland, which appeared vulnerable to invasion, proved for centuries to be virtually unconquerable. Succeeding English monarchs were to discover that control of one area did not guarantee control of a neighboring region.

As when Christianity first arrived in Ireland, the Irish did not abandon their traditional ways and adopt the foreign feudal ways. Rather, the foreigners took on native Irish customs. The original Norman colonists found themselves an isolated and scattered minority surrounded by *Túatha* and Gaelic chieftains. Almost immediately the pull of the native Irish culture was too strong for the Anglo-Normans. Few women had traveled with them, and many of the first-generation newcomers married Irish women. This circumstance proved to be a solid basis for future ethnic identity. After King John's death in 1216, English interest in Ireland declined and the Norman settlers in Ireland were left to themselves. Those English who held Irish land as absentees living in England rarely visited their Irish holdings. Almost within a generation the Norman settlers assimilated to the ways of the Irish, becoming "more Irish than the Irish themselves." Intermarriage with Irish families meant the English quickly became absorbed into the indigenous culture. The Norman settlers adopted Irish customs, the Brehon Laws, and most especially the Irish language. So complete was the integration that Norman names such as FitzGerald, Burke, Walsh, Butler, Joyce, Moore, and others became quintessential Irish names.

## A MATTER OF LAW

During his visit to Ireland in 1210 King John introduced English law into Ireland. Whether he intended English law to extend to the native Irish as well as his English settlers is not clear, but by the time of his grandson, Edward I, in the latter part of the century, the native Irish had no rights in English law. The Irish could gain access to the courts only by the purchase of charters from the monarch in England. This was beyond the economic means of most. The new settlers initially formed an elite class holding their lands by royal charter and living under the protection of the transported English legal system. Their settlement in Ireland was defined and fortified by the backing of institutional privilege and exclusiveness.

Distrust of English methods ran deep among the native Irish who continued to be committed to the ancient Brehon Law system. The survival of the ancient laws of Ireland throughout this period was in part an expression of resistance to the English presence and a clear indication of attachment to the indigenous culture. These laws remained customary with the Irish in their relationship with one another and in their daily life. The Irish Brehon Law system dated to ancient times, before the arrival of Christianity in Ireland in the fifth century. The laws were originally part of an oral tradition, passed on from generation to generation through an elaborate system of law schools. They were first written down around the eighth century A.D., and the many surviving texts depict a complex system of justice. The laws were instigated and administered by a caste of lawyers known as Brehons, from an old Celtic word meaning a judge or judgment. The Brehons made and administered the laws.

The Brehon Laws were so integral to Irish society that it is probably accurate to say that they represented the nucleus of Irish culture. As a study they tell us much about the indigenous culture. Irish law was community based, reflecting a tribal society where the crime of the individual was the responsibility of the group or extended family. Victims were typically compensated with goods.

There were no jails in ancient Ireland, and it was the Brehon's responsibility to determine the amount of compensation for each crime. Irish laws were not male centered. Under Irish law women had more rights than they would under English law—for example, a married woman retained legal ownership of goods she brought into the marriage. A major difference between these laws and English law lay in the making and administering of the law. Traditionally the Irish kings played no role in this. The Irish judges, or Brehons, made, administered, and interpreted the law. Some Brehons were attached to the various Irish courts, some were roving judges who traveled the country serving the disputes of ordinary people when the need arose. Many Brehons held their titles from hereditary succession. The law was a much respected profession, and from ancient times certain families were experts in the Irish law system. Two of the most prominent families in Irish law were the MacEagans and the MacClancys.

## EVERYDAY LIFE IN MEDIEVAL IRELAND

From the information we have of the period we can get some idea of everyday life for ordinary people. At the heart of work for most people lay farming. New farming methods brought an agricultural revolution to Ireland, especially in the southern and eastern parts of the country where the manorial system was being established. This was an uneven development and applied to the areas held by the new arrivals. In this system, part of the land was held by the lord and part was divided into fields held by tenants. Large fields were divided into strips so that each tenant would have a share in both good and bad land. These tenants paid rent to the lord or landowner. New European methods of crop rotation and fertilization were introduced. A large amount of land was given over to tillage crops such as wheat, oats, barley, and rye. Cattle and sheep were also raised; from ancient times cattle had formed the backbone of the Irish economy. Apples were a popular fruit for baking and eating fresh, and apple orchards were commonplace throughout the country. Domestic beehives were kept for the production of honey, a custom dating to antiquity. Barley was grown and used in brewing beer. For those in the middle to high range of the social scale, bread was a staple food, and bakeries were common in towns. Porridge, made from oatmeal, was the essential food of those who were not as well off.

During the initial years after the Anglo-Norman invasion, trade between Ireland and England increased and a merchant class developed in the towns. The towns rapidly expanded with trading centers and homes. The inland towns were built with protective walls around them. Stone walls with large entrance gates were built around some of the former Viking towns, including Dublin and Limerick. With so much building, the appearance of the countryside changed radically during this time with castles, manor homes, mills, and new churches dominating the landscape. While it is difficult to assess prosperity, based on the evidence of agricultural production and the relatively low population Ireland was prosperous during the early medieval period, aside from periods of crop failure and disease.

The Brehon Law system governed much of everyday life. This was most noticeable regarding marriage practices. In spite of the various reforms of the Irish church, Ireland still remained outside mainstream European Christian life. In Ireland throughout the medieval period a secular-style marriage, based on Brehon Law, was the norm. These marriages permitted divorce, and it was not unusual for men and women, especially those of the better off classes, to have a series of spouses. Children from these various marriages were all considered eligible for inheritance.

## THE NATIVE IRISH FIGHT BACK

Although the small colony expanded and thrived economically for the first century after the invasion, all was not peaceful. The good fortune that the invaders enjoyed during their early conquest did not last forever. There were many reasons for this change in fortune. One was the question of land ownership, which to the native Irish was an unresolved issue. The Irish kings had lost their traditional status with the arrival of the Anglo-Normans, but future generations did not automatically accept this. The sons and grandsons of those who had been displaced sought to retrieve some of what had been lost. Many struggled to rid the country of the invaders, or at least to minimize their presence. *The Annals of Connacht* record in 1247 that "the Galls [foreigners] of Connacht had not experienced in many a long year the like of the war that the sons of [Irish] Kings waged against them in this year." In a similar vein the *Annals of Ulster* proclaim in 1247 that "Great war was made by Toirrdelbach (son of Aedh Ua Conchubhair) and by the sons of the Kings [of Connacht] against the Foreigners this year and many towns were burned and many Foreigners slain by them." By the following year the English king's representative in Ireland had to lead an army into Leinster "to attack the [Irish] Kings' sons who were spoiling and ruining the Foreigners."

As the Irish became familiar with the habits and mores of the newcomers, they also learned how to challenge them. From the mid-thirteenth century fortune began to change for the English in Ireland. Irish resistance took effect, and further expansion into new territory became impossible for the invaders. The new generation of Gaelic chieftains was adroit at learning the skill of European warfare. They quickly revived in the face of neglect and low numbers on the Norman side. In some areas the Irish actually forced the English settlement to contract. Some of the land the Normans initially won began to return to Gaelic hands, most especially in areas where the native Irish were a significant force. In Kerry, for example, the MacCarthys and the O'Sullivans forced the Norman FitzThomas family off the land they had seized and confined them to the northern part of the country. Some years later in 1270, the annals record that Aedh O'Connor and an Irish army were victorious against an army led by the king's justiciar, d'Ufford, and Walter de Burgo. Much of Connacht was held once again by the Irish royal family, the O'Connors. Within a generation the O'Neills and O'Donnells of Ulster once more took control of their traditional lands as Anglo-Norman influence waned in the north and the west. This was strategically significant for Ireland's future. The O'Neills would remain a potent and powerful force in Irish society to Elizabethan times.

## IRISH PARLIAMENT ESTABLISHED

The Normans developed a parliamentary system initially to address the issue of taxation. The earliest-known assembly of this legislature occurred in June 1264. The administration did not meet on a regular basis but gathered together as the need arose to address particular concerns. Although taxation was the main point of discussion during the early years, within a short time it became obvious that parliament had to expand its powers and concerns. By the latter part of the thirteenth century the country was perceived by the English to be in an increasing state of lawlessness. With so many successful counterattacks of Norman settlements, the English authorities believed that order had to be established throughout the country. With the expressed desire of asserting social order, a parliament was summoned in 1297 in Dublin. It was a fairly elaborate affair, obviously intended to yield serious results. The justiciar represented the king of England; earls, barons, archbishops, and bishops were all in attendance.

The parliament's surviving proceedings offer a clear picture of the perceived issues of the day. Those attending the assembly were there to determine why law and order had broken down so badly and to find a way to fix the problems. The opening statement of this parliament noted that its purpose in assembling the "chief persons of this land" was "in order to establish peace more firmly." Not surprisingly, the native Irish were considered a major problem. They were described as attacking the borders of the lands held by the Normans to "perpetrate robberies, homicides, and other mischiefs upon the English and return through them without arrest, hue and cry, or hindrance." One of the causes of these constant disturbances, according to parliament, was the settlers' inability fully to guard the land they had seized. As a result, unprotected land was falling back into the hands of the native Irish, who were becoming vigilant in resecuring any undefended territory.

The Norman settlers also came under rebuke from this parliament but only to the extent that they had neglected to maintain their own customs. Many of them were contemptuously described in the parliamentary record as becoming "degenerate in recent times, dress themselves in Irish garments and having their heads half shaven, grow the hair from the back of the head . . . [thereby] conforming themselves to the Irish as well in garb as in countenance." As unimportant an issue as this might seem, behind this statement lay what became a serious impediment to total English control. The twin problems of Irish incursions into Norman territory and Norman assimilation were ongoing difficulties for the English authorities. Although the parliament was astute in outlining the problems and a legal system was firmly established, this did little to alleviate the many problems that the colony faced. Ireland was by no means completely under English control. The native Irish continued to dominate in many areas and continued to attack areas held by the Norman settlers.

## BEYOND THE PALE

With the persistence of the Irish in reclaiming native land and the assimilation of so many Norman families, English authority waned in many parts of the country. Eventually the English influence and authority centered only on the area surrounding Dublin, which became known as the Pale, from an old English word for boundary. The city of Dublin and its immediate area comprised this garrison; the great castle at Trim marked the outer limit of this boundary. Beyond the Pale, as the expression goes, lay the "wild Irish," still living as they had since ancient times, following Gaelic customs and laws, and, most important, speaking the Irish language.

The reason for this accepted contraction was complex. The English found themselves in a difficult situation. For one, it was expensive to attempt to gain and hold control over the entire country. England had little money to spend in Ireland because of its almost constant war with France over French territory. Thanks to Norman assimilation outside of the Pale area, it became virtually impossible to extend English culture and English rule. Maintaining authority in the Pale became the compromise solution that gave the English control over the main port and capital as well as a claim to administrative control of the island.

## A GAELIC REVIVAL

As English influence waned throughout the country, an interesting phenomenon occurred. In spite of Irish success in containing further English incursions and in regaining some lost territories, the Irish had a strong sense that something of the past was being lost, something of immense value. A revival of interest in pagan pre-Christian times took hold. Festivals were organized throughout the country, and large numbers of people are recorded as attending. People traveled many miles to attend and participate in these festivals. Music, poetry recitation, and myth-telling were popular entertainments. The enthusiasm for ancient times extended to new writing.

Much is owed to the scholars of this period because it is thanks to their enthusiasm that so much information has survived from earlier times. Their commitment and dedication to the Irish past knew no bounds. The old mythological sagas that were first recorded in the sixth to eighth centuries were rewritten in the fourteenth century and newly appreciated. This era was a golden age for Irish bardic poetry. Hundreds of old poetic tales were written down, and Irish music took on its modern form. The Irish language of this time is considered very poetic and the rhyming patterns highly sophisticated. It was a language now shared by the Hibernicized Normans and Irish alike; so much so that one of the chief poets of the period, Gerald FitzGerald, was of Norman descent. This assimilation with the native culture would result in serious difficulties for the authorities in England whose main desire was the establishment of a loyal population in Ireland. As the English repeatedly discovered, trouble within the Irish kingdom was never far away. Resistance to English political control would be perennial.

## THE SCOTTISH WARS
## SPILL OVER INTO IRELAND

The English continued to show little interest in directly addressing issues of discontent in Ireland. The Pale area, with the city of Dublin at its nucleus, became more established as the only region that the English could control. When Edward II came to the English throne in 1307, his only apparent interest in Ireland was as a source of money and soldiers to help his campaigns in Scotland. This was not a new role for Ireland. The Irish exchequer was long established as an important source of income for the Crown. Records indicate that from 1203 to 1307 the Irish exchequer furnished an astonishing £90,000 ($80 million in today's dollars) to the "King's wardrobe" alone. The Scottish campaigns were especially expensive and took an enormous toll on the Irish economy. It is fair to say that the English attempt to conquer Scotland almost bankrupted the Irish exchequer. Great sums of money left the country not only to finance the king's expeditions but also to settle his debts. All of this placed enormous strain on the Irish economy as evident from accounts of the period describing unmaintained castles, overgrown highways, and a general feeling that money was not available for building or repair.

Irish interest in the Scottish wars took a more immediate turn when Robert Bruce, king of Scotland, began asking for Irish help in his war with the English invaders. The Scottish king kept reminding the Irish chieftains of their common Gaelic origins and suggested that by uniting their efforts much could be achieved. There were indeed strong cultural ties between the two societies. It was the *Dál Riada* kings of Ireland who had originally settled Scotland and become the kings of Scotland. Even the name "Scotland" is derived from the Roman Latin term "Scoti" meaning the Irish. Calling on these cultural ties, the Scottish king devised a plan. In a famous undated letter written by Robert Bruce, which he fraternally addressed to "All the Kings of Ireland, to the prelates and the clergy, and the inhabitants of all Ireland, our friends," he urged Irish support for the Scottish struggle so that both countries could unite and rid themselves of the English menace. Some of the Irish thought that this was an idea whose time had come and greeted the letter with interest. When Robert Bruce scored a major victory over the English at Bannockburn in 1314, some Irish chieftains decided to accept his suggestion, and the idea of an Irish-Scottish cooperative gained momentum.

## EDWARD BRUCE—KING OF IRELAND?

The Uí Néill chieftain, Donal Uí Néill (O'Neill), invited Bruce's brother, Edward Bruce, to Ireland in a gesture of cooperation with the Scots. Edward Bruce landed at Larne, County Antrim, in May 1315, and was almost immediately given the title "King of Ireland" by the O'Neills and other Irish chieftains. Edward had apparently asked for this title, and the Irish seemed willing to confer it. The O'Neills were the most prominent of the old Irish Gaelic families and had long considered themselves the first family of Ireland. For centuries before the English invasion they had claimed the title of high king and controlled the most sacred site in Ireland, the hill of Tara. It is not surprising that their leader should claim the right to establish Ireland as a kingdom separate from England and the right to confer the title King of Ireland on Edward Bruce. Yet Donal O'Neill was a shrewd man who knew the workings of European diplomacy. To back up the granting of this title O'Neill wrote to Pope John XXII in 1317 asking him to agree with Edward's title as King of Ireland. The pope was the final arbiter in such matters at the time, and O'Neill knew that for the campaign to succeed the papacy had to approve.

But as O'Neill was to discover, ancient rights were no guarantee of political success. O'Neill's letter is passionately written, shows much political savvy, and is of the clear opinion that much of Ireland's problems lay with the English presence in Ireland. O'Neill was explicit about the legitimacy of his right to establish a separate Irish kingdom and to banish the English. He explains that before the English invasion of the twelfth century, Ireland had been a devotional and free country—"it was they (the native Irish) not the English or natives of any nation who eminently endowed the Irish Church with land, ample liberties and many possessions, although at the present time she is, for the most part, sadly despoiled of those lands and liberties by the English." O'Neill further argued that the English invasion was illegal because far from encouraging the Irish to be more Christian by their example the behavior of the English in Ireland was immoral: "where they were bound to implant virtues and root out the weeds of vice, they have cut out by the root the virtues already planted and of themselves have brought in vices." This is a clear repudiation of the initial English justification for the invasion that they came to Ireland to "reform" Irish morality.

The letter also serves as a remarkable document for those who argue on the side of a strong Irish national identity in the medieval period. There is little doubt that O'Neill is expressing this. Although Ireland could not claim political unity, the manuscript serves as evidence for a strong sense of cultural unity. Unfortunately the pope did not offer a helpful response. Partly this had to do with the time and events within the papacy itself. The papacy was undergoing a period of confusion and exile from Rome, and the pope was actually resident in Avignon, France. Ireland's problems had no priority.

## FAILURE OF THE BRUCE INVASION

Robert Bruce, on hearing that his brother was not achieving much progress in Ireland, decided to put aside his war with the English for a time and travel to Ireland to ensure that the war effort there received reinforcement. Unfortunately the English managed to gain support within Ireland among the Norman settlements, strongly defending against the Bruces. Their failure to take Dublin proved central to the lack of success for the Bruces. The citizens of Dublin, in defending the city, pulled down church walls to use them to build up the city walls. Ultimately the combined Scottish/Irish army was defeated, and Edward Bruce was killed in October 1318 in County Louth. By the time of Edward's death, there were mixed feelings in Ireland about the wisdom of the Bruce interference in Irish affairs. The *Annals of Clonmacnoise* refer to his death with the bitter words, "Edward Bruce, destroyer of all Ireland in general both English and Irish, was killed by the English in main battle by their valor in Dundalk." The annalist also proceeds to accuse Edward of being rash in battle, hinting that he did not like his brother's involvement in Ireland and was afraid that Robert would win the glory that Edward thought his.

Since the Bruce invasion Irish scholars have puzzled over the motives behind it. Were the Bruces simply helping the Irish rid the land of the English, or were they intending to turn Ireland into a permanent Scottish conquest? Or was the invasion a political ploy, which, if successful, would have forced the English king Edward II to acknowledge Robert as rightful King of Scotland? Seán Duffy, in *Ireland in the Middle Ages*, suggests that "what we witness in the events of 1315–18 is a Scottish attempt to win support for their struggle with England by exploiting similar sentiment elsewhere."

What can be said indubitably is that the episode exposed the fact that all was not going well for the English in their Irish conquest. Far from the Irish adopting and respecting English ways, it was the invading Anglo-Normans who assimilated Irish ways. As they began to realize that their rule in Ireland was vulnerable, the English acknowledged this assimilation as a serious problem. The Bruce invasion wreaked havoc with the collection of taxes, always an issue for the English authorities. They lost much revenue as many lands returned to Gaelic hands, which meant that taxes were not paid to the Crown. The contraction of English-controlled lands was exacerbated by the Bruce wars. An indication perhaps of how vulnerable the English position had become is the fact that in 1328, for the first time since the invasion, the annals reference a Mac-Murrough being inaugurated King of Leinster "in the Irish fashion." This indicates that the old ways had neither died out nor been successfully outlawed. Reportedly the Irish nobility of Leinster gathered together and elected Donal MacMurrough their king. In a highly symbolic gesture the new King of Leinster ordered that his banner be flown and placed within a few miles of the city of Dublin, declaring that he wanted to lead a conquest of all Ireland. This reconquest was not practically possible, but the fact that this development occurred indicates that a serious Gaelic resurgence was taking place in Ireland. This vulnerability was aided by the fact that some of the landowners were absentees living in England who were paying little attention to their Irish possessions. Vast areas of Irish land remained unprotected.

## SEGREGATING IRELAND— THE STATUTES OF KILKENNY

Eventually in an attempt to bring some regulation to the seemingly unpredictable situation within the colony, in 1366 a group of laws known as the Statutes of Kilkenny was passed. The laws originated in London but were presented in Kilkenny because the Irish parliament had been moved temporarily from Dublin to the Anglo-Norman Butler family base. The purpose of these laws was to separate the native Irish from the Norman settlers and create a true English colony within Ireland. A segregated society is what they clearly hoped to achieve. The statutes were astonishing in the naiveté they displayed.

From the perspective of London, the problem in Ireland was that the original Norman settlers had intermarried with the Irish and were becoming, for all intents and purposes, culturally indistinguishable from the Irish natives. The English believed the settlers had mixed far too freely within Irish society, which resulted in losing their cultural perspective. Most important from the English point of view, they lost their allegiance to the English monarch. It was hoped that the statutes would redress this situation and prevent any further departure from English ways by the Norman settlers. There is no doubt about the intention of the statutes. These laws forbade the Anglo-Normans from mixing with the Irish, from practicing Irish laws, from dressing in the Irish fashion and, significantly, from speaking the Irish language. The question of language in Ireland was a dispute that was to last for many centuries, for language was seen as central to cultural identity. As one English official phrased it, "If the tongue be Irish, the heart must needs be Irish too." The decree was not without some teeth. To reinforce these laws the statutes declared that anyone found speaking the Irish language would face loss of their lands. In the case of anyone who did not own land, "then his person be then taken by some of the officers of our lord the King to the next jail."

Some of the laws were directed toward the native Irish, who were essentially told to stay away from Norman areas of settlement. The Irish were to be excluded from clerical positions, and "no Irish were to be admitted into any Cathedral or collegiate church by provision, collation or presentation of any person whatsoever." The proscription also extended to entertainment, and it was forbidden that "Irish poets, storytellers, harpers and any other Irish minstrels shall come amongst the English." The fear was that Irish poets and minstrels might act as spies. The laws were sometimes very explicit in what they wanted to express. Not only was intermarriage between members of the two communities forbidden, but so was any type of sexual relationship. The concern here seems to have been with the danger of producing a mixed race either inside or outside marriage. Purity of race was believed to be the only way loyalty to the English Crown could be assured.

The obvious design behind these laws was that Ireland would become segregated, with the indigenous Irish population a separate ethnic entity from the Norman settlers. One Irish historian has referred to it as an early attempt at apartheid, and in many ways it was. But the statutes proved impossible to enforce because the two communities were already so socially and culturally intermingled that separating them was an unrealistic hope. Intermarriage had already occurred on such a scale that it would have been impossible to reverse it. Because social partition was not viable, the laws were essentially ignored outside of the Pale area. Even within the Pale, the laws concerning language were the most successful.

Nevertheless it is foolish to dismiss the Statutes of Kilkenny as unimportant because they were unworkable and ineffective. Sociologically and historically they are of immense interest. They were radical in what they attempted to do, and the political intention they reveal is disconcerting. They plainly illustrate a pattern that would have similar manifestations not only in Ireland but in other parts of the world. From an Irish perspective, they display a disturbing depreciatory attitude to the Irish and to Irish culture that would continue to fester among English authorities throughout the following centuries.

## RICHARD II VISITS HIS IRISH LORDSHIP

As an indication of English concern for Ireland, Richard II decided to visit his Irish lordship to bolster his position there. He was the first English monarch since 1210 to do so, and he did it with much pomp and glamour. Obviously subscribing to the theory that nothing succeeds like excess, Richard arrived in the port of Waterford in 1394 with a large, impressive army and a battery of elaborately dressed courtiers. *The Annals of Dublin* claim that Richard arrived "with an army of 30,000 foot and 4,000 horse" soldiers. This commanding display of strength was meant to convince the Irish and the rebellious settlers to submit fully to his authority. The king and his entourage of arms and courtiers traveled throughout the rich grassland area of Leinster in an attempt to make allies or converts of those who might have previously opposed him. Richard must surely have felt that he was successful, especially when he got the powerful King of Leinster, Art MacMurrough, to promise allegiance. Also, in large part because the English were holding his grandsons hostage, Neill Mór O'Neill submitted. Predictably, this forced covenant and others fell apart soon after the king left Ireland. Allegiance to the English king remained capricious.

Still persistent and obviously hopeful, in 1399 Richard returned to Ireland. This proved to be disastrous for him as his Lancastrian cousins in England seized on the opportunity to take the throne of England. Ultimately Richard's tactics failed in Ireland. He had the double misfortune of failing to establish his kingship firmly in England, heralding a series of wars among the English over the succession to the English throne.

# [ 2 ]

# *The Recalcitrant Colony: FitzGerald Power in Ireland*

THROUGHOUT most of the 1400s the English paid little attention to Ireland mostly because of the Wars of the Roses, an internal struggle in England over the monarchy. The House of Lancaster was in a bloody dispute with the House of York, with each attempting to gain permanent control of the English throne. Also, the long dispute with France known as the Hundred Years' War (1338–1453) meant that there was enough confusion in England to make Irish affairs a fairly low priority. As a result of this turmoil in England, the Irish were left more or less to their own devices, and the country settled into what could be described as a peaceful accommodation between the native Irish and the newcomers. The adoption by the Norman settlers, now more properly described as Gaelo-Norman, of native Irish culture continued, as did intermarriage. The communities coexisted in harmony, sharing a language and many customs in common.

As a way of anglicizing Ireland, the English attempted to impose certain legal changes to the Irish way of life. These were not entirely successful. The survival of the old Brehon Law system now posed a problem for the authorities, who realized that the imposition of English law was the only way to bring the country under control. The question of titles and the Irish system of inheritance were continuing problems for the English. Under the old Irish Brehon Laws the head of an Irish *Túath*, or family, was given the designation or prefix "The" as in The O'Neill, The O'Donnell, The O'Connor. Under English law these titles became illegal and were to be supplanted with English titles such as earl or lord, indicating allegiance and subjection to the English monarch. This is why so many Irish chieftains held English-style titles. They had been required to do so in order to show submission and loyalty to the monarch. Many Irish ignored the singular significance of these English titles and also held their ancient Irish titles. The system of inheritance was a thorn for the English administrators too. Under Brehon Law the Irish mode of inheritance was not based on the inheritance rights of an eldest son. Instead the Irish practiced an ancient custom whereby on the death of a chieftain or local king a new leader was voted on following a group discussion. This system was declared to be contrary to English law, which required that the eldest son inherit and forbade local assemblies determining leadership. Conflicts of culture like these were a source of stress between the English administrators within the Pale and the reality of life in Ireland.

## BEYOND THE PALE

Outside the Pale a mixture of Norman and Gaelic families lived in the old Irish manner. The Gaelic language, Gaelic customs, and Gaelic law flourished. Kenneth Nichols, in *Gaelic and Gaelicized Ireland in the Middle Ages*, asserts that "The notion that late medieval Ireland was sharply divided on the basis of the national origin of the ruling lineages is one that cannot survive an investigation of the actual facts." The Gaelic culture remained strong even in the areas of Norman settlement. Nichols explains that many of the Gaelo-Norman families "would to an outside observer have appeared indistinguishable from their purely Gaelic neighbors." The English did not have the money or the manpower to do anything directly about this, and the job of administrating English rule fell to the Norman settlers. As a result of this policy three powerful Gaelo-Norman families emerged as power brokers. In the century that lasted from 1400 to 1500 the prominent families in Ireland were the FitzGeralds of Munster, the FitzGeralds of Kildare, and the Butlers of Ormond, now known as Kilkenny. The ostensive duty of these families was to act as protectors of English interests in the country.

This was the English understanding of the situation in Ireland. Consequently the king would appoint one of these Gaelo-Norman lords in Ireland to be his representative, or lord deputy, to support his interest. Yet in spite of their position as representatives of the Crown, the families had completely absorbed the Irish culture and had developed a strong identity with Ireland. These families had become so culturally Irish that they even practiced the ancient Gaelic custom of placing their children with Irish foster parents and, in spite of the Statutes of Kilkenny, they spoke the Irish language. That the Statutes of Kilkenny had not solved the problem of integration had not yet occurred to the English authorities. They continued to regard the Gaelo-Norman families as protectors of English political interests. The myth would eventually unravel, to the consternation of the English. In the meantime Ireland was left to develop its own social order.

Significantly many old Gaelic families still held their lands and continued to be important forces in Irish life, even if they were politically ignored by the English. The O'Donnells and the O'Neills still owned most of the lands of Ulster. The O'Briens remained powerful in Munster, and the O'Connors, though somewhat reduced in status from their high-kingship days, held more than a third of Connacht. Although in the eighteenth and nineteenth centuries in Irish history Connacht came to be regarded as a remote place somewhat detached from the main events of Irish history, in medieval times it was an area of some importance, being neither economically backward nor politically remote. The continued O'Connor dominance played an important role in the politics of the period. These Gaelic families were an unknown quantity to the English authorities, who relied on the Gaelo-Normans to ensure that the native Irish did not become too powerful.

This made the position of lord deputy a potentially powerful one. To the English it was implicit that whoever held the office of lord deputy would keep the Gaelic Irish in check. This was a far more formidable task than the English realized. Gaelic Ireland had never had a centralized monarchy like the one in England. By tradition it was a politically decentralized country in which many independent rulers took care of their own interests and local areas of influence. The English attempted to gain a foothold over this precarious situation by a divide-and-conquer approach. Part of the ongoing system of government since the invasion had been to ensure that local chiefs continued to dispute with one another so they would rely on the chief governor of Ireland for protection. Of course some chieftains mattered more than others. Important Irish lords such as The Uí Néill or The O'Connor or The MacMurrough were perceived as having a certain status and were therefore given a broader berth by the English authorities. They were nevertheless viewed with a degree of caution.

## THE IRISH LIFESTYLE

From what we can learn from correspondence and commentary on life, the average family in Ireland at this time still observed strong Gaelic traditions and a social ethos dating to pre-Norman times. This culture permeated all aspects of daily living. Dress was determined by a person's wealth or social status, but the style was distinctively Irish at all levels of society. Wealthy people wore a long, elegant mantle, often belted, with a tunic underneath with wide, hanging sleeves. The men wore cone-shaped caps on their heads made of frieze, a coarse woolen cloth, and heavy hose on their legs. Women's dress is described as brightly colored, with skirts sometimes embroidered elaborately with silk threads. On their heads the women wore a folded hood usually made of linen. Poorer people usually went bareheaded and with few garments but with the protection of the heavy Irish wool cloak which could be pulled up over the head against inclement weather. All these garments were traditionally Irish and are indicators of how little English culture had actually penetrated the country. It remained a source of irritation to the Crown that the English dress "code" was not adhered to. But little could be done about it, and the English had other issues at home to keep them busy.

The fifteenth century witnessed a housing boom in Ireland, and many families built attractive homes or added to those they already occupied. Like clothing, housing varied with wealth and status. Large, impressive castles were the homes of the wealthiest families, both Gaelic and Norman. One of the most magnificent castles built by a Gaelic family was the O'Donnell home in Donegal. The O'Donnells were major landowners in the region, and their main castle, Donegal Castle, reflected their wealth and status. The restored remains of this medieval castle can be seen today in Donegal town. In the 1500s an English official described the castle as "one of the grandest I ever saw in an Irishman's hands." Although for years the castle was just a roofless abandoned ruin, it has been reroofed, and restoration work in the 1990s has revived strong resonances of the time when the O'Donnells were the most prominent family in the area.

Slightly down the social ladder from the castles were the tower-houses. In the early fifteenth century it became fashionable to build a tower as accommodation for the landowner who was rising in status but could not quite afford to build the larger traditional castle. Tower-houses were a source of great prestige for their owners, and a number of these homes were built during this time. The popularity of these homes is obvious from a parliamentary order in 1429 which actually awarded a grant to build them and set out such details as size and design permitted by the grant system.

Poorer people lived in small houses, mostly made out of timber and straw, built in their fields. These would have provided little more than basic shelter, but in good times the poor would have had enough room for storage, an important part of survival. With plenty of food the poor would have enjoyed a reasonable standard of living. To bolster their living conditions, people on the margins of society maintained another Gaelic tradition—raiding. Raiding neighboring territories on a small scale for bounty remained a part of Irish economic life as it had since ancient times. The difference now was that the raiding was frequently committed against the Gaelo-Norman settlers, and many of the economically poorer Gaelic families depended on the spoils for their survival. Raiding the Pale area had become almost a sport for the native Irish.

## THE RESILIENT IRISH CHURCH

One of the most noteworthy aspects of Irish life during this time was the persistence of the old tradition of hereditary succession in the priesthood and in bishoprics. The Irish church proved itself as resilient as Irish society to outside influence. Although the diocesan model was established, the so-called reforms of the twelfth century had not transformed the nature of the church. Irish Christianity continued its idiosyncratic ways. Clerical celibacy had never been firmly established in Ireland, and there are extensive references in the annals to the sons of bishops and the sons of priests inheriting their fathers' positions.

Like the English, the papacy paid little attention to Ireland during this long period. The Irish returned the favor by ignoring Rome. The actual daily practice of religion was rare and the sacraments scarcely ever received. Steven Ellis describes the religious situation in Ireland at this time as "a worsening religious climate." The Irish church continued to have an independent ethos and lacked a strong centralized administration. It would not be until the nineteenth century that a strong Roman-model Catholic church would develop in Ireland.

## POLITICS IN MEDIEVAL IRELAND

Within the climate of English inattention, two Norman families emerged as political rivals for the governance of Ireland. Politics in fifteenth-century Ireland was dominated by the actions of the Butler and FitzGerald families. The Butlers owned vast lands around the area of Kilkenny, Tipperary, and Waterford and had essentially made the region into a small state within the island. Their splendid castle, a great symbol of their power, still stands in Kilkenny today, and, until the 1970s, the Butler family lived there. Like the other Gaelo-Norman families, they were closely intermarried with Gaelic families and fairly integrated into Gaelic society. The Butlers controlled the Irish House of Commons in Dublin in the early part of the fifteenth century by filling it with their own family members. When not enough family members were available they used their household servants. Unfortunately their dynastic rule ended in 1452 with the death of their leader, known as the "White Earl," who took up residence in England in order to support the Lancastrian side in the Wars of the Roses. This unfortunate choice ended in his execution. All this paved the way for another and more dynamic Gaelo-Norman family to emerge in Ireland as the major power broker.

## GARRET MÓR FITZGERALD—THE GREAT EARL

By the end of the fifteenth century the chief political family in Ireland were the FitzGeralds of Kildare. Under the guidance of the great head of the family, the colorful and energetic Garret Mór FitzGerald, they established themselves as the foremost political dynasty in Ireland. Born in 1457 to this affluent family, Garret Mór FitzGerald was destined to cast a long shadow over medieval Ireland and the relationship of the colony to the English Crown. For most of his long and eventful political career, which spanned from 1478 to 1513, Garret Mór held the office of Lord Deputy of Ireland. This was granted to him from the English king. He also held the title the 8th Earl of Kildare.

Now in ruins, Maynooth Castle in County Kildare was one of the most important of the FitzGerald residences in Ireland in the fifteenth and sixteenth centuries. (*Carmel McCaffrey*)

From an early age Garret Mór made use of many cunning devices to expand and consolidate his power. He possessed a keen sense for networking with the right people. With military tactics, careful friendships and alliances, and the encouragement of beneficial marriages for his own family, he created a small province for the FitzGeralds around their lands in Kildare. The castle of Maynooth in Kildare was their main stronghold, but Garret also managed to be given the beautifully forested Leixslip Castle by the king, and Garret also built the splendid castle at Castledermot. He expanded the FitzGerald lands into surrounding counties and had the Irish parliament grant him further tracts of unoccupied land that had fallen into disuse. The geographical position of the FitzGerald estates in Kildare, so close to the Pale, probably also contributed to his success.

The English reluctantly accepted the special position of this Earl of Kildare who repeatedly proved that he could control Irish affairs. Although he was often described as a thorn in the side of a succession of English kings, they discovered that Garret Mór was a necessary, if troubling, component to their rule of Ireland. Garret Mór is an intriguing figure who comes across as a charismatic man whose personality filled every room he entered. He had six daughters, all of whom married into prominent Irish families. One of his daughters married into the O'Connors, the former kings of Connacht, who still held extensive lands and continued to be socially important in Ireland. His sister was married to the Earl of Tyrone, The O'Neill, which meant that close ties were established with the powerful O'Neills. He also had strong relationships with many minor Gaelic septs who trusted him and supported his leadership. Part of his income came from the taxes he extracted from Gaelic families of lesser lordships such as the MacDermots, the O'Rourkes, the O'Farrells, and the O'Reillys, all of whom paid him for guaranteed protection.

In addition to his political shrewdness he was an inquiring intellectual with a wide range of interests. He was well read, and his extensive library at Maynooth Castle took up a large area of the second floor of the keep. A surviving list of the books there shows it contained works in Latin, French, and Irish. Yet he was no recluse unconnected or oblivious to the lives around him. Like all the FitzGeralds he was integrated into the indigenous Irish culture and enjoyed participating in Gaelic entertainments. Politically astute, Garret Mór possessed the ability to keep the English relatively happy with his position as lord deputy while he simultaneously maintained the affection and respect of the Gaelic Irish. He seemed to have garnered the best of all worlds; well liked by the local people in Maynooth, he had the loyalty of both Gaelic and Gaelo-Norman lords.

## THE INDEPENDENT IRISH PARLIAMENT

Garret Mór never attempted to make himself an independent ruler of all Ireland, nevertheless separatist ideas among the Irish were evident. Under the influence and vibrant personality of this great earl, the Irish parliament had been flexing its muscles. But it is fair to say that this was not a new departure. As far back as 1460 the Irish parliament had asserted its independence with its "Declaration of the Independence of the Irish Parliament," sometimes referred to informally as the "Home Rule" Bill—but not to be confused with the nineteenth-century bills of similar title. The bill states rather audaciously that "the land of Ireland is, and at all times has been corporate of itself by the ancient laws and customs used in the same, freed of the burthen of any special law of the realm of England." It was a gallant statement for the Irish to make and, as they were to discover, an even more daring aspiration to act upon. Subsequent events in Ireland would attract the attention of the English king and alert him to the dangers of this free-thinking Irish spirit.

While events in Ireland were seemingly settling into a climate of social accommodation, significant political changes were coming to England that would impact Irish affairs. The Wars of the Roses were finally settled when in 1485 the first Tudor, Henry VII, gained the English throne. The Tudors came to power in the midst of much uncertainty and bloodshed, and the succession of Henry VII was not completely accepted in England. This first Tudor king therefore thought it necessary to establish his kingship and his future lineage. He was not about to stand by and allow any threat to his throne to go unnoticed or unanswered. Ireland would soon grab his attention.

## THE IRISH CROWN AN ENGLISH KING— THE TUDOR KING IS NOT AMUSED

Within two years of his accession, Henry VII had reason to be concerned as word from Ireland reached him that the Irish had crowned the young usurper, Lambert Simnel of York, King of England. Henry's surprise and anger at this startling event must have been enormous. This was no small deed done on a remote hilltop by a small rebel band but the work of the Irish parliament in concert with Irish nobles and prelates. Garret Mór FitzGerald had decided that Simnel had a legitimate claim on the English throne and had him crowned King of England, France, and Ireland. The ceremony took place on May 24, 1487, in Christ Church Cathedral. Simnel claimed to be the nephew of Edward IV and took the title Edward VI. Shortly afterward, the Irish parliament confirmed the legitimacy of his title. The Irish were announcing not only that they had the right to declare and crown the king of England but also that their parliament was independent and could make its own laws. The farce continued when, backed by Irish troops and German mercenaries, Simnel attempted to invade England. Henry easily thwarted Simnel's effort at Stoke. When news of Irish actions reached the pope, he was as outraged as the king and commanded the bishops of Ireland to give allegiance to Henry VII.

Henry did not fail to see the meaning behind the Irish actions. The Irish were saying that they had the right to make whatever laws they wanted. There was no doubt that FitzGerald's action in having Simnel crowned was treasonous against the king. It was equally obvious to Henry that Ireland's constitutional position in relation to England was becoming a matter that needed addressing. Henry may have been furious but was cautious not to act too rashly. He understood that FitzGerald power in Ireland had to be challenged with care but also with resolution. He did not dare risk all Ireland rebelling. Alongside the tempering of Irish parliamentary power went the need to establish the English presence more firmly. With these concerns in mind, Henry formally outlined the boundaries of the Pale in the statute of 1488. The inhabitants of the outer limit of the Pale were required to build a six-foot bank in order to repel the ongoing problem of Irish raiding and incursions into the Pale area.

With a strong sense of ferocious absurdity, and probably to display his contempt for an unworthy rival, Henry gave Simnel a job in his palace kitchens, rather than executing him. It was a clever way to degrade the pretender in rank. But Henry went even further. In what can only be described as a scene right out of *Fawlty Towers*, in 1489 Henry VII summoned the Irish temporal lords to England and had Lambert Simnel wait on them at a banquet. We can only imagine what such a reunion must have felt like and how Henry must have enjoyed watching.

## THE TUDOR KING ACTS

In spite of his public face, Henry took the attempt on his throne quite seriously. In July 1490 he summoned Garret Mór to London to discuss the Irish situation. Garret, ever brazen, did not bother answering the summons until June 1491, and then it was only to explain that he was "too busy" with his own affairs to attend. His disregard for the king's power and position was palpable. Indeed his busy life seemed to offer its own very colorful moments. His enmity with his political enemies, the Butlers, entered Dublin legend. A supposedly heated discussion between Garret Mór and "Black James" Butler in 1492 led to a reputed skirmish in the Dublin streets, when Black James fled and took refuge in the chapter house of St. Patrick's Cathedral. Garret is said to have pursued him but finding the door locked cut a hole in it to stick his hand through and offer a truce to his Butler rival. This is said to be the origin of the expression "to chance your arm." In addition to this much-talked-about incident, which reportedly reached the king's ears, Henry was frustrated in his attempt to have Garret Mór bring the O'Neills and the O'Donnells of Ulster into line and behave like taxpaying subjects of the Crown.

## POYNINGS' LAW—
## CURTAILING THE IRISH PARLIAMENT

Because the king knew a serious threat to his control of Ireland existed, he made a decision that would affect relationships between the two countries for centuries. Henry decided to send a representative to Ireland who would severely modify the status of the Irish parliament. His name was Sir Edward Poynings, and he was a good choice for the task at hand. Poynings was considered a loyal servant and soldier of the king who had fought alongside the Tudor in his battle for the English throne. He arrived in Ireland in 1494. Henry's order to Poynings was to reduce Ireland to "perfect obedience," not an easy task. Above all, Henry wished to guarantee against another threat to his throne. Poynings understood the draconian measures that had to be taken. With the power vested in him, he took the necessary steps to ensure that any future risk to Henry would be eradicated. He summoned the Irish parliament and laid down new rules for that recalcitrant body. These regulations became known as Poynings' Law. Under the terms of this new decree the Irish parliament was told that it could meet only after it had the king's permission and that laws passed in Ireland must also be passed by the English parliament before they became law in Ireland. Furthermore all prior legislation passed by the English parliament must now be law in Ireland. The Irish parliament effectively ceased to have power.

Garret Mór was not deterred by any of these changes to the Irish legislature and remained a law unto himself. He employed Scottish mercenaries, known as Gallowglasses, as his own private army who stood outside the parliament in Dublin to protect him. The presence of these Gallowglasses also added to the prestige and mystique of the man. Henry VII tried to dismantle Garret's hegemony by having him removed as lord deputy and replaced by an English official. This action was not successful. The resulting outburst of lawlessness and protest throughout Ireland was too much for Henry to control. The eruption of civil disturbance was organized by Garret, who had called for it as a protest against his demotion. Such was his power in Ireland that his mere request became a command to the Irish. Henry simply could not respond to the mayhem that ensued. The financial commitment of sending so many troops to control many different parts of the country would be too great for him. In 1496 he restored the great earl to the post of lord deputy with the laconic words, "If all Ireland cannot rule this man, then he shall rule all Ireland!"

## THE TUDORS GET SERIOUS ABOUT IRELAND

Although Henry VII failed in his attempt to gain political control of Ireland, he set the stage for success of the dynasty he founded. For the FitzGeralds and Ireland the Tudors proved to be politically difficult to thwart. Part of their ambition involved an absolute determination to control Ireland. During the sixteenth century Tudor monarchs would politically dominate Ireland, using whatever force and, ultimately, expense were necessary to achieve their goal. Ireland would be the first step in the use of violent tactics later employed in the establishment of a major world empire.

Henry VIII succeeded to the throne in 1509 upon the death of his father. The monarchy was now secure for the Tudors. Henry was young and confident. He was an ambitious, clever man who understood the necessity of transforming the different regions under his control into one unified, centralized state. Improved shipbuilding technology and the threat of invasion played an important role in this need for transformation. France and Spain had become powerful enemies of England. The English feared that one of them would attempt to invade Ireland, using it as a base for an attack on England. Spain especially was perceived as a threat after it united in 1516. With this in mind and his own ambitions paramount, Henry VIII was determined to enforce his military and political influence in Ireland and bring the country under his control. He also knew that local magnates like the FitzGerald dynasty would have to be confronted and if necessary destroyed. He therefore began to turn his attention to Ireland.

## GARRET ÓG FITZGERALD

In 1513 Garret Mór died and Garret Óg (the younger) succeeded his father as the Earl of Kildare. True to the maxim that the apple does not fall far from the tree, the son proved himself an equally difficult man for the English king to manage. The FitzGeralds' wealth and influence had increased, and their homes at Maynooth and Leixslip were among the most lavishly furnished of the period. Decorative tapestries hung on the walls, and the castle at Maynooth, today a large imposing ruin, is said to have contained an excellent collection

The son of Garret Mór, Garret Óg
FitzGerald, 9th Earl of Kildare, proved
himself equally impossible for the Tudors
to control. (*Duke of Leinster*)

of gold and silver. The library had been improved over the years, and by the 1520s contained more than thirty-four Latin texts and thirty-five French texts as well as many Gaelic and English books. Garret Óg's income of two thousand Irish pounds placed him among the ten most affluent Tudor families in England and Ireland.

His relationship with Henry VIII was complex and by no means entirely contentious. Garret Óg played the role of intermediary for the king. He did his job well in that he was comfortable in both Gaelic and English cultural life. The king knew that he could not hope to overthrow the Gaelic families who remained steeped in their old customs and traditions and still occupied their traditional lands. Yet Henry equally knew that he needed to reduce the FitzGerald influence in Ireland and that he had a formidable task ahead of him. The Dublin Palesmen and the king suspected that the FitzGeralds had a partiality to Gaelic ways and were too Irish in their lifestyle. They were also far too arrogant and dismissive of the royal prerogative in the use of their power. One of the main issues between the king and the FitzGeralds centered on the appointment of officials to positions of political power. Like his father before him, Garret Óg appointed local administrative officials and sheriffs. Controversy arose regarding where the king's control lay and the limits of FitzGerald power. As an expression of his own expanding power, Garret Óg took it upon himself to grant in his own name pardons of felonies without any reference to the king as supreme overlord. He further offended the king by allowing the Gaelic Brehon Law custom of administering fines as punishment for felonies. Henry had few options at his disposal to rein in FitzGerald power. He made an attempt by appointing English officials to strategic posts in Dublin. This strategy had little effect.

## CONTROLLING IRELAND— AN EXPENSIVE PROPOSITION

Henry then attempted to mount a more significant challenge to FitzGerald by summoning him in January 1519 to London. This was supposedly in response to complaints emanating from the Pale that Garret was abusing his power as lord deputy. Henry dismissed Garret Óg from his post, placed him essentially under house arrest in London, and then sent the Earl of Surrey to Ireland to review the situation and to offer his assessment. The state of Ireland was a shock to Surrey who quickly realized that the Irish were not going to be controlled easily. In fact Surrey thought the native population was incorrigible, and his report was an uncomfortable wake-up call for the king. Surrey reported that to subdue and control Ireland "it would take an army of 6,000 men supported by artillery and munitions from England. Fortresses would have to be built to control each section of the country successfully occupied." Henry could not meet this cost, so he tried another tactic. He attempted to appoint one of the Butlers to the position of lord deputy in 1522, but the FitzGeralds immediately organized a chaotic series of lawlessness around the country. Although detained in London, Garret was in close contact with his family in Ireland and was able to control events in Ireland remotely. With a great network of relatives among the ruling families, nothing seemed impossible for the FitzGeralds. Reluctantly Henry was eventually forced in 1524 to restore FitzGerald as lord deputy.

The FitzGeralds immediately celebrated this victory with a prominent ceremony in Christ Church Cathedral followed by a large banquet at their mansion in Thomas Court, Dublin. The FitzGeralds knew how to throw a party that would serve as an opportunity to retain friends, win friends, and spin their own agenda. Among the notables attending this celebration was the O'Neill chief, Conn O'Neill, a signal to the king that the FitzGeralds were on excellent terms with one of the most important of the Gaelic lords.

Unfortunately this was not the end of the debacle. Later in the 1520s Garret Óg was again detained in London while Henry attempted to find a resolution to his own inability to govern Ireland. Again the earl directed affairs from England, and in an elaborate scheme he had Lord Devlin, the king's representative in Ireland, kidnapped and held by The O'Connor, his son-in-law. Devlin was held for several months, and the ransom was a demand for the restoration of a FitzGerald to the position of lord deputy. The parliament in Dublin was thrown into such chaos by this event that members requested the return of Garret Óg as the only man who could restore order to the country. After attempting to subdue Ireland without FitzGerald, Henry VIII was once again forced to admit that Garret Óg was a necessary if troublesome adjunct. Henry reinstated him and calm was restored. The situation was not one in which Henry liked to find himself. When he judged the time to be right, he took action against the FitzGeralds.

## THE ENGLISH REFORMATION

The peace and stability that the Tudors hoped to bring to England was shattered in the 1530s by an event that at first must have appeared fairly routine and innocuous. It involved the king's personal life. Like the lives of many royals, Henry's life had its complications. He had been married to his wife, Queen Catherine, since 1509. Born in 1485 in Aragon in Spain, Catherine was six years older than Henry. The marriage had taken place when Henry was seventeen years old and his bride twenty-three. She had previously been married to his older brother, Arthur, Prince of Wales, who was heir to the throne. Tragically Prince Arthur had died at a young age, leaving a very young widow.

Both his father, Henry VII, and the courtiers of the time pressured the young Prince Henry to marry his brother's widow. They requested a dispensation from the pope because canon law forbade a man from marrying his dead brother's wife. The pair became engaged in 1503 when Henry was twelve years old and Catherine was eighteen. The papal dispensation was eventually granted, and shortly after Henry ascended the English throne in 1509 the pair married. They had only one child, a daughter, Princess Mary. All other pregnancies for the queen had ended unhappily in miscarriages and stillbirths. As the years went by and no male heir was born, Henry became increasingly restless and frantic about the future of the monarchy. He became convinced that the lack of a male heir was a punishment from God for his marriage. The marriage, he concluded, was invalid.

Meanwhile in Europe trouble was brewing within the Christian church: a German monk, Martin Luther, protested against those religious practices he considered unorthodox and heretical. Because of Luther's actions, reform of the Christian church and its authority was an urgent topic in many parts of Europe. Henry saw himself as a deeply religious man, and in 1519 he wrote tracts defending the pope and the church against Martin Luther's attacks. He was rewarded for his faithfulness to Rome by the pope granting him the unique title "Defender of the Faith." To this day the British monarch retains this title. But the new wave of change sweeping European Christianity would eventually find expression in England as events there would bring the issue of the pope's authority to the forefront of English politics.

## HENRY VIII'S REQUEST FOR AN ANNULMENT

Sometime in the mid-1520s Henry VIII met and fell in love with Anne Boleyn, whose sister had been one of Henry's mistresses. Anne was determined not to follow in her sister's footsteps and told Henry that only marriage was acceptable to her. Henry had already been contemplating an annulment from his wife, and eventually he would attempt to bring this about. The absence of a male heir troubled Henry. He continued to believe that his marriage was not pleasing to God and therefore invalid. With this conviction Henry applied to the pope, now Clement VII, for an annulment to his marriage, which would make him free to marry again.

This was not a radical request. Annulment was a fairly routine practice among Europe's royals. Henry's sister had been granted an annulment a few years earlier. In response to Henry's request in 1528 the pope dispatched an envoy to England to assess the validity of the marriage. Henry's basis for the annulment was the breaking of canon law by the dispensation. He claimed it was against God's will and had resulted in his heirless marriage. There is little doubt that Henry believed he would succeed in his request. Cardinal Wolsey assured him that he had excellent grounds. There is equally little doubt that the pope gave it careful and probably positive consideration, as a document in the Vatican exists today that shows the first draft of a marriage annulment for the English king. Unfortunately for Henry, the Spanish had different ideas and more influence with the pope.

## THE SPANISH HAVE A WORD

Henry's wife, Queen Catherine, had been a Spanish princess before marrying the English heir. She was the aunt of the present king of Spain, Charles V, who also held the title of Holy Roman Emperor. Henry's action of asking for an annulment meant that he was removing a Spanish princess from the English throne, but even more significantly he was disinheriting his daughter, Princess Mary. With annulment the marriage is declared to be null and void, and children born of the marriage are therefore illegitimate. If her parents' annulment were approved, Princess Mary could not inherit the throne of England. The Spanish were enraged at what they saw as an affront to their family, and an envoy was sent to the pope to put forward the Spanish view.

The Spanish position was strong. They had the advantage of having sacked Rome in 1527. At that time the Emperor Charles had imprisoned the pope for a period of six months. The pope remained more than a little afraid of the Spanish emperor, and as a consequence it was not difficult for the envoy to convince the pope not to annul the marriage. Nevertheless the pope prevaricated for a number of years. When the papal decision refusing annulment finally came in 1533, it was done more with the purpose of not offending the Emperor Charles than with the point of legal principle it formally expressed. It also came too late to have any effect because the

English hierarchy had already ruled in favor of the annulment, and Henry had already married Anne Boleyn. The English church would eventually split with Rome on the issue of papal authority.

## THE FITZGERALD REBELLION

These were tumultuous years for Henry VIII. With so much political uncertainty in England over the issue of his annulment, Henry was not in a position to tolerate any insubordination. When he turned his attention once again to Ireland, he decided to take serious action to ensure that the Irish were firmly under his control. Henry embarked on a course of action that would eventually remove the FitzGeralds from the privileged position they had enjoyed for almost a century. In late 1533 he summoned Garret Óg FitzGerald to London to investigate the charge that the FitzGeralds were trying to move the main administration in Ireland from Dublin to their castle in Maynooth. Garret was more reluctant than ever to travel to London. He was suffering from a mild but lingering gunshot wound sustained in a dispute defending the O'Carrolls. Although he was ill disposed to take the journey, he traveled to London in February 1534 to meet with Henry and his secretary Thomas Cromwell who apparently developed a particular dislike for the rambunctious Irish earl.

When he left Ireland, Garret put his deputyship into the hands of his twenty-seven-year-old son, Lord Thomas FitzGerald, better known as "Silken Thomas" because of his penchant for wearing silk. The story of Silken Thomas and his actions is a well-known narrative, but the old theory that his flamboyant, rash personality was responsible for ill-advised decisions no longer holds. Recent scholarship, most especially the work of Steven Ellis, has shed clearer light on Lord Thomas and the rationale behind his behavior.

While in London, Garret Óg sent secret word to his son to take whatever actions he deemed necessary to retain the FitzGerald position. The young lord probably acted on this advice and the concern that his father's position in London was tenuous. Previous experience had shown that when a FitzGerald was called to London it usually resulted in the loss of the lord deputyship. Silken Thomas gathered the FitzGeralds and their allies with the intention of initiating a rebellion against the Crown. He must surely have believed

A stylized drawing of Lord "Silken" Thomas FitzGerald challenging Henry VIII's power in Ireland. (*Linen Hall, Belfast*)

that he would succeed. Over the past half-century every challenge to their authority in Ireland had resulted in a FitzGerald success.

On the morning of June 11, 1534, the young Lord Thomas FitzGerald rode into Dublin accompanied by 1,000 men. He immediately went to St. Mary's Abbey where the king's council was in session. Accompanied and protected by about 140 of his horsemen guards, he entered the chamber and in a purposely public, flamboyant, and dramatic gesture he surrendered the sword of state, indicating his open rebellion against the king. He stated that he was resigning his position as Vice Deputy of Ireland and that he was renouncing his loyalty to the king. The objective was to get Henry to recognize that he needed the FitzGeralds to govern Ireland and any attempt to harm Garret Óg or remove him from the office of Deputy of Ireland would not result in success for the king. The young lord also made some outspoken remarks about Henry being a heretic because of Henry's recent remarriage against the ruling from Rome.

Because of these remarks it is sometimes claimed that the FitzGerald rebellion was purely a religious one, but the situation in Ireland at the time was far more complex. These comments were made more with the aim of attracting Spanish or papal help. In any event this help did not materialize. Religion was only one factor in the Irish struggle to retain control over their affairs. From the beginning of the English incursions in the twelfth century, one of the principal complaints the Irish had against the English involved the ownership of land and its accompanying access to wealth. Religion was now becoming a weapon in that struggle.

Although previously dismissed as impetuous and foolish, the actions of Thomas FitzGerald were quite calculated. In many ways it was a typical FitzGerald action accomplished with the possible aim of showcasing power. The recent biographer of Silken Thomas FitzGerald, Laurence McCorristine, contends that Silken Thomas publicly laying down the sword of state "bears all the hallmarks of an organized medieval public relations exercise." It was not done so much as a threat of actual violence as a demonstration of the FitzGeralds' indispensability. The withdrawal of FitzGerald support was a powerful warning to Henry that he could not fail to notice. The action was also a defensive reaction to the position in which the FitzGeralds believed themselves to be. Their status as the primary political family in Ireland was under threat. Drastic and dramatic action was necessary to protect it. Unfortunately the tactic did not work. The possible expectation that Henry was too busy with other affairs to answer an Irish threat with anything other than capitulation was groundless. The Tudors were a more ruthless and ambitious dynasty than anything previous. In addition, as Steven Ellis points out, Henry could not perceive the threat from Lord Thomas as other than a serious challenge.

## END OF THE FITZGERALD DOMINANCE

In response to the news from Ireland, Henry ordered Garret Óg arrested on June 29 and sent to the Tower of London. This action escalated events in Ireland. From August to October 1534, Silken Thomas FitzGerald and his forces bombarded Dublin Castle, the center of English administration. Accounts of this attack vary from heroic deeds to betrayal in the ranks of the Irish. As a mark of how seriously he took the attack, and how unprepared he was to initiate a military response, Henry's initial reaction was to suppress all news coming from Ireland concerning the rebellion. He even forbade his council from discussing the matter. Laurence McCorrestine comments that "a policy of disinformation and censorship of Irish news was maintained throughout the summer of 1534." Henry might have needed time to think, yet one of Silken Thomas FitzGerald's problems was his failure to gain support from enough of the Gaelic Irish. He also did not gain the hoped-for support from overseas. His revolt was doomed.

Henry appointed an English lord deputy, Lord Skeffington, who arrived in Ireland with a well-equipped army of 2,500 to quash the revolt. Henry wanted results, and he got them. The English army attacked the FitzGerald home base at Maynooth Castle with heavy artillery and soon penetrated and knocked in its walls. The FitzGeralds were crushed. The rebels were quickly defeated and the leaders captured. The English forces even sought out the FitzGeralds who had not been involved in the conflict. Some of Silken Thomas's uncles were arrested in Dublin while attending a banquet. Henry believed that the FitzGeralds constituted such a threat to his kingdom and his reforms that he could not risk leaving any of them at large. In 1537 Silken Thomas and his five uncles were executed. Garret Óg had already died in the Tower of London, probably from his wound. Within two short years the FitzGeralds were a broken power in Ireland. This degree of state-ordered aggressiveness was a new approach, one which was to become the established norm. Uncompromising political determination backed up with the force of arms would henceforth play a major role in the conquest and control of Ireland.

For the first time the English realized that the Norman settlers possessed a strong sense of Irish identity. The policy of trying to keep both communities apart was abandoned in favor of more direct English rule. The guiding principle became one of violent reprisal against anyone who attempted to rise against Crown interests. Although the Kildare FitzGeralds were regranted their lands and titles in 1554, their political position was never what it had been before the rebellion. It was determined that from this time forward the rank of lord deputy, the top political appointment in Ireland, was to be held by an Englishman and, except for small intervals, this was so. Lord Grey, who was appointed lord deputy for Ireland in 1536, wrote a report to Henry explaining how he saw the Irish situation:

> Your Highness must understand that the English blood of the English [twelfth-century] conquest is in a manner worn out of

this land . . . and contrary-wise, the Irish blood ever more and more without such decay, encreaseth.

## HENRY VIII, KING OF IRELAND

The FitzGerald challenge to his power left Henry feeling vulnerable. In May 1536 he convened the Irish parliament in order to declare him head of the Irish church as had been done in England. Then in 1541, as a symbol of his political control, Henry had the Irish parliament formally declare him King of Ireland. The previous title of Lord of Ireland was no longer sufficient. He also introduced the harp as the emblem of Ireland on his coinage. English troops were sent to guard Dublin Castle, where they remained until 1922. Despite these changes, no all-Ireland operational government emerged during this time. English political power in Ireland still remained only a partial reality. Within Ireland there was as much tribal and political variance as ever. Beyond the Pale lay the recalcitrant Irish, still not quite conquered.

# [ 3 ]

# Princes of Ireland: O'Neill and O'Donnell

❋

WHEN HENRY VIII DIED in 1547 a number of heirs had claims to the throne. Although his many marriages and annulments left behind some confusion, in the final analysis each child of his marriages succeeded him as monarch. Henry's son Edward VI ruled briefly, and in 1553 Henry's daughter Mary I succeeded Edward. Mary's rule was not a happy one, as she tried unsuccessfully to restore her kingdom to the Roman Catholic church. Nor were her wars successful. Her loss of Calais in 1558, just months before her death, left England with no continental possessions for the first time since 1066, the arrival of the Normans. In spite of Mary's failure the Tudors were by no means a spent force. She died late in 1558 and was succeeded by the Tudor heir who would make the most lasting impression. This was Henry's second daughter, Elizabeth.

Elizabeth I was Queen of England and Queen of Ireland from 1558 until her death in 1603. Spain had become the most powerful country in Europe, and Elizabeth and her court were anxious to challenge this power and establish English supremacy. She firmly reestablished the Protestant religion. This was clearly stated by the government in Dublin as the Anglican Church of Ireland became the state religion. One of Elizabeth's persistent fears was that the Spanish would invade Ireland and proceed to launch an attack on

England from there. For Elizabeth the threat of a Spanish invasion of Ireland was to be guarded against at all costs. The Irish would pay those costs. The English queen's concern was that the Irish nobility must renounce their own ideas of independence, relinquish their ancient Gaelic titles, and declare themselves to be tax-paying subjects of the Crown. This policy was known as "surrender and regrant" because it involved a surrender of Irish lands to the Crown and then a regranting of these lands to the Irish. Significantly chieftains would no longer own their own lands because land would be held by the Crown in feudal fashion. This was the real issue and the nub of the Crown's problem. The continued Irish refusal to comply with this policy, or their decision simply to ignore it, led to one of the most devastating and bloodiest periods in Irish history.

## THE BIRTH PANGS OF EMPIRE

Elizabeth faced serious challenges to her plans to subjugate Ireland and transform the country into a Crown possession. The issues involved were broad and complex. The difference between the two societies, English and Irish, which had been apparent from the initial incursions in the twelfth century, now came to the forefront. Irish customs and law differed greatly from those of England. Ireland had a strong cultural tradition going back thousands of years, to which the Irish law system was central. Irish law was not about to give way easily to English law. The Irish law system, Brehon Law, had withstood the arrival of Christianity in the fifth century and the later English invasion and was still flourishing beyond the Pale. Elizabeth's specific issues were the Irish mode of inheritance and succession rights. Cultural differences such as these caused the most serious friction.

It was apparently unthinkable for the English to regard Irish society as equal to their own or to consider that there could be anything of value in it. In this they were absolutely convinced of their own cultural superiority. This sense of preeminence made it impossible for the English to accept the validity of Irish culture. The Irish, on the other hand, were adamant that their way of life was, in the words of the author Sean O'Faolain, "as valid, as honorable, as cultured, as complex as [the English culture]." Faced with what seemed like an implacable situation, Elizabeth resolved to remove the Irish chieftains from land ownership and supplant them with English landowners who would be loyal taxpayers. She concurrently decided that military action was the only way to achieve this goal.

The political and social background to this situation was a phenomenon not confined to Ireland. This was also the period of European expansion into the New World and the development of what Seán Duffy refers to as "justification theories, by which the wholesale annihilation of indigenous societies was explained away as the inevitable and necessary progress of civilization at the expense of peoples who were [considered] no better than primitive savages." This philosophy saw sizable native populations in the expanding colonies forced to accept the "civilizing" influence of European masters. Ireland was the first country to experience the appearance of large English armies sent to conquer and dispossess the native population. In this sense Ireland could be described as the first step in the building of empire: a proving ground or template for what became the accepted solution of using an army to subdue an unwilling population.

## ELIZABETHAN BLOODBATH

Elizabeth's decision to use military might to bring Ireland completely under her control and end the independence of Irish chieftains was a financial commitment that her father had been unwilling to make. The result was a bloodbath as Ireland literally became a wasteland of carnage and butchery. During the 1570s and 1580s Elizabethan armies steadfastly and forcibly established English rule in the provinces of Munster and Connacht. With ruthless aggression and brutality they dispossessed many Gaelic families: the O'Sullivans of Kerry, the McCarthys of Cork, and the O'Connors and O'Flahertys of Connacht were among the major Irish septs who suffered massacre, defeat, and loss of lands. No Irish dynasty escaped Elizabeth's resolve as her armies sought to establish a loyal colony in Ireland. Even the Gaelo-Norman settlers were attacked with fury when they revolted against the brutality of the invading militia. In 1569, when James FitzMaurice FitzGerald, Earl of Desmond, opposed Elizabeth's Irish policy, his soldiers were crushed and his Munster lordship supplanted by English lords.

The transference of Irish land to English ownership was paramount to the strategy of conquest, and Elizabeth distributed these Irish lands among her favorites at court. Sir Walter Raleigh was initially granted 12,000 acres and later 42,000 acres, including the beautiful castles of Lismore (near Cork) and Waterford. According to tradition, it was at this time that the potato came to Ireland, when Raleigh introduced it to his estates in Cork. When Raleigh fell from favor during the reign of James I he was forced to sell these estates, but his holdings suggest the vast acreage that was handed out during this period. Raleigh was eventually hanged in London. These were very brutal and dangerous times, when loyalty and ambition played pivotal roles in personal destinies.

## RELIGION AS A WEAPON OF RESISTANCE

Thrown into the mix of all this land seizure was the question of religion. In 1560 the Irish parliament, under direction from the Westminster parliament, issued a decree called the Act of Uniformity. This document declared that the Irish church must conform to the Anglican Book of Common Prayer. The act was an attempt to eliminate the Catholic church in Ireland. The form was clearly laid out:

> that all and singular ministers in any cathedral or parish church or other places within this realm of Ireland, shall from and after the feast of Saint John Baptist then next ensuing, be bounder to say and use the matins, evensong, celebration of the lord's supper and administration of each of the sacraments, in all their common and open prayer, in such order and form as is mentioned in the said book.

This new church took the name the Church of Ireland, but in its early stages it was distinctly Anglican in ethos. To ensure loyalty to the new state religion, churchmen, especially bishops, were to be English by birth except in places where too few Englishmen could be found. The new religion did not find much favor among the ordinary citizens of Ireland, but this had little to do with actual religious fervor. Truthfully, the Irish church was not in a strong position before the Reformation. Contrary to popular myth, the Irish were not solid devotees of Catholicism. Surviving documents show that orthodoxy was not a compelling component in the lives of ordinary people. But the arrival of this new covenant, accompanied as it was by the brutal Elizabethan method of land conquest, made accepting the religious reforms an unlikely response. Given the violent processes employed by the Elizabethan armies, nothing the English were trying to impose would engender cooperation from the Irish. Unable successfully to combat the Elizabethan armies, withstanding the imposition of a new religion became a weapon of resistance for the Irish.

At the heart of the matter between England and Ireland from Tudor times to the twentieth century lay the issue of authority. Although from the Tudor period religion came to play a role in that struggle, it was not the basis for the problem. From the time of the first English invasions the Irish had continued to express the desire to control their own destiny. As the English strove to build a world empire, their ambitions clashed with the Irish resolve to maintain a degree of self-determination.

## IRELAND'S PRINCES

Amid the attempted destruction of a way of life and the wholesale annihilation of so many of Ireland's ancient families, there was to be one final stand by the Irish chieftains. In the 1590s the Ulster chiefs, under the leadership of Hugh O'Neill, known as the Great O'Neill, Earl of Tyrone, stood between Elizabeth and her total conquest of the island. Elizabeth recognized that their power had to be broken if she were to control Ireland. Elizabeth also knew that they would not bend easily to her will. Feudal allegiance to the English Crown would not come naturally to the obdurate O'Neills or indeed to many of the Irish chieftains. Elizabeth concluded that her only solution was to drive them forcibly off their lands.

Hugh O'Neill had been born in 1550 into the ancient family which had held its land in Ulster since prehistoric times. At one time the O'Neills had been high kings of Ireland, and had claimed that prestigious title for hundreds of years. They considered themselves an independent entity, free of the English monarchy's control. Their claims to autonomy were set forth in a manuscript known as *Ceart Uí Néill,* or the Rights of the O'Neill. This document asserted full rights over Ulster for the powerful O'Neill dynasty. As a result of placing military posts in the south Ulster region, the Crown was now encroaching on these ancient rights and territories.

When the young Hugh's father, Matthew, was killed, Hugh became a ward of the Crown. It was once believed that as a youth he lived for a time at Elizabeth's court, where he attended services in the new religion and learned to be a loyal subject of the queen. Hiram Morgan, in *Tyrone's Rebellion,* questions this belief, as he claims there is insufficient evidence for it. O'Neill's reference that he was "educated among the English" may simply refer to his having lived in the Pale during his youth. Morgan also points out that the description of O'Neill being caught in a cultural identity crisis is not accurate and is a modern assessment of that period. Morgan asserts that at the time "things were not that black and white." What is significant is that O'Neill was known personally to Elizabeth and was quite familiar with English courtiers and English aspirations. There is evidence of Hugh O'Neill attending the English court with other young Irish lords in the years 1567 and 1568. He was a man comfortable in both worlds, Gaelic and English. He was ambitious from an early age, and he made an importance alliance with the O'Donnells when in 1574 he married Siobhan O'Donnell, daughter of Sir Hugh O'Donnell, Lord of Tirconnell. The English authorities grew wary of the alliance between O'Neill and O'Donnell and within a few years unsuccessfully attempted to cause trouble between the families. Divide and conquer was to be the hallmark of English governance throughout their empire.

## THE O'DONNELLS OF ULSTER

The O'Donnells were an important family in Ulster who held extensive lands, mostly around the area of southern Donegal and Sligo. Sir Hugh O'Donnell was their chieftain. His young son, Aodh Ruadh, or Red Hugh, earned a reputation for valor when, as a young prodigy in 1584 at the age of twelve, he took part in his first military action. With other members of the O'Donnell family he participated on the side of the O'Gallaghers in their feud with the O'Rourkes. This early experience earned him a reputation as a brave and fearless fighter. In 1587, as a gesture of friendship toward the O'Neills, he was betrothed at a young age to Rose O'Neill. Red Hugh's future looked bright, but his growing reputation as the potential head of the O'Donnells made him a target for the English authorities.

The English had good reason to be watching the O'Donnells. Sir Hugh was proving to be difficult for the English to control, and his growing alliance with the O'Neills was not a welcome sign. At this time the English were attempting to anglicize Ulster by placing sheriffs in the area as a way to establish English law. This was resisted throughout the province. A union of the O'Neills and the O'Donnells strengthened Irish defiance. Having conquered the rest of the country by military force, the English found Ulster difficult to bring under their control, and Elizabeth at first showed reluctance to confront the Ulster chieftains in battle. In spite of various attempts by the lord deputy at alliances, political maneuverings, and divisive policies, nothing had worked to England's advantage. So a plan was devised to cause the O'Donnells distress and bring Sir Hugh to heel.

## THE MAKING OF AN ENEMY: HUGH O'DONNELL'S STORY

In September 1587, under orders from the queen's representative John Perrot, the lord deputy, the young Red Hugh O'Donnell was kidnapped. He was seized along with two young friends, Art Mac-Sweeney and Hugh O'Gallagher. The three had been enticed aboard a ship at Rathmullen on Lough Swilly, where they were encouraged to drink wine but found that the invitation was not a friendly one. No sooner were they on board the ship when the hatches were closed, and they set sail for Dublin. The three teenagers were then taken to Dublin Castle and imprisoned there. The Four Masters, the Irish chroniclers (see Chapter 4), tell of the capture and declare that when Red Hugh was brought to Dublin there was great happiness and "the Lord-Justice and the Council were rejoiced at the arrival of Hugh; though, indeed, not for love of him." Red Hugh O'Donnell was a great prize. He was placed in the strongest part of the castle, the Birmingham Tower.

As bizarre an action as this might seem, in fact this was not an unusual practice. The authorities, especially under Perrot's deputyship, made a habit of kidnapping and holding sons of the Irish nobility in order to intimidate the parents. The taking of the young O'Donnell was the talk of Ireland and generated anger. The wily plot had been planned some months previously and was employed to put pressure on the stubborn Sir Hugh O'Donnell. The plan did not altogether work. While O'Donnell remained obstinate, his son's kidnapping broke him. The youth remained imprisoned for more than three years, and the story of his escape is one of the great adventures in Irish history. Lughaidh Ó Clérigh, who wrote a biography of Red Hugh shortly after his death, gives breathtaking details of the courageous young O'Donnell's escape from his prison inside the tower at Dublin Castle.

## ESCAPING FROM DUBLIN CASTLE

A first attempt at escape by the young Red Hugh ended in failure and recapture. But on Christmas night 1591 he escaped again with two young O'Neills, Henry and Art, who were also imprisoned. They managed to remove one another's shackles and then let themselves down by a rope which they hung from the castle privy. Quietly they jumped down into the ditch that surrounded the castle and quickly climbed out of the trench to the opposite side. Soon they were walking freely through the streets of the city. They had immediate help because Hugh O'Neill had sent a servant to meet them once they had cleared the castle boundary. Because it was Christmas night the gates of the city were open late, and they all simply walked out. Once outside of Dublin "they leaped over the strong palisade that was outside of the city." They immediately made for Glenmalur, south of Dublin in County Wicklow. They aimed to seek refuge with Fiach MacHugh O'Byrne, but the weather was against them as it was a particularly hard winter's night. According to Ó Clérigh's account: "That night it was snowing, so that it was not easy for them to walk, for they were without sufficient clothes or coverings, having left their outer garments behind them in the privy-house, through which they had escaped."

It was a difficult journey for the young men. The night was dark, the weather was bad, and they were poorly clothed. Art O'Neill became exhausted and ill and could not go on. The bad conditions in which the youths had been kept at the castle are blamed for their unhealthy condition. Hugh O'Donnell, himself

The old wall and gate of Dublin city,
dating to the early thirteenth century,
through which the young Hugh
O'Donnell made his escape from captivity
in Dublin Castle. (*Carmel McCaffrey*)

weary, put his arms around his friend and tried to help him walk. But it was hopeless for Art, who could barely stand up. He lay down to rest, and his friends stayed with him. Meanwhile O'Byrne heard of the breakout and sent some of his servants to meet the escapees and help them reach his house. The servant found the youths lying down, exhausted, and practically covered with snow. Art O'Neill had died from exposure and was buried close to where he lay. Red Hugh survived, and the rest of the small group managed to get to O'Byrne's house where they were well received. They rested at last, but Red Hugh was anxious to get home. After a few days' rest he was again on the road and made his way to his father's castle at Ballyshannon, County Donegal. The escapade was not without incident for Hugh. He had hurt his feet getting out of the castle at

Dublin. Then his shoes had fallen off because the straps became wet in the damp and snow, and the bitter frost had given him chilblains and frostbite. As a result his feet were badly damaged, and he was in much pain. When he finally returned to his home, castle doctors had to amputate his two big toes.

Unwittingly the English had created a problem that would return to plague them. The experience of years of captivity left the young O'Donnell with a deep hatred and distrust of the English. Although he crept from Dublin Castle without a sound the English were to find that Red Hugh O'Donnell did not go quietly into the night but would prove himself a formidable enemy. In the ensuing years the O'Donnells became stalwart allies of the O'Neills, forming a critical alliance to stand up to English expansion into Ulster. In May 1592, by the wishes of his father, Red Hugh O'Donnell was inaugurated The O'Donnell, chief of the O'Donnells. He was only about twenty years old, but his life experiences gave him an older perspective. As a leader of the O'Donnells he showed himself to be a charismatic, passionate man who committed himself to whatever cause he adopted. He would ultimately gallantly attempt to defend Ireland from the most aggressive military assault in the country's history.

## THE GREAT HUGH O'NEILL STEPS UP

Although Hugh O'Neill was not born in direct succession to the title of Earl of Tyrone, he would eventually be granted that title in 1587 by Elizabeth. From all reports he was a much respected man. His personality is often described as being courteous yet cautious, cool, sagacious, affable, and as one observer described it, "never acting on passion." He was considered as good a diplomat as a soldier. He inspired great loyalty among his followers, and historically he must rank among the most truly remarkable figures in Irish history. His stronghold was his home at Dungannon Castle, destroyed by the English after O'Neill's defeat. The castle is believed to have been built in the fourteenth century by the O'Neill family and remained their primary residence until the early 1600s but the O'Neills had much older homes. Dating to around 200 A.D. was their great fort of Grianan Ailech the remains of which still stand today.

Perhaps not so surprisingly, Hugh O'Neill's spirit was with the Ireland of old; the society that could trace its roots back to antiquity. The O'Neills had always held a prominent position in that world and Hugh O'Neill's loyalty was clear and evidenced by his actions. Although in his early career he seemed to acquiesce to English actions, he most likely did so to gain time to launch a serious attack on their incursions into Ulster. He fought the English efforts to anglicize Ireland because he did not wish to see the old Gaelic social order die. For all the influence the English court might have had on him, he chose to remain with his people and keep to the old traditions. In 1595, in what can only be described as an affront to the queen, he allowed himself to be inaugurated The O'Neill in Tullaghoge, the ancient ritual site of O'Neill inauguration. The ceremony was conducted according to the rite of Brehon Law and was widely reported in Ireland and in England. The queen was not amused. This illegal title under English law meant that O'Neill was essentially declaring open rebellion against English rule. He also held fast to the "old religion," probably more out of a sense of it being in the interest of Ireland not to conform to the Anglican rite. Spanish help would be more likely if the Irish remained Catholic. The Gaelic leadership in Ireland was aware of this fact. In this they had the support of the ordinary people, who showed no interest in adopting the religion of the reformed church. Religious fervor was not really the issue here; the heavy hand of the Elizabethan armies won few friends in Ireland for any part of the policy that they sought to establish.

For years the young lords of the Maguires and the MacMahons had been engaged in small battles to keep the English out of Ulster and had formed a federation with other Irish chieftains. They had also made contact with Philip II of Spain and hoped to enlist his help in fighting the English incursions. This was the beginning of what came to be known as the Nine Years' War, the protracted Irish fight to drive the English out of Ulster and eventually out of Ireland. When it became clear that the English were resolute about anglicizing Ulster and ousting the Gaelic lordships, O'Neill joined forces with the Ulster chieftains in 1595 in open rebellion. Almost immediately O'Neill assumed the leadership position. Red Hugh O'Donnell, who was now the O'Donnell chief, also joined in, and the scene was set for one of the greatest struggles to be mounted by the Irish against an English army.

## THE NINE YEARS' WAR

Hugh O'Neill had been planning for armed conflict and organizing his people to take on the Elizabethan armies for a number of years. His reputation as a cunning tactician is strongly supported by the way he accomplished this task. With the use of covert, clever strategy he discreetly developed a well-trained army of about ten thousand. Because he held the English title of earl, he had been permitted to have a certain number of soldiers in the queen's pay whom he switched frequently. Thus he was able to train a large number of men at the queen's expense. In an equally adroit move he purchased huge quantities of lead which he claimed were for reroofing. He then had the lead made into bullets. The weapons of the Irish were as advanced as O'Neill could make them. Guns were a relatively new technology, and O'Neill wanted his army to be trained in this expertise. In the mid-sixteenth century the Spanish had shown all of Europe what could be achieved with guns, and it was now obvious that no war could be fought without them. O'Neill acquired the most modern weaponry available to him, especially matchlock calivers and muskets. In teaching his people about guns, O'Neill reportedly gave them out to those who could demonstrate they could use one. The contemporary commentary notes, "All here, even the farmers, ploughmen, swineherds, shepherds, and the very boys have learned to use this weapon." Under the Great O'Neill's steady leadership, Ulster was united in purpose and organized brilliantly for war.

## VICTORY FOR THE IRISH
## AT THE YELLOW FORD

The enormous effort and preparation paid off when Hugh O'Neill and the Irish forces won a decisive battle against the English army. In August 1598 the Battle of the Yellow Ford was fought near the Blackwater River in southeastern Ulster. The English were attempting to advance in the area and decided to march forth in a column extending about a mile long. The Irish army of O'Neill, O'Donnell, and Maguire was waiting for them hiding in the hills, behind trees, and in the bog areas. When the Irish sprang their attack, the English were hardly able to respond. Confused and with little knowledge of the territory, they had not planned well. To their own expressed surprise, the badly defeated English army scattered and fled south to the Pale. It was the greatest victory by the Irish against an English army, and it alarmed Elizabeth terribly, not least because many of her soldiers deserted to join the Irish side. The forces were roughly equal at about six thousand men each, but the casualties were not. More than twelve hundred English were killed compared to two hundred Irish. King Philip II of Spain wrote to congratulate O'Neill on this great triumph and offered further help. Elizabeth could not ignore the victory or the possibility of Spanish military intervention.

Although at first she prevaricated, in 1599 Elizabeth sent a force of about twenty thousand men to Ireland and appointed Robert Devereux, Earl of Essex, lord deputy of Ireland to lead the army. This was a massive campaign. Essex was confident of quick victory over the Irish. In response Hugh O'Neill defiantly put his forces on the Blackwater River and declared a large part of Ireland free of English control. In spite of his huge army, Essex's campaigns in Ireland turned out to be desultory and mismanaged. He landed in Dublin, but instead of moving north to confront O'Neill he marched his forces around the southern part of the country in what he termed a show of strength. In doing so Essex totally misunderstood and underestimated his enemy. By marching around in this manner he left himself wide open to surprise hits from the Irish. His army suffered attack after attack in ambushes by an enemy who knew the countryside and the terrain. Many of Essex's soldiers were killed, and many more deserted in the face of such terrible odds.

## ESSEX AND O'NEILL MAKE A TRUCE

Frustrated, Essex finally marched north and made a truce with O'Neill in a famous meeting when the two met alone by a riverbank. Rumors about their conversation were rife at the time. It was even said that they discussed splitting the two countries between them, with O'Neill taking Ireland and Essex becoming King of England. Elizabeth was now in her late sixties, and rumors like this were endemic. Whatever the two men discussed, their truce was strictly against Elizabeth's wishes. In her fury on hearing about it, she sent Essex a letter ordering him back to the battlefield. With his depleted forces, Essex was reluctant to confront O'Neill in battle, and kept the truce. He eventually crept out of Ireland with only four thousand of the men with whom he had arrived. His failed campaign in Ireland had cost the British treasury £300,000, a sizable sum in those days. It serves as an example of the political uncertainty of the time that Essex was later discovered to have been involved in a plot to seize the English throne. Although at one time he had been a great favorite of hers, Elizabeth had Essex arrested. Politics in Elizabethan England held no place for sentiment or past achievement. Essex was sent to the Tower of London and in early 1601 was beheaded there.

The Great Hugh O'Neill, who defended Ulster against the Elizabethan armies. (*Lord Dunsany*)

To the Irish, O'Neill was now the great hero of Ireland's resistance. The Battle of the Yellow Ford meant that the English were now expelled from their garrisons in south Ulster. O'Neill then publicly challenged the notion that the English were bringing in a better, more civilized way of life. In a proclamation he declared, "I will employ myself to the utmost of my power . . . for the extirpation of heresy . . . [and] the delivery of our country of infinite murders, wicked and detestable policies by which this kingdom was hitherto governed." This was a clear condemnation of English policy in Ireland. Around the same time as his proclamation, O'Neill wrote up his "Articles Intended to be Stood Upon by Tyrone." Drawn up in November–December 1599, O'Neill promised to permit the Catholic religion to "be openly preached and taught throughout Ireland" and that "all Irishmen that will may learn, and use all occupations and arts whatsoever."

## MOUNTJOY ARRIVES IN IRELAND

Elizabeth recognized that the situation in Ireland now required decisive action against O'Neill. In place of the hapless Essex, the queen sent Charles Blount, Lord Mountjoy, to Ireland as lord deputy with an army of three thousand foot soldiers and three hundred cavalry. His specific mission was to break O'Neill's power and bring Ulster, the remaining outpost, under the Crown. At first Mountjoy was no more successful than Essex, and his initial attempt to take Ulster in October 1600 failed dismally at the Moyry Pass, commonly known as the Gap to the North. O'Neill deployed the same methods he had used at the Yellow Ford: stay on the defensive and attack the enemy on the march. Familiarity with the area helped the Irish beat back the English attempt to take the pass and proceed on to Armagh. In the end the English retreated to Dundalk and the Pale without establishing their desired military post at Armagh. In spite of this success O'Neill knew that he could not last forever against an English army that could easily replace its numbers and repeatedly reattack. With this in mind he decided to arrange for Spanish help. He also had the full support of the O'Donnells, led by the dynamic Red Hugh. O'Donnell's memory of his imprisonment in shackles in Dublin Castle was vivid, and as a result he hated and distrusted the English. He would risk anything to see Ireland rid of them.

## SPANISH ENCAMPMENT

Although Philip II of Spain had died, his successor Philip III was equally anxious to help the Irish. Convinced that O'Neill's campaign was a Catholic cause, he was happy to offer the Irish his military support. O'Neill decided to take the Spanish offer of help and arranged for a Spanish army to arrive in Ireland. After much correspondence the Spanish chose as their landing destination the small port of Kinsale on the southern coast. Situated about thirteen miles south of Cork City, today the harbor town of Kinsale is a picturesque area considered ideal as a holiday destination. Yet this seemingly modest small town once witnessed what many consider to be the death knell of Gaelic Ireland. Varied historical perspectives notwithstanding, the Battle of Kinsale is one of the colossal tragic notes in Irish history. Under the command of Don Juan de Agila, the Spanish army of 3,500 landed at Kinsale harbor on September 21, 1601. Almost immediately Mountjoy learned of the landing and gathered his forces to fight what he knew was to be a decisive battle. The English army numbered around 7,000. The Spanish encamped within the wall of Kinsale but were shortly surrounded by the English forces, who encircled the town on the north side. In spite of this, the Spanish held the town.

The choice of Kinsale as a landing place was agreed upon by the Irish and the Spanish. The Spanish were concerned about the size of their fleet and needed a harbor that could accommodate them. The weather also had to be considered, with winds a decisive factor in the final decision. O'Neill, who had originally wanted a landing on the northwest coast that would have been easier for his forces to reach, finally acquiesced. The landing at Kinsale turned out to be a disastrous decision. Hugh O'Neill had easily held Ulster against the English army because he knew the terrain very well. The forests and bogs of that region were home to him and he had the advantage there, but he was less familiar with Munster. O'Neill, O'Donnell, Maguire, and the other Irish chieftains had to march three hundred miles with their soldiers in order to link up with the Spanish army on the southern coast of Munster. They left in separate contingents. O'Donnell was accompanied by three MacSweeneys, O'Rourke, MacDermott, and leaders from north Connacht. O'Donnell's heroic march entered folklore as the glamorous champion marched his army over snowbound mountains, twice successfully dodging English attempts to stop him from reaching his destination. The Irish still celebrate his famous march in song with "O'Donnell Abu."

## THE BATTLE OF KINSALE

The armies of O'Neill and O'Donnell met on December 15 just north of Kinsale. Exact figures for their army are sketchy and vary with different accounts, but the combined forces of the Irish were probably around ten thousand, including three thousand cavaliers. The Irish army camped behind the English, who were now hemmed in on both sides. O'Neill's instinct was not to attack the English in the open but wait, perhaps to starve them out or draw them into a position where the Irish would have cover. Taking a different view, the less cautious O'Donnell and other Irish leaders argued for attack. Against his better judgment, O'Neill reluctantly agreed to a surprise attack on the English camp, with the plan that the Spanish would then sally forth into a formal battle. The Irish assault began before dawn on Christmas Eve, December 24, 1601.

Mountjoy saw the Irish approaching and launched an immense cavalry counterattack. The report that Mountjoy had been informed of the Irish attack beforehand is disputed by some historians. The Irish forces fought well, but their plan of attack was not well coordinated. By attacking as they did they were forced to fight in the open in formal-style battle, which proved to be catastrophic for them. It was quickly apparent that they could not match the English cavaliers and soon retreated. One source describes Hugh O'Donnell running around the rear of the retreat urging the Irish not to give up and to reenter the battlefield. It was in vain.

The Irish lost the battle almost before it started. Within a few hours it was all over. One of the major bewildering aspects of the battle was the lack of Spanish contribution. Communication between the Irish and the Spanish was apparently appalling. Incredibly the Spanish missed the signal (a musket shot) to enter the battle and consequently never participated in major combat. They claimed they did not hear the call. When the English set off noises to celebrate their win, the Spanish came forth, too late.

## "SO MUCH AS WAS LOST THERE"

Because of its great significance for Ireland, the Battle of Kinsale attracted its own historiography. Much debate surrounds the question of why the Irish lost a battle when they seemingly had so many advantages. Disagreement between the leadership on how to attack was a damaging factor, as was the disastrous failure of the Spanish to come forth, but the fact that the Irish army had to march so far to engage with the enemy added to the confusion and lack of apparent preparation for the actual battle. According to the contemporary account of Ó Clérigh, Irish losses were few, yet the sense of the real loss is palpable: "Though there fell at that defeat at Kinsale so few of the Irish that they would not miss them after a while . . . yet there was not lost in any defeat in recent times in Ireland so much as was lost there."

Although defeated, O'Neill's effort and genius in training his army for battle were admired even by his enemy. Lord Deputy Mountjoy, writing after the battle, lauded O'Neill's skill in preparing his men: "So far from being naked people, as before times, they were generally better armed than we, knew better the use of their weapons than our men, and even exceeded us in that discipline which was fittest for the advantage of the natural strength of the country, for that they being expert shot, and exceeding in footmanship all other nations." Yet the Irish were defeated. A new era was about to begin for Ireland.

The defeat at Kinsale was more than a bitter disappointment for the Irish; it marked the end of a way of life. The Great Hugh O'Neill, the last of the strong Irish chieftains, returned to Ulster with a heavy heart. The pain can only be imagined. According to Ó Clérigh's account, Hugh O'Donnell "was seized with great fury, rage and anxiety of mind; so that he did not sleep or rest soundly for the space of three days and three nights afterwards." O'Neill advised O'Donnell to go to Spain to Philip III and get rest and succor from him with the intention of obtaining more forces.

## A ROYAL FUNERAL FOR AN IRISH PRINCE

Red Hugh O'Donnell left for Spain within days of the defeat and was warmly welcomed by the Spanish king Philip III. O'Donnell's spirit of determination and his energy had not deserted him. He still believed that Ireland could be taken from the English. He paid homage to King Philip and then asked him for help in launching another attack on Ireland, which O'Donnell felt would be a success. Before the request could be fulfilled, Red Hugh mysteriously fell ill and died shortly afterward. The belief is that he was poisoned by an agent of the lord deputy. The Spanish honored him as a prince of Ireland, and Philip gave him a royal funeral. It is worth quoting the Four Masters to get a sense of the high esteem in which Philip of Spain held him:

> His body was conveyed to the King's palace at Valladolid in a four-wheeled hearse, surrounded by countless numbers of the King's state officers, Council, and guards, with luminous torches and bright flambeaux of beautiful wax-light burning on each side of him. He was afterwards interred in the monastery of St. Francis, in the Chapter precisely, with veneration and honor, and in the most solemn manner that any of the Gaels had been ever interred in before. Masses, and many hymns, chants, and melodious canticles, were celebrated for the welfare of his soul; and his requiem was sung with becoming solemnity.

Red Hugh O'Donnell was only thirty years old.

## THE FLIGHT OF THE EARLS

Submission did not come easily to O'Neill. Ultimately he was forced to surrender to Mountjoy in March 1603 at the Treaty of Mellifont. O'Neill did not know that Queen Elizabeth had died just days earlier. Even his submission has a fable attached to it. At the signing of the treaty Mountjoy took his seat at the head of the table, and the Irish sat to the side. When one of the Irish leaders remarked to O'Neill that he ought to be at the head of the table, O'Neill is said to have replied, "Where The O'Neill sits *is* the head of the table." The historical truth of this story is irrelevant; the sentiment that carried it to future generations says much about native feelings for the Great O'Neill.

Although O'Neill was confirmed as Earl of Tyrone and Rory O'Donnell, Red Hugh's successor, was made Earl of Tirconnell, their real status in Ireland was greatly reduced. There were to be no more autonomous lordships living in the old Gaelic manner. The lands of their people were taken by the Crown, and the earls were reduced to the ranks of mere subjects of the monarch, with no local power. The status of an independent Ulster was lost and the area, like the rest of Ireland, was divided into counties. The English-style county system in Ireland had been first introduced in the twelfth century by the English; it now became the geographic system for the entire country as the old traditional Gaelic regions disappeared. Realizing that English rule over Ireland was a reality that they could neither alter nor accept, the last of the Gaelic leaders of Ireland decided to leave for the Continent.

On a very poignant day in Irish history, September 4, 1607, the Great Hugh O'Neill, Rory O'Donnell, Cuchonnacht Maguire (who

Recently restored, Donegal Castle was once the elegant stronghold of the O'Donnell family. The O'Donnells lost it and their traditional lands after the Battle of Kinsale. (*Carmel McCaffrey*)

was Lord of Fermanagh), and nearly one hundred of the elite of the Gaelic aristocracy of Ireland, sailed away from Lough Swilly in northern Donegal and entered legend. Their tragic departure would be forever known as "the Flight of the Earls." It is one of the great watersheds in Irish history. The Irish princes never returned to Ireland, and their remaining lands were seized by the Crown.

## EXILE—THE FIRST IRISH DIASPORA

It is not clear whether Hugh O'Neill intended to return to Ireland invigorated by a new army. Evidence from letters suggests this, but whatever his intentions on leaving, he never returned. There was to be no continental help for the situation in Ireland. Yet this does not invalidate the motive for his departure and exile. It is not difficult to understand why the leadership left. The traditional power of the Gaelic chieftains and lords had been so eroded by the English conquest that they likely thought that they had no role to play in their country's future. Their ability to provide any meaningful leadership, protection, and prosperity for their people had been taken away. The English now ruled Ireland and controlled the future of the island. To stay in Ireland under such reduced circumstances where they were little more than chattel of the Crown was unthinkable for the Gaelic leadership. Exile seemed to be the only option.

By leaving they were also spared some of the painful aftermath of the defeat. In a symbolic gesture of the permanence of his victory, Mountjoy vandalized the ancient ritual site of Tullaghoge and smashed the inauguration seat of the O'Neills. He also captured and destroyed the O'Neill home of Dungannon Castle after Hugh O'Neill's departure. To add insult to injury, he then hung the flag of England, the St. George's Cross, from the tower. These apparently petty acts of vengeance toward a formidable enemy must have been felt necessary by Mountjoy finally to establish supremacy, both psychically and psychologically, over the defeated chieftain.

## THE DEATH OF O'NEILL AND A WAY OF LIFE

In 1616 Hugh O'Neill, undeniably one of the greatest heroes of Irish history, died in Rome. O'Neill and the other Gaelic aristocrats then quietly disappeared from Irish history—but not from the hearts and memories of the people they left behind. Their actions ensured that they would be remembered. Although they could have accepted the English conquest and become comfortable subjects of the Crown, they decided against this. Their decision to challenge the English and the anglicization of Ireland gave them a place of honor in the history of their country. By defending their way of life they forced Elizabeth to effect a violent and bloody military conquest, thus ensuring that her reputation in Ireland would be forever sullied and debased. The decision to fight for the survival of the old Gaelic order guaranteed that Ireland was not left with a dead past that had been willingly abandoned by her leaders, but a memory of heroes to be cherished.

The defeat at Kinsale marked the beginning of an entirely new way of life in Ireland. The dispossession of lands and the downward spiral of Gaelic society took on a momentum that was impossible to stop. Ireland was conquered. The old order with its myriad of bards, minstrels, and Brehons would cease to exist. Brehon Law was successfully outlawed and died out. It was the end of a once-vibrant culture. With the loss of status and wealth of the old Gaelic aristocracy there would be no one to patronize the Gaelic high poets, and their rank was greatly diminished. Other poets would follow, but they would herald a different era in Irish-language writings. The Gaelic language became the language of the poor as the English language spread among the educated Irish. One of the last of the great ancient bards, Daibhi Ó Bruadair, wrote in anguish (here in translation):

> The high poets are gone and I mourn for the world's waning, the families of those learned masters are emptied of sharp response.

The English conquest of Ireland appeared complete. The lands of the ancient chieftains now fell into the possession of new owners, with the English monarch in control. In Ulster a terrible experiment would follow—the plantation of the province—sowing the seed for the present-day conflict in the north of Ireland.

# [ 4 ]

# The Plantation of Ulster and the Erosion of Gaelic Ireland

❋

AT THE DAWN of the seventeenth century Ireland was in a state of disarray. There had been almost constant violent conflict for about eighty years. Whole families had been forcibly driven out of their homes, and most people did not remember a time of peace. Many of the native Irish chieftains were dispossessed of their traditional lands and were now tenants on their own property. Chieftains who considered themselves earls and princes were reduced to lives of poverty and servitude. Those who retained their land were subject to the Crown and were politically powerless in the face of invasion and so much foreign influence. Ordinary Irish people, who by long tradition had rights to land ownership, were now reduced to the level of vassals or serfs to the English Crown. A sense of disconnectedness with the past became dominant among the native population. All of this resulted in social disintegration.

## "NEVER IN THE WIFE"

One of the central features of ancient Irish culture was Brehon Law. Previous attempts to eliminate the old Irish law system had

failed, but with the physical removal of so many of the Irish aristocratic class it was now possible to eradicate the native system. The
authorities now condemned Brehon Law as barbarous and uncivi-
lized and orders went out that it was to be replaced by English common law. In 1606, under English government decree, Ireland was
placed under the English law code and Brehon Law specifically
outlawed. Some important distinctions were spelled out so as to ensure clarity regarding the new code. The Irish system of succession
was described as "inconvenient and unreasonable" because it relied
on a debate and an election on the death of a leader and not on primogeniture. Under the new law the eldest son must automatically
inherit as sole successor to property. Regarding the position of
women, the new common law stated that women could not hold
property independently of their husbands. Brehon Law was condemned because it endowed women "with the power of disposing
of such goods without the assent of their husbands." Now under
English law it was "resolved and declared by all the judges that the
ownership of such goods is adjudged to be in the husband and
never in the wife, as is the common law in such case." Irish women
thus lost their ancient rights to property ownership.

## THE EMPIRE WRITES BACK— THE GAELIC SCRIBES

Into this uncertainty came another struggle. Power over the written
word and the assertion of "truth" became part of the propaganda
war. This is an issue which has dogged all historical writings, but it
is one which is of particular significance to Ireland. History is indeed written by the winners, and the English Elizabethan writers
wasted no time in writing the "history" of Ireland accompanied by
the most pejorative comments and scathing attacks on Irish culture. A plethora of contemporary English authors, including Edmund Spenser, Richard Stanihurst, Edmund Campion, and John
Hooker, took it upon themselves to write their versions of the history of Ireland. From the Irish point of view, these English writers
wrote to justify the conquest.

    It soon became obvious to the Irish scribes that historical writ-
ing about Ireland was henceforth destined to reside in the hands of
the conquerors. Irish culture and customs would also be wide open

to unfavorable commentary by these vanquishers. The English authors of the Elizabethan conquest, and indeed for centuries afterward, wrote the history of Ireland from their own perspective, justifying their joint claims to sovereignty over the island and the written record of that history. These claims did not go unchallenged.

The assertion of privilege by English authors was met with a colossal response from Irish authors who wanted to set the record straight. Their efforts were indeed heroic, and future generations owe them much. In response to what amounted to a collapse of the old Gaelic way of life and to the many erroneous charges of barbarity in Irish society, Irish scribes began to compile and write the history of Ireland. To counteract what they considered spurious accusations in English writing of Irish savagery, crude social behavior, even bizarre ritual practices, they wrote in a detailed and systematic manner. Drawing on contemporary sources and accounts in the Irish annals kept for almost a thousand years, Irish scribes faithfully recorded the history of Ireland. They worked with a sense of purpose for a doomed civilization and sought to put forward a necessary alternative record to what they perceived as the bogus history being written by the conquerors. Chief among the Irish authors of the 1600s were the historians known as the "Four Masters" and Geoffrey Keating. The Four Masters were the Franciscan monk Brother Micheál Ó Clérigh and his three associates, Lughaidh Ó Clérigh, Fergus O'Mulconry, and Peregrine O'Duignan. Writing in the Irish language and consulting the written and oral evidence available to them, they left carefully documented records. Their major work is *Annála Ríoghachta Éireann*, or the *Annals of the Kingdom of Ireland*. Produced in 1632 it took more than two hundred years before the work was translated into English and published.

With equal fervor Geoffrey Keating wrote his *Foras Feasa ar Éirinn*, or *The Basis of Knowledge Concerning Ireland*, which he completed in about 1634. Keating compiled the lore and history of Gaelic Ireland in a lyrical literary style. Writing in Gaelic and Latin, Keating, like the Four Masters, consulted the monastic annals and the Brehons who were still living. In his introduction to his work he categorically states that the purpose in writing is to set the record straight so as to ensure that Ireland's illustrious past be recorded "lest so honorable a land as Eire, and kindreds so noble as those who had inhabited it, should pass away without mention or report of them." Giving a strong sense of his own time and the widespread feeling that the record of Irish history was being tainted, Keating emphatically declares that his work is a response to those English authors, whom he names, who are writing in a prejudiced and pejorative way about Ireland's past. Attacking their work, he claims that the English "have displayed no inclination to treat of the virtues or good qualities of the nobles among the native Irish who then dwelt in Ireland; such as to write on their valor and on their piety." Keating proceeds to write eloquently about the native Gaelic way of life with its emphasis on helping the lesser off in the communities and "insomuch that it cannot truthfully be said that there ever existed in Europe folk who surpassed them, in their own time, in generosity or in hospitality according to their ability." As for the support of literature and poets by the Irish, Keating asserts that he will "bear witness [to] the literary assemblies which were proclaimed by them, a custom not heard of among any other people in Europe."

Gaelic authors were unable to print or publish their work at the time they wrote. This medium was reserved for the English authors only, but the Irish had another way of getting their message preserved. The old tradition of writing out manuscripts by hand was still an active pursuit in Ireland. By using this means these Irish scribes saw to it that their witness to the history of Ireland was kept alive for future generations. The works of these Gaelic authors are considered the most authentic and extensive records of early Irish history and serve to counteract the English version of events. Yet it would be some time before their work was appreciated. The Irish version of events was for centuries relegated to the closets of what became a hidden culture. From this time on a dark curtain descended on Gaelic Ireland and its history. A poet of the period lamented that the books of Gaelic Ireland were "unjustly abandoned and decaying in corners." A long chain of English rulers climbed onto the Irish stage and took control. Years of struggle lay ahead.

## O'DOHERTY'S INSURRECTION

Elizabeth I died the very week that Hugh O'Neill surrendered, and a new era began. Elizabeth never married and left no direct heir.

The throne of England went to her cousin King James VI of Scotland. James's right to succession came from his English great-grandmother, who was the sister of Henry VIII, Elizabeth's father. Thus the first Stuart came to the throne and took the English title of James I. His government welcomed the departure of the Irish elite from Ulster, and the lands that they left were confiscated in December 1607 by the Crown.

At first the Irish felt hopeful at the accession of a Stuart and thought that they might be shown some tolerance because James's mother, Mary Queen of Scots, had been a devout Catholic. They hoped this might suggest some leniency for them. This hope was short-lived, and an effort by Cahir O'Doherty to restore some Gaelic lands was unsuccessful. O'Doherty's story is typical of the confusion some of the Irish experienced at this time about where they fit with the new order.

O'Doherty had actually been on the side of the English but found himself falsely accused of treason and arrested. When he applied to the lord deputy for help he got none but was released on bail. Sir George Paulet had been appointed the governor of Derry, and during a negotiation over land he struck O'Doherty in the face. This was the last straw for O'Doherty, and he declared he would endure the English no more. On April 18, 1608, he and his men rose in revolt, seized Culmore Fort, and attacked the city of Derry the following night. Derry was set on fire, Strabane was burned shortly after, and the rebellion looked like it might spread across all of Ulster, as some of the O'Cahans and O'Hanlons also came out in revolt. The English quickly put down the uprising, and O'Doherty was killed at the Rock of Doon, near Kilmacrennan. The O'Doherty insurrection and the support he received from other Ulster Irish added credence to a plan that had been taking shape for some time. The English believed they needed a more permanent solution for the unwilling and potentially rebellious subjects in Ireland. The plan they devised was the plantation of Ulster.

## EXPANDING TERRITORIES

It is important to understand events in Ireland within the context of broader British ambitions and experiences. By this time the British Empire was beginning to develop, with all its consequences for people around the world. Overseas possessions were expanding, and individual human rights were not a consideration in the imperial process of any of the European powers. The English slave trade began in 1562 when Captain John Hawkins, an English trader and naval commander, traveled to West Africa. Hawkins was one of the chief architects of the British navy. He sailed from West Africa to the Caribbean, where he then sold approximately three hundred native Africans whom he had captured in Africa. The British were fighting the Spanish over establishing colonies in the Caribbean at the time, and slave labor was important in building up the settlement. In another significant development, on December 31, 1600, the British East India Company was founded by Royal Charter granted by Elizabeth I. The company business, centered on India, had been established ostensibly to contest Dutch and Portuguese supremacy in the spice trade. This sole commercial aspect did not last long. Very soon the British East India Company also acquired auxiliary and military functions that rapidly exceeded its commercial activities, and British colonialism began in earnest. The East India Company became a major force behind British imperial expansion throughout the seventeenth and eighteenth centuries. Questions about Irish loyalty were not about to interfere with this newly expanding and ambitious empire. A solution had to be found to eliminate the threat of any further trouble in Ireland.

## THE PLANTATION OF ULSTER

The idea evolved among James and his courtiers to physically drive the remaining native Irish off the recently seized lands of Ulster and replace them with people from the Scottish lowlands and northern England. This "plantation" of new people was seen as a way of securing a population loyal to the Crown. It was believed—rather foolishly, as history records—that lasting peace in the region could be achieved only in this way. Lord Chichester, who had been made the new lord deputy of Ireland, thought the entire country might be transformed into loyal subjects using this system. He saw the departure of the earls as the perfect opportunity for "a plantation of the whole realm, and especially the fugitive counties." His plan for the entire country was never carried out, but the "fugitive counties" of the north were planted with people invited to come to

Ulster to displace the native population. Besides, it was widely known at the time that England and the Scottish lowlands were overpopulated, and this scheme gave the impoverished people of these countries the chance to obtain land cheaply. This solution proved to be so destructive for the province of Ulster that four hundred years later the social turmoil it caused has yet to be resolved.

## GUIDELINES FOR THE ULSTER PLANTATION

The information on the nature and guidelines for the plantation are contained in a parliamentary document known informally as "The Printed Book" of 1610, which spelled out the conditions for settlement. First and foremost it was to be a Protestant settlement, as this was seen as the only way to ensure loyalty. The anti-Irish nature of the document is striking. The native Irish were referred to throughout as the subordinate "mere Irish" and were not to be appointed to any position of power or authority in the disposition of land. Those given the lucrative contract for such disposition and the settlement of land were the "undertakers." It was categorically explained in rigid legal language what exactly the undertakers were to do and how the entire business of resettlement was to be conducted. Undertakers were first required to prove their Protestantism by taking the oath of allegiance before a judge and were to vouch also for the religion of their own families.

The new settlers were to be brought in from Scotland and northern England. These who were invited to come were mainly lowland farmers involved in arable farming and cattle-raising. Because of poor economic conditions in Scotland at the time, many of these people had in fact been landless. They were happy at the prospect of a better life. The potential settlers, or planters as they are sometimes referred to, were offered a lucrative arrangement to entice them to come. The seized territory was broken up into precincts, and these were divided into farming estates. Land taxes were to be low, about half the usual rate of the time, and the planters were to be granted exemption from taxes for the first four years. Estates of land ranging in size from one thousand acres to as many as two thousand were distributed. It was specified that each one-thousand-acre estate could have no more than twenty-four tenant families on it.

It was then immediately declared in law that no "mere Irish" were allowed to settle on these acres of confiscated land. Additionally, no one taking the land could hire the Irish in any way. Craftsmen and laborers were to come in from Scotland so that the entire community would be comprised of newcomers. Anyone found violating the law and hiring the native Irish would lose their property. Segregation was the basis for settlement. In each county that was planted, native Irish were segregated into defined areas set aside for them. Their tax rate was twice that of their new Protestant neighbors. Furthermore anyone who would take the oath of allegiance to the Crown was to be allowed to immigrate into Ireland as part of the plantation. This was a way of ensuring a Protestant settlement and avoiding even the outside chance of Catholics coming in from abroad. There was provision for a few of the native Irish—who were described as "deserving Irish"—to retain part of their traditional lands, but the terms were so harsh that these Irish soon faced financial difficulties. Feelings against Catholicism were fired up and included even an order to destroy the Catholic pilgrimage center of St. Patrick's Purgatory at Lough Derg, though this did not happen.

## THE PLANTATION TAKES HOLD

Between 1610 and 1630 more than forty thousand immigrants settled in Ulster. The area being planted covered the modern counties of Armagh, Tyrone, Donegal, Derry, Fermanagh, and Cavan. Counties Down and Antrim were excluded because successful private plantations had already been established there with a group of handpicked families from Scotland who would remain loyal subjects. Besides the population changes in Ulster, major physical changes were also occurring there. The undertakers, who were the most privileged of this new group, were required to build principal residences and place adequate defenses and bawns (Irish-style earth or stone fortresses) around their homes within three to five years or risk heavy fines.

To discourage reprisals and to act as possible defenses against a hostile native population, one of the laws stated that "the said undertakers, their heirs and successors, shall have ready in the house at all times, a convenient store of arms." The Protestant tenants were also to build stone homes to be clustered around this principal residence. As to the natives, they were to be given "an allowance of timber" to build homes in the areas to which they were assigned, but were warned that "there will be a proviso or forfeiture of their estates if they enter into actual rebellion." Woodland was cleared to make way for more land. The clearing of woods had started under Elizabeth as the developing British navy required wood for shipbuilding. Across the region small tilled fields replaced the open pastures of previous times.

Within a generation Ulster had changed physically, socially, and politically. In a bitter irony for the native Irish, the territory that was the last great symbol of the free and independent spirit of Gaelic Ireland became the most British part of the island. The monarchy achieved loyalty, but at a great price. In the twenty-first century, peace has yet to come to the region. The economy in the province was in the hands of the new Protestant settlers, and Belfast, the new town given a charter by King James in 1613, became the center of that Protestant economy. Catholics were excluded from this new community and, more important, from the economic life of the province. Those few Gaelic lords who had been granted land found it hard to survive and soon found themselves heavily in debt. Altogether native Ulstermen received less than a quarter of the lands that were distributed. And the amount of land in their hands steadily eroded as more and more land went to the planters.

## DANGER SIGNS IN ULSTER

It is an understatement to say that from the beginning the plantation was not a success in the way the framers had envisioned. For one thing, the native population remained a sizable and highly disgruntled community. In counties Donegal, Cavan, Fermanagh, and Derry the native Irish Catholics remained a majority. In spite of the initial plan to keep the two communities absolutely separate, not enough "support" families came in to Ireland to act as servants and laborers to the new landowners. This created a gap in the system because the planters could not exist without people to take on these servile roles. With no other option open to them, the native Irish became the underlings of the planters. The two communities therefore daily lived side-by-side but worlds apart.

From the beginning there was a great cultural divide between native and planter. The settlers never assimilated into the native culture. Unlike the Vikings in the ninth century or the Normans in the twelfth, the Ulster Protestants did not absorb their new surroundings and adopt an Irish identity. Separated by the very laws that brought them in, they remained a culture apart. Worse, they developed a kind of siege mentality. From their arrival in Ireland the planters were acutely aware of the size of the native population and the widespread hostility toward the plantation. Nor were they made to feel welcome by the authorities in Dublin. Many of the Scottish settlers were dissenters from the Anglican church. The "Black Oath" imposed in 1639 required that all Presbyterians swear to obey the king in all matters. In spite of being Protestant, their Presbyterianism put their absolute loyalty in doubt. Almost from the beginning of their coming to Ireland they were a people who felt their position was tenuous.

## THE COLONIAL PROCESS

The idea of settling a territory with people whose loyalty could be guaranteed was not unique to Ireland. It was fairly typical of the colonial process—Newgate prison, near London, helped populate the states of Virginia and Maryland in the new territories in America. English convicts were routinely transported to the new colonies in order to create an English population that would be culturally in sync with the mother country. In the Irish case, however, the native population was substantial compared to the new settlers, and the memory of land seizure and dispossession was to form an important part of the native psyche.

Although today religion is the feature most often expressed in describing the dividing lines of the communities, in fact it was not initially the most significant demarcation, nor the origin of the problem. The harsh process of plantation was largely at fault. Removing entire families from their homes and livelihoods and replacing them with new owners was a cruel act. The sense of dispossession was strong among the displaced population. Different ethnic origins and religious affiliations combined with this harsh reality to develop the fault lines in Ulster. Future generations of Catholics would struggle to redress what they saw as unlawful possession. On the other hand the planters would believe that they had rights of ownership and worked hard to build a new life for themselves.

## BEYOND ULSTER

Outside the Ulster region, things did not go well for the dwindling Catholic aristocracy. The position of the Protestant officials in Ireland had been greatly strengthened by so many Protestants settling in the country, and Catholic protests were given short shrift. When in 1613 the Lord Deputy Chichester asked for suggestions for items to be included in the upcoming parliamentary session, he rejected a request by six Catholic lords to consider abolishing the oath of supremacy. A Catholic could not take the oath because it involved a denouncement of the pope. After Chichester ignored this request, the Irish lords immediately wrote directly to the king with their grievances.

In their letter to the king they attempted to explain that the oath of supremacy was alienating good and loyal Catholic subjects by excluding them from positions of power, most especially in the legal profession. They argued that Catholics were not inherently disloyal, an allegation they believed was implied by the insistence on the taking of the oath. As a consequence of this requirement, they explained, Catholics were losing jobs throughout the country. The letter went on: "Your majesty's subjects here in general do likewise very much distaste and exclaim against the deposing of so many magistrates in the cities and boroughs of this Kingdom [Ireland] for not swearing the oath of supremacy in spiritual and ecclesiastical causes." The insistence on the taking of this oath for many offices, they explained, "did so much more alienate and affright and disquiet the minds of your well-affected subjects here especially." They continued that those being removed from their positions were quite fit to fulfill their posts but were being replaced by those "comfortable in that point [the taking of the oath] but otherwise unfit and uncapable to undertake the charges." The letter had some effect, and a number of boroughs were changed. But it remained a difficult time for Catholics as increasingly their religion relegated them to the status of second-class citizens. A more violent expression of this frustration was to occur, led by none other than a new generation of O'Neills.

## THE O'NEILLS ARE DOWN BUT NOT QUITE OUT—THE REVOLT OF 1641

The decade of the 1640s saw affairs in Ireland come to a boil. A myriad of political events, both Irish and English, converged to create a situation where unlikely alliances were forged by the Irish in various attempts to restore land titles and religious tolerance. There were now three branches of Christianity in Ireland. The original Gaelic population had for the most part remained Catholic as had the Gaelo-Norman settlers, now sometimes referred to as Old English. The Anglican Church of Ireland was the established church. Although all the cathedrals and church buildings had changed to the new religion, it remained a minority religion of the ruling class. The new planters who had moved to the Ulster region were Presbyterian and were not members of the established church. They were viewed with some skepticism by the Church of Ireland and were often referred to as "dissenters" or "nonconformists." It is thus historically incorrect to think of Irish Protestantism in monolithic terms. The divisions between Protestants in the early centuries after the Reformation were as real as the division between Catholics and Protestants.

## THE DEMANDS OF THE REBELS

The insurrection of 1641 was organized by a group of disgruntled Catholic aristocrats who were attempting to draw attention to the distress in which they found themselves. The leaders of the rebellion declared their loyalty to the Crown and claimed to wish to safeguard the monarch from growing Puritan influence in the English parliament. Within Catholic Ireland it was believed that the threat from a Puritan parliament was greater than any threat from the Anglican King Charles I, who was sympathetic to Catholicism. In a proclamation published in 1641 and called "The True Demands of the Rebels of Ireland," the Irish explained the reasons for the rebellion. First and foremost they declared their belief in "the Catholic and Apostolic Roman Church" and asked for religious freedom.

Sir Phelim O'Neill, one of the chief organizers of the 1641 rebellion. (*British Museum*)

Quickly they moved on to economic issues, requesting "that all lands and livings be restored unto those owners if yet living, or their undoubted heirs, and very nearest of kin that were taken away either in Queen Elizabeth's or King James' days." It is hard to ignore the very obvious reference to the plantation. The self-described "rebels of Ireland" were mostly dispossessed or demoted Catholic gentry of Ulster and their supporters. The group was led initially by Sir Phelim O'Neill, Rory O'Moore, and Lord Maguire.

Sir Phelim O'Neill was born in Ulster in 1604 to the aristocratic O'Neill family. He was too young to remember the events that led to the departure of so many of his family members, but he was well aware of the history of his own people. He was not a marginalized personality with little credibility; Sir Phelim was an elected member of the Irish parliament for Dungannon and had studied law at the Lincolns' Inn, Dublin. He became disenchanted with the lack of constitutional support for the evicted Catholics of Ulster. Removed from their lands, their financial and political situation was increasingly hopeless. O'Neill's frustration led him to take more direct action. A rebellion was planned, but it was probably doomed from the start because he was not a military commander and had no military experience.

The plan that was devised was that forces led by O'Neill would lead a rebellion throughout Ulster beginning with the taking of Charlemont Castle on October 23. Simultaneously Rory O'Moore would take Dublin Castle on the same date. The Dublin scheme was foiled, but O'Neill managed to seize Charlemont Castle by arranging to be invited there as a guest. At first the uprising was somewhat limited, but within a short time the whole of Ulster was in an uproar.

## CATHOLICS MASSACRE THE SETTLERS

Many of the Ulster Catholic families were involved, and the rebels were more successful than they could have imagined. A swarm of Irish family militias swept across Ulster: the Maguires took over Lisnarick, the McCaffreys easily took the town of Archdalestown, and the McMurrays took Garrison. Armagh, a significant strategic point, fell to the rebels. The leaders had depended on the support of the Gaelic families in the area, and they got much more than they anticipated. Soon the rebellion was out of control. The upsurge of spontaneous support turned the uprising into a massive bloody campaign far beyond anything the organizers had anticipated.

Phelim O'Neill's brother had declared that "no Scotsman should be touched," and the O'Reillys told supporters "not to meddle with any of the Scottish nation, except they give cause." These cautious remarks were in vain. Catholics who worked as servants and laborers to the planters and had not been a part of the initial rebellion joined in to make it a bloodbath. In the space of two days, October 23–25, 1641, thousands of Protestant men, women, and children were massacred by angry Catholics. The actual numbers have been in dispute for centuries, and the only point that historians agree on is that casualties numbered in the thousands. There is no mistaking the passion behind the behavior of the protagonists as they pursued their prey. The victims were stripped of their clothes and often beaten to death, and some were driven naked out of their homes to die later of exposure. Some were driven into rivers where they drowned. The attacks were mostly directed at those who were the direct beneficiaries of the plantation.

The revolt and its consequences would seem to have been an inevitable consequence of the plantation that had gone on for twenty years at the beginning of the century. Whatever the ultimate intentions of the rebel leadership, they could not halt the violence once it started. Historians argue about the widespread reason for this bloodbath, and some suggest that there were many other factors involved. The exclusion of Catholics from public office was one. The rise of Puritan power in England might have constituted a further threat to the Catholic position. Yet it seems impossible that the dispossessions did not play a major role in the uncontrolled passion and hatred behind the gruesome events of those few days in October. The widespread anger that found cathartic expression in the actions taken by the native Irish against the settlers can only be understood within the context of land theft and the bitterness over so much loss. That the beneficiaries and living symbols of this loss were in view daily must have rankled greatly.

## THE REBELLION SPREADS, AND OWEN ROE O'NEILL JOINS IN

News of this carnage quickly spread to England, where it filled broadsheets. Exaggerated rumors of the numbers killed were widely reported. The English parliament responded by sending in an army to crush the rebellion—unsuccessfully. Determined to push on with their cause, the leaders of the insurrection gained traction the next year when they were joined by Owen Roe O'Neill, nephew to the great earl, Hugh O'Neill. News of his participation was greeted with joy in Ireland.

Owen Roe O'Neill was born about 1590 and was just a boy when he left Ireland. He had risen to the rank of colonel and general in the Spanish army. He remained aware of events in Ireland and was eager to take part in the rebellion. Because of other military commitments on the Continent he was not able to be in Ireland when the revolt broke out in 1641, but Phelim kept him informed of events. He arrived in the summer of 1642 and landed on the coast of Donegal close to his ancestral homelands, bringing with him a large supply of arms, ammunition, and two hundred Irish officers who also had experience in foreign wars. Unfortunately those he was to lead in Ireland had none. He was well received in Ulster where many of the Irish considered him their natural leader. Owen Roe O'Neill was immediately appointed commander-in-chief of the rebel forces in Ulster.

By this time the other provinces of Leinster, Munster, and Connacht had also joined in, as had some of the Catholic clergy. In March 1642 Edmund O'Reilly, the Catholic archbishop of Armagh, gave the Catholic church's formal approval of the rebellion. This was to have significant results. It was under the guidance of the Catholic clergy that a federation was formed. The only sense of organization in this affair seemed to come from the clergy. Calling themselves the Confederate Catholics of Ireland, a gathering was organized in October 1642 of all rebels and clergy at Kilkenny. They declared themselves to be the governing body of Ireland. The confederation set out their aims for a restoration of Catholic lands and religious freedom but also stressed the king's prerogative. This was an important declaration because in England serious political divisions were occurring as Parliament was challenging the king's position. In Ireland the influential James Butler, Earl of Ormond, of one of the old Gaelo-Norman families, defended the king's cause and formed an Irish royalist army. These were mostly made up of Church of Ireland members, and they formed an alliance with the confederates who believed that the king's side held better expectations for Catholics.

Hope for the cause was given a boost in 1645 when Giovanni Battista Rinuccini arrived as papal nuncio with a large supply of arms and money from Pope Innocent X. Rinuccini took control of the confederates, but this proved to be a mistake. He alienated the Irish royalists, and the confederate army failed in an attempt to take over Dublin. Dublin was of strategic importance to the control of Ireland and was the rebellion's first failed target of 1641. Ultimately the rebellion collapsed mostly because of mismanagement. The revolt and brief attempt at self-government ended. Yet this did not end the unrest in Ireland; it resulted in a slight hiatus before the Irish were to suffer large-scale slaughter under Oliver Cromwell. Events in England had overshadowed Irish affairs throughout the 1640s, but now internal English politics were about to overwhelm the Irish situation.

## OLIVER CROMWELL—
## THE KILLING OF THE KING

The English Civil War had its origins in the English Reformation. Although the English church had broken with Rome, some thought that too much of the flavor of Roman practices remained and ought to be cleansed. The Puritans were a growing influence in English Christianity but were generally viewed as troublemakers by the established Church of England. The basis of Puritan belief was that the Bible was the literal word of God and that salvation was obtained by hard work. They viewed excess pleasure and luxury as sinful. This would eventually bring them into conflict with what they perceived as the royal family's opulent lifestyle and the liturgical trappings of the established church.

Charles I came to the English throne in 1625 upon the death of his father James I. He is often described as having a relaxed view of Christianity but of being autocratic and aristocratic in nature. He believed in royal supremacy and sometimes conducted his affairs in a high-handed manner. With the growing Puritan influence in the House of Commons, the king was soon on a confrontational path with its members. To make matters worse, his wife was the French Catholic Queen Henrietta Maria, who had a strong sense of the rights of kings and constantly urged Charles to stand up to those who might oppose him. She was also trying to persuade the king to grant toleration to Catholics. The Puritan members of Parliament became openly critical of the king and highly suspicious of his queen.

As king and Parliament cruised toward a collision course the king decided to take action to protect himself. In January 1642 Charles failed in an attempt by his guards to arrest his leading Puritan opponents inside the House of Commons. This was an outright attack on parliamentary privilege and, not surprisingly, enraged members of Parliament. The king had an intense opponent in the person of Oliver Cromwell. A modest country squire born in Huntingdon in 1599, Cromwell was the driven leader of the Puritans. He believed fervently in his mission as an emissary of God, and most of his actions reflected this. As a young man he became a religious zealot while studying at Cambridge, and his faith soon influenced his thinking and appearance. He was austere in composure and manner and wore dark or black clothes. These attributes were hallmarks of the Puritan style. The women wore simple black dresses with their hair up, and generally eschewed any type of decoration. Cromwell entered Parliament in 1640 when he was elected to represent Cambridge City. His magnetism and ability to speak convincingly gave him a commanding presence in the English parliament. He became a leading figure for the Puritan cause. The Puritans demanded that the king recognize the power of Parliament over the monarchy. When it became obvious that the king would not cede power and would use the army to maintain his position, Cromwell amassed an army to take on the king's men.

## THE ENGLISH CIVIL WAR

In August 1642 Charles I raised his standard at Nottingham and declared that he would defend the monarchy and his religion against all attack. This was a direct reference to the parliamentarians and is considered to be the beginning of the English Civil War. The two armies, the Puritan parliamentarians and the king's army, first faced each other in October 1642 at the Battle of Edgehill. Although that confrontation ended in stalemate, other bloody battles followed. Cromwell developed his army into a well-trained modern force and gave it the name the New Model Army. In the end it defeated the king's men, and Charles was arrested.

At his trial before Parliament, Charles was accused of trying to assemble a foreign army, including some Irish, to help him retain the English throne. The charge for this was treason. What remained of the Irish aristocracy had indeed supported Charles against the Puritans. With their own interests in mind, the Irish had promised the king an army to fight Cromwell and Parliament. It was thought among the Irish that of the two the king, with his Catholic wife, would be more favorable to the Irish cause. Puritan hatred of Catholicism was endemic, and the Irish had good cause to fear a Puritan government.

When the king was found guilty of treason and beheaded in Whitehall on January 30, 1649, Parliament became the sole form of government. The Puritans were in control of the House of Commons, the monarchy was abolished, and a Commonwealth was declared. The remaining members of the royal family, including Charles's eldest son, fled to the Continent. England became a republic.

## CROMWELL IN IRELAND

Having secured England for Puritan rule, Cromwell now turned his attention to Ireland. He had long held a grudge against the country and wanted retribution for the 1641 slaughter of Protestants, an event much publicized in England. Gruesome details of the horrific bloodbath and gross exaggerations of the numbers killed had been widely reported. The continuing revolt in Ireland and support for the king's cause would have to be eradicated. At a general council at Whitehall in March 1649, when Cromwell was asked about his plans for Ireland, he answered that he intended to bring the army there out of "duty to God . . . for all the world knows their [Irish] barbarism." He viewed the 1641 massacre as proof of evil and ungodliness in the Catholic Irish and professed strong feelings of revenge. He also stated that his hatred for the Irish was not confined to those of the Roman faith only. He had little respect for the Anglican Church of Ireland—"in a manner they are as bad as Papists"— and considered the liturgy and services of that church too close to Roman practices. The support of the Church of Ireland for the king's position also infuriated him. Other issues figured in his Irish campaign: Irish revenues were an economic asset for England's coffers, so bringing the country under control was a necessity.

Cromwell landed in Ireland in August 1649 with a well-trained army of 20,000 men and a large navy to support them. He did not formally disestablish the Church of Ireland, but he immediately removed most of the religious symbols from church buildings. His troops took control of both Protestant cathedrals in Dublin and Trinity College. He stabled his horses in St. Patrick's Cathedral and is said to have publicly burned the Book of Common Prayer, denouncing it as a Mass book. Many Catholic and Church of Ireland clergy went into hiding. Cromwell and his army then went on a rampage throughout the country, burning Catholic churches and wreaking havoc. Cromwell's actions in Ireland are burned into Irish memories to this day. On September 11, 1649, he attacked the town of Drogheda and slaughtered approximately 2,700 people. This figure is thought to be close to the total population of the town. In fact, many of the slaughtered included English army officials acting on behalf of the king to protect the town.

A printed version of a letter that Cromwell sent to the House of Commons at the time has survived and confirms the Drogheda carnage. Cromwell asserts that "many inhabitants" were among those killed by his forces at Drogheda. There can be little doubt that he believed the massacre was God's justice. He was well satisfied with the bloody result and remarked, "I am persuaded that this is the righteous judgment of God upon those barbarous wretches who have imbrued their hands with so much innocent blood," a reference to the 1641 massacres. He also reported audaciously that captured Catholic priests "were knocked on the head promiscuously."

A second massacre was carried out on Wexford town a month later when about 2,000 people were killed. Cromwell's opponents could expect little mercy from God's emissary. Under Cromwell's army Ireland became a wretched place. Contemporary descriptions of orphaned children wandering the roads were rife. Hundreds were rounded up and executed, including Sir Phelim O'Neill. Owen Roe O'Neill died suddenly of apparently natural causes in 1649, but rumors of his poisoning were widespread at the time. The only real disaster for Cromwell in Ireland occurred in May 1650 at Clonmel. When his army breached the town wall, they walked into a trap set by Hugh Dubh O'Neill, nephew of Owen Roe, who was defending the town. As many as 2,500 of Cromwell's men were killed, making it the worst defeat the New Model Army had suffered anywhere. Irish historians note that Cromwell was conspicuously silent about Clonmel in his dispatches.

## CROMWELL'S SETTLEMENT OF IRELAND

The Cromwellians were relentless in their punishment of those who opposed them. Vast areas of land were seized by the Cromwellian army, and Catholics were removed from their lands in those parts of Ireland where previously they had been left undisturbed. Only landowners who could prove that they had been constantly on the side of the parliamentarians were spared. Cromwell returned to England in June 1650 and never left Britain again. But his campaigns in Ireland were the final death knell for a significant number of Irish landowners. In 1652 the Act of Settling Ireland was passed by the English parliament. Under this act landowners who had been disloyal to Parliament were to lose their lands. One hundred five named rebels or Irish royalists were to be cleared from their land or forced to move west of the Shannon River to Connacht, a measure known in Ireland as the "To Hell or Connacht" bill. The English army had not been paid for its campaign in Ireland, and this was a way to compensate them. Lands in ten counties were to be divided among the army, many of whom were mercenaries. These counties included Armagh, Down, Antrim, Laois, Offaly, Meath, Westmeath, Limerick, Tipperary, and Waterford. Under the arrangement about 2,000 acres per man were distributed. In spite of this largess, many soldiers received nothing for the wars in Ireland.

Significantly, this new wave of dispossession did not result in a new onslaught of immigrants into Ireland on the scale of the Ulster plantation. Practically all of Cromwell's soldiers sold off their land to wealthy English landlords. While a few of these came to settle in Ireland, most did not. The majority continued to live in England while holding land in Ireland. Irish rents would support the lifestyle of these new absentee landlords. Some Irish-based landlords bought this available land, thereby adding to their estates. In spite of the law, not all Irish landlords ended up west of the Shannon. Nevertheless the Cromwellian land seizures resulted in a dominant class of mixed origins, many of whom had little interest in the affairs of Ireland. These "squatters," as they came to be called in local vernacular, formed the backbone of the Irish ruling class for the next 250 years.

## RESTORATION OF THE MONARCHY

For a while the Puritans retained a firm hold on England, but rifts soon began to appear in their ranks. They were heavy-handed in their dealings with ordinary people and the popular culture. They ordered theaters closed and coffee houses shut down in an effort to impose a simple but austere lifestyle. They also banned all royalist publications in order to stop information that might offer another viewpoint. In spite of these efforts, disagreement among them grew, and the country became restless with the enforced rigorous lifestyle. When Cromwell died in 1658, there was no one who could hold the government together the way he had. The Puritan influence in Parliament receded.

The Restoration of the monarchy came about in 1660 when Charles II, son of the beheaded Charles I, was invited by Parliament to return from exile to become the new king of England. The Commonwealth established by Cromwell was abandoned, and many of the Puritans left for the New World and settled in the American colonies. At first Charles announced that he would restore the Catholic lands seized from the Irish, but this proved a difficult thing to do as most members of his court now owned lands in Ireland and were not about to surrender them easily. Charles did not wish to take on some of his senior courtiers. As a result of his diffidence, most of Cromwell's damage stood. The Irish who lost their land never recovered their property, and Catholic land ownership remained low.

## RELIGION IN THE LATE 1600s

After 1660 the Catholic church was able to reestablish itself in Ireland due to the influence of the Jesuits, who were formed in the previous century as part of the Counter-Reformation. The Jesuits found Ireland to be a challenge as they sought to establish a more ritualistic church. The Irish church had always been an irregular church, and the actual practice of Catholicism was lax to nonexistent. Kinship relationships mattered most, with religion playing a secondary role. Many pagan practices survived from ancient times and frequently took the place of a more formal religion. Yet Catholicism was kept alive by the acceptance of many clergy of these irregular practices and by an unwillingness on the part of many Irish to convert to a religion that was introduced by the English aggressors.

Nevertheless the Protestant population almost doubled during the years 1652–1672, and by the 1670s it was around 300,000. Two-thirds of these were members of the Church of Ireland which, though it was the religion of the elite, saw itself as representing another version of Irishness and, like the Catholic church, claimed to descend from St. Patrick. Supported by taxation, the Church of Ireland was sure of an income and showed little interest in converting the mass population. It had its intellectual center in Trinity College, Dublin, founded in the 1590s. Approximately one-third of the Protestants were Presbyterians residing in the northern part of the country, but these people were less assimilated into Irish life. Population estimates for the entire country are uncertain, but Sir William Petty estimated a total population in 1672 of 1.1 million. This is now regarded as too low, but exact figures remain unclear.

## THE CATHOLIC THREAT OF JAMES II

When Charles II died in 1685 he was succeeded by his brother James II, who had become Catholic. His years of exile in the French court had influenced James in his religious choice. Later in life he had taken as his second wife the Italian Catholic Mary of Modena. James planned to return his kingdoms (Ireland, Scotland, Wales, and England) to the Roman church. Irish Catholics believed they were in luck, and hope again rose that land titles would be restored. To show his goodwill toward Ireland's Catholics, James appointed a Catholic landowner, Richard Talbot, to be Earl of Tirconnell and head of the Irish army. Talbot was also appointed to the post of lord deputy, making him the highest-ranking official in Ireland. The Irish army was given a complete overhaul, and many Protestant officers were removed and replaced by Catholics. Likewise in other agencies, including positions in the Dublin parliament, Talbot removed many Protestants and replaced them with Catholics. As beneficial as this was for Catholics, James did not move on the issue of land title. The Catholic gentry of Ireland remained hopeful that he would restore some of the land lost under Cromwell. This was not to be.

In 1688 James had a son with his second wife. When this son was baptized Catholic, alarm bells sounded throughout Westminster. James had already aroused fear and suspicion at court. He had alienated the English aristocracy by establishing an alliance with Catholic France. Growing even more brash, he moved against some English bishops and had them arrested for not conforming to the Roman Catholic faith. Now, with the birth of a direct heir, the possibility of a Catholic succession, with its implied allegiance to Rome, became a major concern for Parliament. A solution had to be quickly found. The newborn son had to be disinherited. This was accomplished by breaking the law of succession.

## WILLIAM AND MARY
## GIVEN THE ENGLISH THRONE

James had an older daughter, Mary, from his first marriage. She had been raised Protestant and by now was married and living in Holland with her Dutch Protestant husband, Prince William of Orange. Parliament appealed to William and Mary to come to England and take the English throne. It would not be a simple takeover, and James was expected to resist. With this in mind William gathered his forces and landed in England in November 1688. James tried to defend against the arrival of William's military and the warm welcome they received from the English landholders. Unfortunately for James the army mutinied when the soldiers refused to take orders from their Catholic officers to defend James's position. Isolated by his abandonment by the English parliament and army, James fled to France. In February 1689 William III and Mary II were formally declared to be joint sovereigns of England, Scotland, and Ireland. In Scotland the Scots were outraged at this removal of a Stuart from the throne. The Scottish Highlands were to remain loyal to the Stuart line of James until well into the following century.

## JAMES II IN IRELAND WITH
## PATRICK SARSFIELD

James was not yet beaten, and he managed to arrange for the support of a French army. He was also supported by some Scots who were willing to fight to restore him to the throne. In addition he was in touch with Tirconnell, who assured him of much support from the Irish. The Irish remained hopeful of land restoration under the Catholic king. James decided that the path to the English throne was through Ireland. By now Tirconnell was sixty years old and in ill health, but he was willing and anxious to help James regain the throne. James landed in Cork on the southern coast of Ireland in March 1689 with a French army of approximately three thousand men and officers. Chief among his supporters who traveled to Ireland with him was a young Irish officer, Patrick Sarsfield. Sarsfield had been born in Lucan in County Dublin in 1650 to a wealthy Catholic family. He was the grandson of Rory O'Moore, one of the leaders of the 1641 rebellion. Like the sons of other Irish Catholic aristocrats, Patrick was educated in France where he attended a French military school and then fought in the French army. He then joined James's army in the life guards and in 1688 went into exile with the king. Now Sarsfield was supporting James in his attempt to regain the throne. Sarsfield was an excellent commander and was made brigadier general in the Irish army. James also had with him about one thousand Scots and the few English who still supported him. Within a year he raised about twenty thousand men from the ranks of the Irish dispossessed and the few remaining landowning Irish Catholics. For the Irish this was to be the last stand to attempt recovery of ancient lands and expiate the property dispossessions of the past hundred years.

This Jacobite army marched around Ireland establishing support where it could and found favor in the provinces of Leinster, Munster, and Connacht. Ulster proved more difficult. With so many new Protestant settlers, support for a Catholic king was not high. Protestants' fear of losing their lands and economic position was fundamental to the political climate in Ulster. Derry became a great symbol of Ulster Protestant resistance. The walled city had been under siege from Tirconnell's men from April 1689, and James joined them in an attempt to enter the city. James was not successful and was met with cries of "no surrender." One of his generals eventually advised him to leave, but the situation at Derry did not improve. The siege of Derry lasted for 105 days until the attempt was abandoned by the Jacobites.

## JAMES II'S IRISH PARLIAMENT

James was more welcome when he arrived in Dublin. He summoned a sitting of the Irish parliament which met from May 7 to July 20, 1689. Because Tirconnell had removed Protestants from positions of power and replaced them with Catholics, the Dublin parliament of 1689 had only 6 Protestant members of 260 members. Although to James the main issue was the regaining of the English throne, the Irish had other concerns in mind. There was much discussion on the land issue. The members of the Dublin parliament wanted the Cromwellian settlers thrown out and the land taken by Cromwell restored to the Irish. Ownership of land was central to economic power throughout Europe in the centuries before the Industrial Revolution. Economic survival, for the rich or the poor, depended on land; this is why the issue was fought over so bitterly.

When the Dublin parliament repealed the Act of Settlement, it sent chills through the homes of the Protestant landowners, especially in Ulster. The proceedings of the parliament demonstrate the mood of the Irish people, or at least of Irish Catholics, of the period. The opening words of the Declaratory Act are nationalist in nature and declare valiantly that "his majesty's realm of Ireland is, and hath been always a distinct Kingdom from that of his majesty's realm of England." This is an interesting declaration coming at the end of a century that saw the Irish repeatedly aligning with the monarchy in the hope of having land issues resolved to their own satisfaction. Some enthusiastic Irish even suggested establishing Ireland as a separate kingdom with James as king. This suggestion met with no agreement from James, who viewed Ireland only as a stepping-stone to the English throne. He refused to agree to any law that would break the political ties between the two countries. James was obviously uncomfortable with the situation in which he found himself but needed the Irish in order to battle William.

## PREPARING FOR BATTLE

William meanwhile was aware that James had gathered a large army in Ireland and had garnered much support. William decided that a confrontation was necessary to put an end to any possible threat from James. In June 1690 William traveled to Ireland and landed in Carrickfergus near Belfast in Ulster. He fully realized that his best support would be in that region of the country, among those who did not wish to see a restoration of Catholic lands. He arrived in grand style with a fleet of approximately 300 vessels. As word reached William of the Dublin parliament's enthusiasm for James, William feared that James would declare himself King of Ireland and King of England in Dublin. With so many of the Scots against William, they might also recognize James as King of Scotland, and the entire kingdom would fall into James's hands.

William had sizable support for his side. He had an army of approximately 36,000 troops. Like James, he had a number of French on his side—Protestant French Huguenots who were forced out of France in 1685 when the freedom to practice their religion was revoked. The French Protestants had their own unfortunate history. In the previous century Protestants in France had been slaughtered in what became known as the St. Bartholomew's Day massacre. The French Protestants feared a repeat attack, so in the 1680s many fled. Many of them had gone to Holland and become part of the army that accompanied William to Ireland.

Dublin was the great prize in the battle that would decide the English throne. James had to defend it, and William knew he had to take it. After they landed in County Down, the Williamite forces advanced south to Dundalk in the direction of Dublin. James marched north to meet them at Dundalk. The Jacobite army is estimated to have had 25,000 men. James at first held Dundalk but retreated south of the Boyne River when he was told that William had 50,000 men in the nearby town of Newry. William's forces advanced to the Boyne on June 30, 1690. James and his son-in-law faced each other's army on either side of the river. The Battle of the Boyne took place on July 1 (by the old calendar). It is now commemorated on July 12 each year. It is one of the greatest European battles which irrevocably shaped British history—the winner would hold the throne of England and with it the future direction of British history.

## JAMES'S DEFEAT AT THE BOYNE

The day did not go well for James. His army was poorly trained and undisciplined. For reasons that are not clear, Patrick Sarsfield, James's ablest and most experienced commander, was underutilized by the king. James may have underestimated his value, a costly mistake. Many of James's men were raw recruits, deposed chieftains who wanted a settlement to the religious and land question and believed they had no choice but to fight. They were not regular soldiers, and few had any experience of warfare. The Williamites, on the other hand, were a well-trained and experienced force. They were also commanded by officers who had fought many campaigns on the Continent. James proved himself a bad commander and

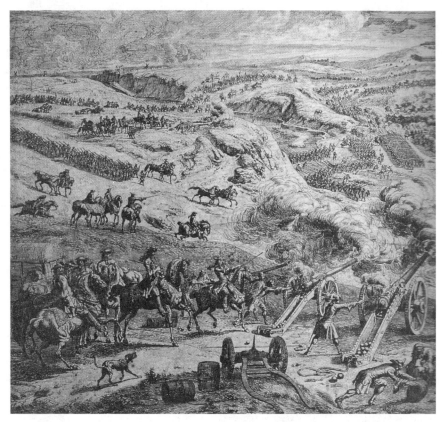

The Battle of the Boyne was the great dividing line in Ireland's history. Following the defeat of King James II, the old Gaelic way of life finally gave way to that of an English-speaking elite. (*National Library of Ireland*)

acted confused in battle. In those days kings were expected to be generals and march at the head of their army. By the end of the day James had fled his post, and his army was in full retreat. There is a story in Ireland that when James fled to Dublin he was greeted at the city gates by Lady Tirconnell, wife of the head of the Irish army. He is said to have commented to her that her fellow countrymen knew how to run well, to which she replied, "So do you sir, in fact I think you won the race."

Shortly afterward William's army pushed farther south and took Dublin and eastern Ireland. James, defeated, left for France about three days later, but the Irish fought on, trying to defend other Irish cities. They hoped they might be able to defend the rest of Ireland, reattack Dublin, and take it back. The Irish were clearly fighting for more than the restoration of James to his throne; they were fighting for their own economic future. The hope that something could be salvaged from the fight was hard to extinguish. In August, when the Williamites were fighting to capture Limerick, Patrick Sarsfield made a daring and successful raid behind enemy lines, which prevented the Williamites from taking Limerick at the first siege of the city. The news of this daring feat secured his reputation as the true lead commander of the Jacobite forces and a hero to the Catholic Irish.

William took stock of the situation and in spite of Sarsfield's success in defending Limerick believed that he was in a winning position. He left Ireland in September, secure in the fact that his forces would ultimately be successful. In this he was correct. The war continued into 1691, and on June 30 William's forces managed to cross the strategic Shannon River. Within a few weeks they had taken the city of Galway. The capture of the city did not come easily for the Williamites because the Irish fought literally to their dying breath, with about seven thousand giving their lives. It was a terrible defeat for them. Limerick remained the last important holdout. Tirconnell was proceeding to prepare Limerick for a second siege when on August 14, 1691, he died suddenly of apoplexy. Immediately Patrick Sarsfield formally assumed the leadership of the Irish army. He defended Limerick until he concluded it was useless to continue, and surrendered. With the fall of Limerick went all the Catholic Irish hopes of regaining their lost land.

## THE WILD GEESE

In October 1691 the Treaty of Limerick, which followed the defeat, was signed. At first sight the terms were generous. Catholics were given the right to worship. They were also granted rights to any property they owned even though they had fought against William. Those who thought the terms seemed too good to be true were correct, because the conditions of the treaty concerning Catholic rights came to nothing. The treaty was never fully ratified by the English parliament. Shortly afterward laws against Catholics would overturn it completely. Nonetheless the military articles in the treaty permitted any of the Irish who wished to be given liberty and transport to go abroad. Many Irish exercised this option. Patrick Sarsfield left in December. About fourteen thousand of the Irish army also departed Ireland. Most of them went to France and, with Sarsfield, formed an Irish legion in the French army—the Irish Brigade. Others who left scattered throughout continental Europe. They are referred to as "The Wild Geese."

In a postscript two years later at the Battle of Landen on July 23, 1693, Patrick Sarsfield was mortally wounded and died on the battlefield in Flanders. When he saw the blood flowing from his body, he is reputed to have said, "Oh, if only this were for Ireland." These words are ubiquitous in Ireland's story: so many of Ireland's heroes died with an "if only" on their lips. The conquest of Gaelic Ireland was now complete, but those who believed this would bring lasting peace were mistaken.

# [ 5 ]

# *Catholic Dispossession: The New Elite*

THE EIGHTEENTH CENTURY in Ireland is a period of great historical curiosity, not the least because there are many varying pictures of Irish life at this time. In spite of the fact that it was a century of peace and prosperity, it was also a politically uneven period. As the century opened the main concern for the ruling class both in England and in Ireland was the curtailment of Catholic power. Although the Catholic upper class had been defeated and removed from their lands, the Catholic religion remained the religion of the majority of people in Ireland. This defeated class of people was anything but quiescent, a fact that gave rise to the fear that a resurgence of Catholic influence would result in a loss of position for the new ruling class, the members of the established Church of Ireland.

In the English parliament the question of succession to the English throne had to be addressed in order to avoid another Catholic threat. Parliament decided that the law had to be changed in order to guarantee a Protestant monarchy. This was done with the 1701 Act of Settlement. Under this act, Protestant succession was secured by proclaiming that in the future no Catholic could sit on the throne of England. This law remains in force to this day. Just as important, this act fully established parliamentary supremacy, finally settling the power dispute between monarchy and Parliament. In keeping with the new parliamentary powers, other changes were made that curtailed the monarch's power. The Settlement Act prohibited wars without Parliament's consent. Judges were no longer under royal control and punishment. Under the new terms, to be removed from office a judge had to be formally impeached by both houses of Parliament, with no royal pardon.

As an assertion of its supremacy Parliament claimed the right to name the actual royal succession. William and Mary had no children, and the Crown passed to Mary's younger Protestant sister Anne. Under these new laws, James's Catholic children with his Catholic wife, Queen Mary, were barred from the throne. The Stuart line was essentially eliminated, and the Crown was to pass—after Queen Anne—to the descendants of Sophia, granddaughter of James I and niece of Charles I, who had married into the German Protestant House of Hanover. Parliament had successfully eliminated the accession of any more Catholic monarchs. In 1714 the first Hanover, George I, came to the English throne. He was of German birth and spoke not a word of English. In addition to this handicap he had imprisoned his wife and had two German mistresses. In spite of these flagrant social disadvantages he managed to hold the British throne until his death in 1727, when his son became George II. The Scots continued to recognize the Stuart line through James III, the son of James II, and for much of the eighteenth century the English feared a Catholic Stuart restoration achieved through Scotland.

## CURTAILING CATHOLIC POWER

This fear manifested itself especially through laws aimed at preventing a reinstatement of Catholic political power. In order to protect the Protestant preeminence in the English and Irish parliaments, a series of laws was passed to make it impossible for Catholics to gain political control. These laws are known as the Penal Laws. One of the earliest of them was passed in 1692 when Catholics were excluded from the Irish parliament in Dublin. With one stroke, Tirconnell's work in reestablishing Catholics to power was wiped out. This exclusion was achieved by requiring those who wished to sit in parliament to take oaths denying the doctrine of transubstantiation—

central to Catholic communion rites—and all papal power. Part of the required oath reads:

> I do solemnly and sincerely in the presence of God profess, testify and declare, that I do believe that in the sacrament of the Lord's supper there is not any transubstantiation of the elements of bread and wine into the body and blood of Christ, . . . and that the invocation or adoration of the Virgin Mary, or any other saint, and the sacrifice of the mass, as they are now used in the church of Rome, are superstitious and idolatrous.

A similar law was passed in the English parliament in Westminster. This oath meant that Catholics could not sit in either the London or the Dublin parliament without giving up their religion. The Penal Laws extended further than parliamentary membership. Just about all government positions of any consequence were closed to those who would not take the Oath of Allegiance accepting the English monarch as head of the Church of Ireland and denouncing the pope's authority. Catholics could not be members of municipal corporations, nor could they sit on grand juries. Further laws prevented Catholics from bearing arms or owning a horse valued at more than five pounds. Ownership of land remained an important and central issue as it was the key to economic power. The Protestant Ascendancy, as the ruling class came to be called, was anxious that Catholic ownership of land be eliminated or at least severely curtailed.

## HOW THE PENAL LAWS AFFECTED EVERYDAY LIFE

A parliamentary bill passed in 1704, called An Act to Prevent the Growth of Popery, declared that Catholics were forbidden from purchasing land or taking leases for longer than thirty-one years. Even marriage to a Protestant did not result in Catholic land ownership unless the Catholic spouse converted to the established church. Catholics also were forbidden from making wills, and the law stated that upon the death of a Catholic landowner an estate had to be divided equally among his sons. Ironically the succession of the eldest son was now outlawed for the Catholic Irish. This was no mere whim; it was a way of ensuring that Catholic estates would dwindle in size and Catholic wealth would dissipate. The law stated that should one of the sons become Protestant, he could inherit the entire estate without division. Because of these restrictive laws on land ownership, by mid-century many Catholic landlords changed their religion to the established church. By 1778 a meager 5 percent of the land of Ireland was in Catholic ownership—this at a time when approximately 75 percent of the population was Catholic. Changing religion was not uncommon. In the legal profession there was a religious exodus as large numbers of Catholic barristers and lawyers went over to the established Church of Ireland early in the century in order to continue their professional lives. In the ultimate refutation of rights in 1728, Catholics were denied all voting privileges.

While these laws were directed primarily at wealthy Catholics, they had an adverse effect on Catholic tenants who saw themselves more and more isolated in a world where hardly anyone in a position of authority shared their religion. They had lost their chieftains and aristocracy to the land confiscations of the previous century when many upper-class Irish fled to the Continent in wave after wave of land seizures. Now many of the remaining upper-class Irish were abandoning their religion for purposes of economic survival. This left a huge vacuum in the lives of ordinary tenants who were left with no one in authority to identify with or to trust. The lower classes in European societies had a dependent relationship with their overlords and for the most part trusted them. Not so in Ireland. Because of the many differences in ethnic origins and religion, the new Ascendancy class did not coalesce with the Catholic Irish tenant class. But one institution did. Into the void created by the lack of a trustworthy upper class stepped the clergy of the Roman Catholic church.

## THE SPECIAL RELATIONSHIP OF PRIEST AND TENANT

Catholic priests now began to assume the role of protectors to the Irish tenant class. The special relationship that developed between tenant and priest in Ireland has its origins in this period. This relationship is often described as feudal in nature. It did develop along these lines, but the Catholic clergy were not wealthy overlords. The clergy of this period were for the most part poor and often ill housed. The Reformation parliament in Dublin in the sixteenth century had given all existing church buildings to the Church of Ireland so Catholic church buildings were few and Mass was frequently said on Mass rocks with makeshift shelters. The absence of a sizable wealthy Catholic class left the church impoverished and destitute. A particular drain on any possible resources was the tithe law that required all citizens, irrespective of religious affiliation, to pay 10 percent of their income to the established church. This was later reduced to 6 percent, but it was a highly unpopular tax. Its effect was that Catholics, being mostly of the poorer classes, could ill afford the tax and certainly could not also contribute to their own church. Priests therefore had little income and shared the poverty of their parishioners. Because of these shared experiences, priests were often the only means of sustenance for the poor. The special relationship thrived.

The actual practice of religion was not in itself a real issue in the Penal Laws. There were laws directed against clergy, but these were not effective. At first they appeared to be successful as Jesuits and friars were expelled in 1698. But many of them never left and within a short time many others had returned. Priests were given legal recognition in 1703 and required to register. Registered priests were permitted to say Mass. An attempt was made to stop the pilgrimage to St. Patrick's purgatory in Lough Derg on the grounds that it constituted unlawful assembly:

> Whereas the superstitions of popery are greatly increased and upheld by the pretended sanctity of places especially of a place called St. Patrick's purgatory in the county of Donegal . . . be it further enacted that all such meetings and assemblies shall be deed and adjudged riots and unlawful assemblies and punishable as such.

This law proved impossible to enforce. As a sign that the authorities remained concerned about a Stuart restoration, in 1709 Catholic clergy were required to take an oath against supporting James III's right to the throne. Some of the laws appeared petty. Catholic churches could not have bells or steeples, and clerical garb could not be worn in public.

## DID THE PENAL LAWS WORK?

Laws against Catholic education were more serious. Catholics could not have their own schools or become teachers even in a Protestant school. The law stated that they could not send their sons abroad to be educated, but "hedge schools," where classes were held in the open, soon developed in many rural areas. These hedge schools played an important role in keeping the memory of the lost Gaelic Ireland alive for the lower classes. Higher education suffered most; the most egregious prohibition on education was that Catholics were not allowed a university. The ban on Catholics sending their children abroad for an education was impossible to enforce, and ways were usually found by more affluent Catholics to educate their sons in Belgium, France, and Spain. Catholic worship itself was not forbidden, and legislation against pilgrimages simply did not work. In fact the Penal Laws against religious worship were largely allowed to fall into disuse from about 1716. The main functions of these laws were to prevent Catholics from owning land or gaining political power. In these aims they succeeded absolutely. Catholic land ownership declined considerably, and Catholics were totally excluded from government at any level.

Much was made of the Penal Laws, especially in the late nineteenth century and well into the twentieth. They were frequently used in school history books as evidence of abominable discrimination against Catholics and of a bigotry unmatched anywhere. Exaggerated stories of priest hunting were not uncommon. In recent times such use of these laws for propaganda purposes has come under scrutiny. Some modern commentators have attempted to soften the image of the laws by placing them within the context of their time and stressing the difficulty in enforcing some of the laws, especially those regarding religious practice. While these are valid points, it remains the case that to be Catholic in Ireland during this time was to be completely inferior in the political, social, and economic sense. The Penal Laws constituted a formidable directory of discrimination. While such practices existed in other societies, Ireland's case was unique in European terms. This denial of political participation and economic inclusiveness was being perpetuated against a large majority of the Irish population and would fuel nationalist feelings in the nineteenth century.

## PENAL LAWS AGAINST PRESBYTERIANS

In the north of Ireland the Presbyterians who had arrived in the preceding century were having a mixed experience. They thrived economically but their religion, while Protestant, was an issue for the established church. It is important to note that the term "Ascendancy," as it came to be used in Ireland, referred exclusively to the members of the Anglican Church of Ireland and did not include the Presbyterians of the north. Irish Protestantism was not a monolith. The northern Presbyterians were not considered equal to the members of the established Church of Ireland. They had originally been invited to Ireland because Catholicism was considered a disloyal religion. It was therefore a bitter irony for them that now their religion too had come under suspicion. In Ireland they faced the reality that their particular brand of Protestantism was not good enough to allow them full political participation.

The Anglican church had become suspicious of the nonconforming churches, especially because of the Puritan experience, and wished to guard against any threat to its own position. The High Anglican government of Queen Anne's time in the early eighteenth century was determined to impose serious restrictions on dissenters. This was considered necessary because further Scottish immigration to Ireland led to a doubling of Presbyterians in Ulster between 1660 and 1715. There was an additional fear of the dissenters gaining ground because Ulster Presbyterianism had made some converts from the Church of Ireland. The Presbyterian ministers' simple approach apparently appealed more than the often worldly clergy of the Anglican church, and in Ulster the Presbyterian congregations were growing. Because Presbyterians posed a challenge to the power base of the established church, a series of laws was directed at them too.

In 1704 a clause added to the bill To Prevent the Growth of Popery stated that any person holding public office must, in addition to taking the Oath of Allegiance, produce a certificate proving that he had received the sacrament of the Lord's Supper "according to the usage of the Church of Ireland." This certificate was to be obtained from the minister and church wardens "immediately after divine service and sermon" in a public church. Failure to produce such a certificate would result in a person being "adjudged incapable and disabled in law to all intents and purposes whatever" and not therefore permitted to hold government office, either civil or military. Since Catholics were already excluded from public office, this was undoubtedly directed at Presbyterians. By the 1704 act they could no longer be members of municipal corporations, even in Ulster, or hold commissions in the army or the militia.

Presbyterians felt especially aggrieved by these laws as they had supported William's side at the Battle of the Boyne, ensuring the establishment of a Protestant monarchy. Now they were being excluded from participation in many positions of power. They were also required to pay the tithe tax to an established church to which they did not belong. Eventually they won some inclusion in government when the Toleration Act of 1719 gave them a degree of political recognition. As this act gave them only a limited number of seats in the Dublin parliament, they were not completely satisfied. It took until 1780 for the Ulster Presbyterians to win the right to sit in the county boroughs. As a result of these laws and a general feeling of dissatisfaction with life in Ulster, some of the Ulster Presbyterians chose to leave Ireland in the eighteenth century, many emigrating to the United States. But because they were not restricted by land ownership prohibitions, their economic position was firm. Neither were they as politically outcast as Catholics were by the Penal Laws.

## THE ECONOMY OF THE 1700s

In spite of social and political changes, the eighteenth century was a time of great economic growth and prosperity for the country as a whole. Ireland was predominately rural, and for the most part the economy was based on farming production. Cattle, butter, wool, worsted yarn, and linen were among the most important commodities. Large country fairs became an important part of economic life as they facilitated the buying and selling of farming goods in large quantities. The fairs also became a focal part of social life. Marriages were frequently arranged or romantic matches cemented at these festive events. In particular the country towns of Ballinasloe and Mullingar were famous for their wool fairs. Visitors traveled from all parts of Ireland to participate in and enjoy the festivals. The growing popularity of public houses (known commonly as "pubs") added to the attraction of fair days with music and dancing often rounding out the day's commercial events.

A large industry also grew up around linen production, especially in the northern part of Ireland where flax was grown. In 1711 the Irish Linen Board was formed. This industry grew rapidly as there was no competition for it from England, so it escaped restrictive laws. Although flax was grown in many parts of the country, the bulk of it was to be found in the Lagin Valley in the northeastern part of the country. In the thriving economy many other new industries developed. In 1759 Arthur Guinness established a successful industry when he began a brewing company at St. James Gate, Dublin. A crystal factory was founded in Waterford in 1783 by two brothers, George and William Penrose. Soon Irish glass was being exported from the port of Waterford to Spain and to the new country, the United States.

Improved shipbuilding was making overseas trade more important. Exports formed an important part of the growing prosperity of the country. Agricultural commodities were a major feature of the export trade. Produce and merchandise were transported from all areas of the countryside to the main ports. Transport services improved, and the inland waterways and new roads were central to this development. The 1730s and 1740s saw a rapid acceleration of road building, and from Belfast a turnpike road was built to carry linen to Dublin. Roads leading out of Dublin were built to connect the city with the western part of the country. One road west reached as far as Roscommon. Roads also connected Dublin with Cork in the south and Limerick in the southwest. Many of the new roads built at this time were turnpike trusts, that is, they were built and maintained by a group of trustees who put up the money to build them. Income was obtained from tolls.

Dublin was the main port for imports and exports. Great canals were built to connect many parts of the country with the seaports. Work on the Grand Canal was begun in 1756, eventually connecting the Shannon River with Dublin. Shortly afterward, the Royal Canal was built to accommodate high levels of water traffic sailing from the Shannon toward the port of Dublin.

## THE SOCIAL LIFE OF DUBLIN

Ireland's estimated total population in the early eighteenth century was around two million. In 1725 only one-eighth of the people lived in the towns, but the cities of Dublin and Cork were exceptional in that they grew in size and economic importance. The capital, Dublin, was the center of the booming Irish economy. With the demise of the Pale and the expansion of English control over the whole county, the economic reach of Dublin expanded. The city handled most of the country's banking, both foreign and domestic. This activity gave rise to an affluent class, living mostly in the capital. Inland traveling became easier and popular as people found that they could more easily travel between town and country. Dublin was the center for the first stagecoaches, which traveled to many of the inland and coastal towns.

By the end of the eighteenth century it is estimated that the population of Dublin was almost a quarter of a million. It was an affluent, flourishing city with large fashionable houses and buildings. The aristocracy, who owned large houses on their country estates, now also built large town homes in Dublin. Between 1718 and 1725 the number of houses in Dublin grew from 9,505 to 11,466, an increase of some 20 percent in fewer than ten years.

Many well-known Dublin landmarks were built during this time, and the city developed into the Georgian-style metropolis that it is today. Charles Brookings's map of Dublin published in 1728 reveals much about the city at that time. Large classical-style town homes were built in a homogeneous style in the beautiful squares that still grace the city.

Individuality was expressed with a variety of front-door styles, which remain part of the Dublin landscape. Dublin grew to be the fifth largest city in Europe, larger even than Rome or Amsterdam, and rivaled London in fashion and importance. It was referred to as "the second city of the Empire." As an indication of how fashionable Dublin was, Handel's *Messiah* had its first public production in 1742 in Dublin. Handel was living in Dublin at the time and wrote it as a benefit for Dublin charities, including the new Mercer Hospital. The *Messiah* was presented at the New Music Hall on Fishamble Street, with boys and men from the two cathedral choirs.

At the center of social life lay Dublin Castle. The original fortress, begun in the late twelfth century, now became a magnificent palatial structure symbolizing the elite status of the Protestant Ascendancy class. Brookings's map shows Dublin Castle with new construction well under way. Much of present-day Dublin Castle dates from the Georgian period, including the magnificent state apartments, which were renovated in the 1740s in classic style. Dublin Castle reached its summit in both fashionable and social terms. The viceroy, the king's representative in Ireland, lived at the castle with his family. Successive viceroys encouraged the participation of the Protestant Ascendancy class in castle social life, which became known for its extravagant lifestyle, elaborate rituals, and pageantry. The most important social period in the calendar included the six festive weeks of the castle's balls leading up to St. Patrick's Day, March 17. The castle was highly decorated during this festive time, and lavish dinners and receptions were held. It all came to a climax with a grand St. Patrick's Day ball. Dublin Castle

Built by the wealthy William Conolly, speaker of the Irish House of Commons, Castletown House is the finest example of eighteenth-century Irish Georgian style. (*Carmel McCaffrey*)

remained the focus of Irish social life throughout the eighteenth and nineteenth centuries. Social life of the period reflected a typical European class society, with the wealthy enjoying a privileged position. But in Ireland this division had the further enmity of religious differences.

## MAJESTIC HOMES FOR THE WEALTHY CLASS

It was during the eighteenth-century Georgian period that the Irish Ascendancy class built large magnificent homes on their vast country estates. The most outstanding of these mansions is Castletown House, in County Kildare. It was built for William Conolly, speaker of the Irish House of Commons, who at the time was the wealthiest man in Ireland. Conolly's life did not begin in such plush surroundings. He was born Catholic in 1662 in Donegal, the son of an innkeeper. He was clever and astute and learned early in life how to survive in the Ireland of his day. He changed his religion to the Church of Ireland in order to participate fully in the life of the country and showed himself to be a shrewd businessman. After the Williamite wars he purchased at low cost some of the forfeited estates that became available. He quickly amassed great wealth and entered politics. In 1715 he was elected speaker of the Irish House of Commons. His grand home, Castletown House, was a clear manifestation of his social position and wealth. It was begun in 1721 and is the largest and most splendid country house ever built in Ireland. It is also the most important architecturally because it introduced the sophisticated continental Palladian style which became the hallmark for Irish buildings of the time. Proud of his Irish identity, he is credited with using his power to support Irish interests and with the promotion of Dublin as a great capital city. Conolly instigated the building of the Irish Parliament House on College Green, Dublin, the first of its kind in Europe. Today the building is occupied by the Bank of Ireland.

Classic-style buildings flourished in Dublin throughout this time. Toward the end of the eighteenth century a truly superb vice-regal residence was built in Phoenix Park which was, and remains, the largest municipal park in Europe. Fallow deer were imported to run freely in the two-thousand-acre parkland. Today this building is known as Áras an Uachtaráin, the official residence of the president of Ireland. One of the most interesting homes from this period is Leinster House in Kildare Street, Dublin. Begun in 1745, it was built by the Earl of Kildare, James FitzGerald, as a private residence and was known originally as Kildare House. Today the building houses the Irish parliament. Leinster House is believed to be the model for the White House in Washington, D.C. In 1792 a young Irish-born architect, James Hoban, won the design competition for the White House. He had studied architecture in Dublin and had worked on the Kildare house, and his plans are described as being influenced by the design.

## HIDDEN IRELAND

In many ways there were two Irelands in the eighteenth century: the vibrant Ireland of the new Ascendancy class who spoke English and knew little about the old way of life, and, beneath the surface, another culture—"hidden Ireland," a phrase coined by Daniel Corkery in the 1920s to describe the Gaelic-speaking Irish of the eighteenth century.

The traditional bardic schools of *filí*, or poets, had gradually died out in the late 1600s as the English language spread among the educated population. As time went on, fewer and fewer educated Irish people spoke the Irish language. It was reduced to second-rate status and eventually became only the language of the poor. This brought an end to the great Gaelic tradition in poetry and in harp music. The last of the great harpists, Turlough Ó Carolan, died in 1738. Poets continued to write poetry in Irish. While it can be argued that the poetry was not of the same quality as the *Ollamh* or high poets, it had a vibrancy of its own.

In spite of the social disintegration of the old order, the old Gaelic culture had not completely disappeared. It had been retained by an underclass of people who differed in many ways from the Ascendancy class. They remained Catholic whereas most of the landed class was Protestant, but more important they continued to speak the Irish language, practice many of the old Gaelic customs, and frequently celebrate the old pagan feast days. They represented the remnants of the old Gaelic way of life. The Irish-language poets of the eighteenth century wrote in the vernacular of the people and played a vital role in expressing the experiences of the dispossessed.

The utter confusion and pain felt by this underclass are expressed in the lines of a poem from the period (here in translation):

> Last night as I was lying in my bed, exhausted even in rest,
> I uttered—in my momentary ignorance—my resentment to
>     Christ
> that he handed to the stranger all the lime-fields of Flann
> while the Gael is downcast and ceaselessly robbed and
>     tormented.

The hedge schools played a vital role in the survival of a native Irish national consciousness. They kept alive a sense of tradition and the living memory of an era now gone. These schools and their erudite masters were quite extraordinary and went beyond the teaching of Irish-related issues. Arthur Young, an English traveler who traveled to Ireland in the late 1700s, recorded in his *Tour of Ireland* that "many of the common people speak Latin fluently and I accidentally arrived at a little hut, in a very obscure part of this country, where I saw four lads reading Homer."

In addition to the schoolmasters, the *seanchaí*, or storytellers, told stories handed down over generations and recalled the mythology and history of Ireland long ago. This underclass did not share in the great wealth of the country. Many tenant-farming families lived on plots of ten or fewer acres. They lived in poor-quality housing, and many existed on a diet of potatoes and milk. They raised sheep or pigs. Sometimes they used these animals as food, but mostly they went to pay the annual rent. The poorer tenants were usually to be found in Connacht, west of the Shannon River. In this respect Ireland in the eighteenth century was no different than anywhere else in Europe in that a disproportionate amount of the wealth was owned and controlled by the ruling class.

Not all the tenant class was abjectly poor by any measure. Considering what was to follow in the tragic nineteenth century, this period was a fairly comfortable one for the average rural family. The richer farmlands of Leinster and Munster had tenants who farmed land of up to a hundred acres and produced commodities for marketing such as wheat and dairy products. Families of this class are described as living comfortably according to the European standard of the time. But there were major differences between Ireland and Europe that were not economic. As Nicholas Canny points out, "The most glaring anomaly, and the factor which made Ireland different from all other European societies, was that most landowners and most senior officials were of a different ethnic background and a different religion from the population at large." Tenants continued to view much of the upper class as interlopers. Even those of the Ascendancy class who were of native Irish stock no longer spoke the Irish language and were out of touch with the ancient native culture. The tension and resentment produced by these differences, especially in hard economic times, eventually spilled into the political arena.

## IRISH WRITERS IN THE ENGLISH LANGUAGE

While the high literary tradition might be said to have died in one language, it reemerged in force in English as Ireland began to produce an overabundance of writers in the English language. Anglo-Irish writing—Irish writers writing in the English language—emerged in the eighteenth century. In an impressive contribution to English writing, Ireland in this century produced a long list of authors. These included Oliver Goldsmith, Richard Milliken, Thomas Moore, Edmund Burke, Aubrey de Vere, and Richard Brinsley Sheridan. In philosophy there was George Berkeley, for whom the California city is named. He was the Church of Ireland bishop of Cloyne.

One of the most interesting of them all was Jonathan Swift. Swift was born in Dublin in 1667 and died in 1745, and for more than thirty years he was dean of St. Patrick's Cathedral in Dublin. He lived through many of the violent and political upheavals in the Ireland of the late seventeenth and early eighteenth centuries. He was acutely aware of the subservient position that Ireland held in British political and economic policy and wrote extensively in support of the Irish situation. "Burn everything English, except the coal" was his advice to his fellow countrymen. Swift wrote *Gulliver's Travels* and *Tale of a Tub* while he was dean of St. Patrick's. He was a well-known pamphleteer in Dublin and would distribute his pamphlets outside the cathedral. Two of his rhetorical questions about Ireland read: "Were not the people of Ireland born as free as those of England? Is not their parliament as fair and as representative of the people as that of England?" Swift's tomb in St. Patrick's is a shrine to many. His epitaph, which he wrote himself, famously refers to his earthly "savage indignation."

## SECRET SOCIETIES

During the eighteenth century many secret societies evolved in Ireland with the aim of intimidating the ruling class, especially in difficult economic times during bad harvests. Perhaps as a way of distinguishing themselves, they tended to have remarkable names like Blackfeet, Whiteboys, and Hearts of Oak. Mostly these groups operated in relatively better off areas where the tenants had more to lose in bad times. Whatever their following, these organizations did not present a particularly dangerous threat to the establishment in that they did not coalesce into a major national movement. Frustrated tenants and laborers used threats and sometimes arson against what they considered to be an oppressive aristocracy. Society membership was probably relatively small, but the societies do point to a degree of discontent among the underclass.

Many of the landlords were absentees, and the rents were collected by middlemen, which made them obvious targets for attack. In times of bad harvests, rents could not be paid. Violence sometimes erupted when agents showed up to remove farm animals or scarce produce for rent payment. Members of these secret societies also attacked the collectors of the church tithes, a tax that was particularly resented. The fact that agents were collecting money for a church that few tenants attended engendered these attacks.

## RESTRICTIVE LAWS ON THE ECONOMY

The economy remained strong throughout most of the eighteenth century, but clouds hung over the possibility of healthy economic expansion. Like the American colonies, Ireland suffered under the British commercial system, which demanded that local economic interests be sacrificed for the greater good of the "mother" country. The relationship of Ireland to Britain had long been one of subservience, a position that did not sit well with the Irish of any period. Now a new generation experienced the economic and political reality of always playing second fiddle to Westminster. An effort to rectify this parliamentary inequality was attempted early in the century when the Irish House of Lords proclaimed that the Irish parliament was the highest court with jurisdiction over Ireland. This proved to be a short-lived affirmation. In answer to those in Ireland who had asserted Irish autonomy over Irish affairs, the British parliament passed the Declaratory Act of 1719. It stated categorically that "the said Kingdom of Ireland hath been, is and of right ought to be, subordinate unto and dependent upon the imperial Crown of Great Britain as being inseparably united and annexed thereunto." The statement left little room for maneuver.

Ireland's subordinate position manifested itself especially in how the British parliament dealt with the Irish economy. In keeping with the spirit of this stated superiority, laws were passed restricting Irish economic activity in situations where it might prove to be competitive and harmful to the British economy. These laws were initiated at the request of British manufacturers and farmers. Anxious that the Irish economy not challenge their own products, manufacturing lobbyists launched a successful campaign within the British parliament. As a consequence, laws protecting English interests and curbing Irish exports were passed. One of the most financially damaging laws was the 1699 Wool Act. According to this law, no Irish wool was to be sent to foreign countries or to the British colonies, lest it compete with English wool. Irish wool was to be sent only to England, where heavy import duties were levied on it. This essentially killed Irish wool exports which until this time had been an important commodity for Ireland. The production of wool had also been an important economic asset for the tenant class, whose standard of living declined as a result of the law.

Beef production also came under attack. Beginning in the late 1600s numerous Cattle Acts curtailed the sale of Irish beef and sheep. These laws were even more restrictive than those concerning wool. In order to avoid competition with English beef, the law stated that no Irish beef was to be exported to England or wherever English beef was being sent. Soon the law extended to sheep, pigs, beef, pork, butter, and cheese. The Irish managed to find ways of getting around the restrictive laws, and some of the targeted industries survived. For example, Irish merchants switched to producing salted beef for export as fresh beef and live cattle were restricted. When new markets had to be found for Irish goods, Ireland began to export to continental Europe, where countries were not under the control of the British government. Cork, Limerick, and Galway became leading ports in the export of Irish beef and butter to Europe. As there was no linen produced in Britain, the linen industry in Ireland thrived. Because of the favorable conditions surrounding its production and the restrictions on other products, by 1788 Irish linen constituted 70 percent of all Irish exports.

## THE INFLUENCE OF THE AMERICAN REVOLUTION

The American and French revolutions impacted European ideals by establishing a form of government in which ordinary citizens could participate. Irish political opinion identified with the American cause on many levels. For one thing Ireland had strong connections with America. Northern Presbyterians had established links there through emigration. Catholic families had also emigrated to seek better lives. Among the most prominent was Charles Carroll, a wealthy Irish Catholic who settled in Maryland, where his family became an important part of that state's history. American and Irish society shared much in common. The notion of "independence" from Britain highlighted the similarities between American grievances and the suppressed Irish parliament. The difference was that the Irish desire for independence was seen as a restoration of lost rights as opposed to the quest for new ones.

While it might seem that Catholic Ireland would have been ripe for such ideas, the Catholic church in Ireland at this time was reluctant to take on ideas of democracy. In Ireland the clergy were alienated from these ideals and even feared them because of the anti-clerical policies of the French revolutionaries. Irish priests who had been mostly educated in France witnessed their counterparts and former teachers stripped of power and position. The Irish clergy were resolved that the "French disease" would not infect their parishioners.

Although members of the Ascendancy opposed democracy because it would diminish their own powerful position, some families in the Protestant professional and commercial classes believed that Ireland should become a more politically inclusive country. Many of these people were influenced by the ideals of democracy, but others simply reflected their own sense of fair play. Outside the Ulster region, Protestants and Catholics did not live in strictly segregated areas, and their lives crossed in numerous social ways. Many Irish families, especially those in the Dublin area, were often more mixed in religious affiliation than the composition of the parliament might suggest. Intermarriage between Catholics and Protestants was not uncommon, and couples found ways of quietly accommodating the religious divide within the marriage. Before the twentieth century such "mixed" marriages frequently resulted in sons going to the church of the father and daughters following the mother in religious practice. It was not uncommon to find that members of the Protestant Ascendancy had cousins or even siblings who were Catholic.

This resulted in a degree of support for Catholic rights, which included representation in government. This is not to say that the support was universal, but neither was it totally rejected. Another important factor was the number of wealthy Catholic merchants who had grown rich in the century. The Penal Laws had not excluded Catholics from manufacturing and business, and many had made money in the eighteenth-century economy. These wealthy Catholic families who paid taxes to the state believed it unjust that they were prohibited from participating in government. The tensions caused by these issues contributed to social unease as the century progressed.

# [ 6 ]

# *Patriots and Rebels: Grattan, Tone, and FitzGerald*

THE ISSUE of Catholic rights was underscored by the Irish parliament's concern with its power. Poynings' Law of 1494 and the further restriction in 1719 on the Irish parliament meant that in essence it was a powerless body under Westminster control. The situation was bound to cause friction, and eventually it did. In the latter part of the eighteenth century a group of young parliamentarians began to argue for more autonomy for Ireland. They agitated within the Dublin House of Commons for a more vital government that would not be a puppet body. The group became known as the "Patriots." Their ideas were to some extent influenced by the Enlightenment and the ideals of democracy, but these ideas were not new to Ireland.

The desire for a more independent government had been a feature of Irish life for hundreds of years. This desire had been previously articulated by earlier Irish pamphleteers, especially Jonathan Swift and William Molyneux, both of whom argued for Irish autonomy. Molyneux was himself a member of the Dublin parliament in the 1690s. In 1698 he published a pamphlet called "The Case of Ireland being bound by Acts of Parliament in England Stated," in response to discussion surrounding the Wool Act. He argued that Ireland had a long parliamentary tradition of its own and should not be bound by laws of the English parliament. In a comprehensive analysis in support of the rights of the Irish legislature, he contended "That Ireland should be bound by Acts of Parliament made in England, is against Reason, and the Common Rights of all Mankind." A further grievance for the Irish was the issue of taxation and the amount that Ireland contributed to the British exchequer.

## THE PATRIOTS IN THE IRISH PARLIAMENT

In the 1770s organized opposition to control by Westminster emerged in the form of the Patriot movement. This was more than a nationalist movement because it also involved issues of commerce. Both inside and outside government the subordinate nature of the Irish parliament regarding the laws restricting trade and commerce was harshly criticized and debated. These trade laws were especially egregious to the commercial classes, who considered the restraints on the Irish economy to be unjust and detrimental to the further expansion of the economy. The specific demand from the commercial interests was that Ireland have free access to world trade. This sentiment found legislative expression within the Dublin parliament among young elected members who were frustrated by what they perceived as the Dublin assembly's complacency. As they saw it, the problem lay in how the parliamentary system worked. The commercial classes had little power, and the landlords who held power in parliament were not inclined to promote change. As long as the landlords received rents, they had little interest in the commercial economy or the issue of the subordinate nature of the Irish parliament. In essence the parliament had become something of a country club for the aristocracy. The Patriots wanted more vigorous action. They argued that Ireland, though a possession of the British Crown, was by tradition a separate kingdom and as such ought to be governed according to its own laws and institutions. The Patriots sought an extension of Dublin's power and a lessening of Westminster's authority over Irish affairs. They were not seeking total independence from England but a larger say in how Ireland was governed.

The leader of the "Patriots" in the Irish
House of Commons, Henry Grattan tried
to make the Irish legislature more
independent of Westminster. (*National
Portrait Gallery, London*)

## GRATTAN'S PARLIAMENT

The Patriot party placed itself in political opposition to those who
were controlling the Dublin parliament. The movement found a
leader in the very dynamic Henry Grattan. Born in Dublin in 1746,
Grattan was the son of a Dublin lawyer. He attended Trinity College and in 1772 was himself called to the bar. In 1775 he was
elected to the Irish parliament. Within a few years he was a leading
spokesman for the Patriots within parliament. One of the first issues he had to contend with involved the tensions over the Irish
economy and Westminster control.

The controversy over free trade reached a high point when in
1776 Irish exports to the lucrative markets in the American colonies
were prohibited. In Ireland this caused outrage and calls for a revi-
sion of the law. In response, in 1779 an organized boycott of British
goods in Ireland heightened tensions. In December that year the
British relented and announced a change in the law allowing the

Irish to export to the colonies and specifically allowing for the export of glass and wool. This was a major victory for the Patriots, and an improved economic climate followed. Another important boost came from Grattan's support for grants of financial aid to new industries. This practice had been in place since mid-century, but Grattan enhanced it. The economic historian Louis Cullen notes that "in the second half of the century parliamentary grants were made more lavishly in support of public works and economic development," which led to a greater expansion of the Irish economy. The Patriots within the Irish parliament now believed they were in a position of strength. They would soon flex their muscles over the broader issue of parliamentary independence.

## IRISH PROTESTANT VOLUNTEERS— FIRST IRISH NATIONALISTS

Meanwhile the world outside Ireland was changing as democratic ideas took more tangible form. In 1776 the American colonies revolted, sending waves of hope through Ireland for those who supported a more independent Irish legislature. Ireland was also impacted more directly. The revolution in the colonies caused the British to withdraw troops from Ireland in order to handle the difficult situation in America. Because Ireland lacked its own national army, when the standing British army was withdrawn, volunteer militia groups were set up around the country. The volunteers were formed ostensibly to act should Ireland be attacked. Tensions between Britain and France during this period gave rise to a fear, among the British and some of the Irish landed gentry, of a French invasion of Ireland. The Irish parliament had refused to accept the presence in Ireland of four thousand German mercenaries, as the British government had suggested. Instead the Irish developed a volunteer army.

The volunteers were organized in the countryside by landowners and in the towns by members of the professions. They were therefore not under the control of the Irish parliament. Volunteers supplied their own guns and uniforms, so only the better off were able to participate. Most of the volunteers were Protestant because the penal code forbade Catholics from carrying arms. But in some areas a sizable number of volunteers were Catholic. Approximately

35,000 men enrolled in the volunteers. Although these martial groups were initially to act as substitutes for the depleted regular army, they soon developed into a quasi-independent force that supported Irish free trade and a lessening of British interference in Irish affairs. Under direction from Grattan, a sizable number were also in favor of relaxing the Penal Laws against Catholics. Grattan knew that part of Westminster's policy in directing attention away from its domination was to keep alive the divisions within Irish society. He asserted that "the Irish Protestant will never be free until the Irish Catholic hath ceased to be a slave."

Power would not be surrendered lightly by the British, but they were under pressure for a number of reasons. The war in the colonies was not going well; the Americans were proving to be a formidable challenge for the British army. In addition, the British had to deal with threatening murmurings from the Irish Volunteers in concert with Grattan's Patriots, who were making vocal political demands. The Patriot movement had placed the British government in a difficult position. The British knew that Ascendancy support was an ongoing necessity in maintaining their position in Ireland. Now trouble was brewing among the very people they normally depended upon. They did not wish to disaffect their base in Ireland. Realizing the dilemma and the potential for alienating the British support system, the Westminster parliament renounced its right to make laws for Ireland and overrule any laws made in Dublin. In what seemed like an amazing reversal, in 1782 the Westminster parliament passed the Repeal of the Declaratory Act and gave the Irish parliament full legislative power. With a war with France now imminent, the British did not wish to risk an Irish war. It was not total independence by any means. The Irish parliament remained under the control of the monarch. The king retained veto power, but the centuries-old Poynings' Law was overturned.

## SOME CATHOLIC RIGHTS RESTORED

The British were also reacting to a series of events already unfolding in Dublin. Aided by the reality that a Catholic Stuart restoration was now remote, in 1771 the Irish parliament had begun to pass a number of acts called the Catholic Relief Acts. These acts reinstated many of the property rights, including land ownership, that Catholics had lost under the Penal Laws. They gave Catholics the right to purchase and own land. Permission was granted "for any person or persons professing the popish religion to purchase or take by grant, limitation, descent or device, any lands." Catholic clergy were declared to be legitimate. A new Oath of Allegiance was drawn up in 1774 whereby Catholic teachers could swear obedience to the king while still respecting the pope. This allowed Catholics to teach in schools though their appointment was still under the local Protestant bishop's control. It would be wrong, though, to suppose that all rights would so easily be restored to Catholics. There was considerable opposition to legislating too many changes in the laws and a share in power proved to be the most difficult to gain. Unexpectedly, demand for further change came from London.

In the spring of 1793 the British began a war with France that was to last for twenty years. Westminster was becoming more alarmed at unrest in Ireland and believed it could not afford to face trouble there. The British had real fear of a Catholic uprising in Ireland, leading to an alliance with the French. In this new climate Catholic civil liberties were broadened. In 1793 Catholics who met the property qualification were given the right to vote, and by 1795 Catholics had the right again to bear arms.

Yet democracy was still unevenly applied in Ireland. In spite of the relaxation of some of the Penal Laws, Catholics did not possess full political participation rights. A bill to grant emancipation to Catholics was introduced by Grattan in parliament in May 1795 but was defeated 155 to 84. At the time more than 80 percent of the Irish population was Catholic. Henry Flood, a Patriot who had been a liberal before the time of Grattan and wanted more power for the Dublin government, had reservations about extending power to Catholics. He confessed as much in 1783 when he defended the Penal Laws by saying:

> Ninety years ago four-fifths of Ireland were for King James. They were defeated. I rejoice in that defeat. The laws that followed were not laws of persecution, they were a political necessity. What will be the consequence if you give [Catholics]

equal powers with Protestants? We will give all toleration to religion. We will not give them political power.

## THE LIMITS OF GRATTAN'S ACHIEVEMENTS

The changes brought about by Grattan's parliament were not as
momentous as it might seem. Parliament stalled on the issue of
full participation for Catholics who were mostly of old Gaelic or
Gaelo-Norman stock. More than 75 percent of the Irish House of
Commons was comprised of families who had come to Ireland
since the 1600s. Furthermore the chief government official in Ireland was still the lord lieutenant—as the lord deputy was now
called—and his appointment remained under the control of the
British prime minister. Dublin Castle continued to be a formidable
institution, with the Irish civil service being run by Englishmen
who reported directly to the Westminster government. The head of
the civil service was the chief secretary, an English appointee. In
addition to his role in Dublin Castle, the chief secretary also held
an automatic seat in the Irish House of Commons, where he presented British government policy. Law and order remained under
the jurisdiction of the Castle authorities. Below the chief secretary
were a number of different departments dealing with taxation, fi-
nances, the army, and varying government branches such as the
Linen Board and the Department of Roads. Irish people worked in
these departments but rarely, if ever, did they rise to positions of
real power.

None of this was altered in Grattan's parliament, and Dublin
Castle remained an institution with much power and influence in
Ireland. The electoral system remained the same, and reforms were
not introduced to make the government a more representative one.
In later years nationalists would dub this period "Grattan's Parliament" with a sense of pride in the achievements of Henry Grattan.
Although these years brought forth an expression of Irishness that
impacted the Ascendancy, ultimately more change was needed for
that body to become a true reflection of Irish society as a whole.
Henry Grattan did not fail to see this and became disillusioned
with his ability to effect significant change, especially regarding
Catholic rights in the electoral system. The Protestant Ascendancy
remained the dominant power as Catholics had yet to win the right

to sit in parliament or hold Crown office. Neither the Dublin nor the London parliament had given way on these issues.

## THEOBALD WOLFE TONE AND THE UNITED IRISHMEN

In spite of the concessions won by Grattan and the Patriots, there remained a perception that not enough had been achieved to make parliament more representative of the population at large. This was certainly the view held by Catholics and a section of the Protestant population, who began to seek ways of changing how Ireland was governed. One of the most important of these activists was Theobald Wolfe Tone. His contribution would have a lasting influence on Irish history. Born in Dublin in 1763, he was the son of a coachmaker. His family was Protestant Church of Ireland. Like Grattan, he was educated at Trinity College and was a member of the Irish bar. But he had a much more radical outlook than Grattan and sought to transform how the Irish parliament worked. He also wanted fundamentally to change England's basic relationship to Ireland.

Tone was fully aware of the political situation in Europe and the success of the radicals there. He was impressed by the violent methods used in France and in the new country, the United States, to bring about change: "Nations . . . are vindicating themselves into freedom." Tone was willing to take military action in Ireland: "Ye talk about it yourselves, and do ye think that we will be left behind: If ye will join us, we are ready to embrace you; if you will not, shame and discomfiture await you." Although a Protestant, he had deep sympathy for the Catholic cause. His pamphlet, "Argument on Behalf of the Catholics of Ireland," published in 1791, called for a far more radical approach to Irish politics. He argued passionately on behalf of Catholic liberties and against the system that had denied them basic rights: "Hath a Catholic the mark of a beast in his forehead that he should wander over his native soil like the accursed Cain, with his hand against every man, and every man's hand against him?"

Tone expressed his frustration with and distrust in parliamentary methods when he said, "Have we not sufficient experience, how fruitless all opposition is on the present system?" He argued that too many vested interests in government, on both sides of the Irish Sea, made substantial change impossible to achieve. He was looking for sweeping change, and he believed that he needed to unite the whole of Ireland for this to happen. In the spirit of unity, Wolfe Tone established links between the Dublin radicals and the Belfast Presbyterian radicals. Out of this connection grew the Society of United Irishmen, established in Belfast and Dublin in October and November 1791 by Tone, Thomas Russell, and James Napper Tandy. Tandy had expressed great joy at the revolution in the American colonies. "When America revolted against the tyranny of Great Britain, my heart rejoiced within me," he said.

## THE DASHING LORD EDWARD FITZGERALD

Among the young men who were attracted to the movement was Lord Edward FitzGerald, the twelfth child of James FitzGerald, the twentieth Earl of Kildare and first Duke of Leinster. The FitzGeralds had become Protestant and in the eighteenth century were one of the wealthiest families in Ireland. New information on the life of Lord Edward came to light in the 1990s when the National Library of Ireland managed to procure an extensive collection of letters and papers, many of which had been previously unknown to historians.

Edward FitzGerald was born in 1763, and almost immediately became the favorite child in his family. An early portrait shows him to be a beautiful child with dark curls and long eyelashes. His mother was a great proponent of Jean-Jacques Rousseau, with whom she corresponded. When Rousseau declined her offer to be her children's tutor, she hired one who would make the French philosopher's theories a part of her children's education. Edward was a responsive child who was encouraged to develop his sensitive side. He was considered a good student who eagerly took to his studies. He is described as having a lively interest in the world of ideas and in the new political ideas of his time. The young Edward was close to his mother and the tutor who would later become his mother's second husband on the death of Edward's father. Edward was drawn to the romance of a military career and entered the British army in the Sussex militia when he was sixteen years old.

When it became apparent that his unit would not see much military action, he changed to another regiment.

## AMERICAN INFLUENCES

As he had wished, Edward was sent to America during the Revolutionary War and was wounded in battle in Eutaw Springs, September 8, 1781. In later life he would look back on his time in the American war with the lament that he had fought in America *"against* the cause of liberty." The war greatly influenced him, but probably not in the manner he had imagined before he went. His ideas of military heroism had been tempered with a grounding in American ideals and nationalism. On returning to Ireland he was full of the new ideas the American colonists were fighting for. Elected to the Dublin parliament in 1783, he immediately professed himself to be on the side of Grattan and the Patriots. He was twenty years old at the time of his election. As time went on his politics became more radical, and he spoke out in favor of Catholic rights. This was the urgent political debate in Ireland at the time. He was particularly influenced by the writings of Thomas Paine and stayed with him in Paris when he visited in 1792. The two became close friends. Paine's publication *Common Sense* had been widely distributed in Ireland and was published in the popular newspaper the *Freeman's Journal*. Paine's writings had a profound effect on Edward. According to Lord Edward's recent biographer, Stella Tillyard, it was Paine's *Rights of Man* that "transformed him from a Rousseauist to complete Painite and from a radical to a republican."

These influences led Lord Edward to want a more inclusive government for Ireland, but he could not see constitutional change happening under the existing parliamentary system. He talked freely and openly about his ideas, which put him in trouble on more than one occasion. At a banquet in Paris he made disapproving remarks about inherited titles and was expelled from the British army. His frustration with politics led him to join the United Irishmen. He was a significant recruit for the organization because he brought with him not only his military experience but also the important centuries-old FitzGerald name, with its respected reputation going back to the days of his legendary ancestors Garret Mór, Garret Óg, and of course the heroic "Silken" Thomas.

## THE UNITED IRISHMEN

The goals of the United Irishmen organization were set out in the members' agenda, which they called *The United Irishmen's Plan of Parliamentary Reform*. It was published in March 1794, and its sympathy with the spirit of the Enlightenment is obvious. It proclaimed that every man over the age of twenty-five should be entitled to sit in parliament and that no oath should be used to disqualify any candidate. Emphasizing its commitment to end all religious discrimination, it declares "That no reform is practicable, efficacious, or just, which shall not include Irishmen of every religious persuasion." The United Irishmen also sought to broaden the franchise beyond the norms for the period and pronounced that "no property qualification should be necessary to entitle any man to be a representative." Until that time parliaments in Britain and Ireland had been the prerogative of the landed class, with hereditary succession the norm.

The United Irishmen's plan went far beyond anything that had been proposed within the British or Irish parliament. The organization was suppressed later that year, most likely because of its sentiments, but it did not disband. It went underground and continued as a major force in Irish affairs, a huge organization with committees in every county and provisional committees over them. Ultimately its goal was to free Ireland from English control and "to unite the whole people of Ireland, to abolish the memory of all past dissension, and to substitute the common name of Irishmen in place of the denomination of Protestant, Catholic and dissenter." These words, used by Tone, became the motto of the entire movement, echoing into the twentieth century when Gerry Adams quoted it in 1998 after the signing of the Good Friday Agreement.

## MAKING THE FRENCH CONNECTION

Theobald Wolfe Tone's politics would not be contained within words. He was destined to be a man of action. In 1792 he became secretary of the Catholic Committee, an organization that formed among the wealthy Catholic merchant class. It demanded full participation in government, and it said much about Tone that he, a Protestant, should become spokesman for Catholic aspirations. Tone was in touch with members of the French Directory and convinced them that Ireland was ready for an invasion. In spite of tensions with the British, or perhaps because of them, the French and the Irish had remained on good terms. There were strong emotional links between the two countries from the establishment of the Irish Brigade as a unit in the French army in the late seventeenth century. The Irish upper classes tended to be francophile in taste and sentiment. Many Irish men had traveled to France over the previous hundred years and joined the Irish unit. It was also common for wealthy Irish Catholics to send their children to be educated in France. Moreover the Irish support for the British war with the French was tepid at best—a common refrain was, "What harm have the French ever done to us?" It was therefore not unexpected that Tone would look to France as an ally in the Irish struggle for independence.

The French welcomed the idea of an association with the Irish. A base in Ireland would give them a platform from which they might attack England. With the heightened awareness of the dangers of a French connection with the Irish, British authorities in Dublin Castle were on the lookout. Tone's subversive connections with the French were soon discovered, and he was arrested and allowed to leave Ireland in lieu of prosecution. Tone chose to go to the United States. In 1795 he arrived in Philadelphia. He believed that the New World would act as an incubator in allowing him to hatch his plans. He never gave up on his planned strategy, and he continued his communication with the French. He traveled to Paris the following year and arranged with the French Directory to send troops to Ireland to assist in a rebellion. With support from the French, it all looked promising.

## THE IRISH PREPARE FOR THE FRENCH

Support in Ireland for rebellion appeared widespread, and the authorities in Britain sought to curtail it. The Insurrection Act received the royal assent in March 1796, which effectively put Ireland under martial law. This actually provoked support for the rebel cause as it angered many Irish, especially those in rural areas who felt outraged by the possibility of having their homes entered and searched without apparent cause. Many of the volunteer units were in favor of armed action against the British, and support crossed religious lines. After the repeal of the law against Catholics bearing arms, many Catholics had joined the volunteers and were willing to participate. Their Protestant commanders were also ready. Lord Edward FitzGerald, who by now was heading the military committee, was confident that tens of thousands of troops could be raised in Ireland. With this huge number and a French invasion, success was thought to be certain. FitzGerald, like the other Irish leaders, was convinced that a French intervention was an important component to an Irish rebellion and would undoubtedly bring victory.

Within this seemingly united Irish force, tensions nonetheless existed. The Protestant/Catholic divide continued in Ulster, especially in the southern part of the province where local groups had organized to defend one another's economic interests. A group known as the Defenders formed within the Catholic population in Armagh in order to articulate Catholic grievances. Defenderism represented an organized way of expressing discontent and disaffection, but with the repeal of the Penal Laws concerning Catholic land ownership, suspicion among the Protestant settlers grew that Catholics were planning a restoration of the forfeited estates of a century earlier. The most prominent Protestant band was known as the Peep O'Day Boys. Clashes between Catholic and Protestant groups occurred in the early 1790s. It was after one of these violent clashes in 1795 that the Orange Society was formed. It was named in honor of William of Orange, regarded as the great symbol of Protestant rights.

## THE FRENCH ON THE SEAS

In late December 1796 a French fleet consisting of forty-three ships and fifteen thousand troops sailed from Brest bound for Bantry Bay on the southwest coast of Ireland. The fleet was under the command of General Louis Lazare Hoche, and Tone sailed with him. Tone had won the respect of the French to such an extent that he was made an adjutant general in the French army and was in

French military uniform. Hoche and Tone worked well together and had a high regard for each other. Their plan was to land on the coast of Ireland, combine with the Irish forces, and fire the country into rebellion. They aimed first to seize the port of Cork. They reckoned they could then occupy Dublin within two weeks.

They were attempting an enormous feat which, if successful, would have changed the course of Irish and British history, but luck was not with them. Heavy storms scattered the ships, and Hoche became separated from his fleet. The bad weather prevented them from approaching close enough to the Irish coast even to consider landing. Eventually they were forced to return to France and abort their plans. Undeterred, Tone continued to plan for another French invasion. Hoche's sudden death in September 1797 was a great setback, but Tone pushed ahead with his plan for another attempt at an uprising with French help.

## LORD EDWARD FITZGERALD BETRAYED

In spite of its failure, the Hoche expedition greatly boosted morale in Ireland, and the United Irishmen gained in membership. In a paper sent from his home to the Leinster provisional committee, and headed "National Committee, 26th Feb. 1798," Lord Edward FitzGerald claimed an army in waiting of approximately 280,000 men. By now the French were procrastinating about their continued involvement in Ireland because of the prospect of a truce in their war with the British. The Irish waited for a response from France, but when it did not arrive they decided to take action on their own. Lord Edward FitzGerald mapped out a specific plan with armies' marching from various parts of the country into Dublin to take the capital. He was to lead the attack from Kildare. In preparation for his role as commander, he had an elaborate uniform made echoing the style of the French officials in their revolution. By this time green had been adopted by the Irish radicals as a nationalist color, and Edward's uniform reflected this—a green jacket and green breeches. A scarlet braiding on the jacket indicated revolution. A dramatic green cape hung from the shoulders. In high hopes of success, he also had a uniform made to be worn at the national convention that would take place after the success of the armed rebellion. Alas, it was not to be.

The enchanting Lord Edward FitzGerald, whose arrest and tragic death foreshadowed the failure of the 1798 rising. (*National Portrait Gallery, London*)

This time it was not weather that brought the scheme down but betrayal in the Irish ranks. With the use of spies, Dublin Castle authorities had penetrated the organization, and in March 1798 many of the leaders were arrested. A warrant went out for the whereabouts of Lord Edward FitzGerald. A value of one thousand pounds was placed on his head. After an informer came forward and revealed his hiding place, FitzGerald was arrested on May 19, 1798, in the attic room of a house on Dublin's Thomas Street. He put up a fight, killed one of his attackers, and was wounded in the struggle. He was immediately taken to prison, his family and friends forbidden from seeing him. The details surrounding his death are still a mystery. Initially his wounds were declared not mortal, and he was expected to recover and stand trial. But within a few days the prisoner was delirious. The authorities would not permit anyone, including his family, to visit him. In anticipation of his own arrest and death, he had placed his wife and children in the care of relatives. It took enormous effort by his formidable aunt, Lady Louisa Conolly (of Castletown House), to gain permission for the family to see him. His brother, Lord Henry FitzGerald, Duke of Leinster, and Lady Louisa were allowed to enter his cell only hours before his death. He died in the early morning of June 4. He was deeply mourned by his family and the United Irishmen; his loss to the rebellion was beyond calculation.

Lord Edward FitzGerald was everything an eighteenth-century figure should be. He entered history as a great romantic hero. Dashing and handsome, he had a passion for human rights and a belief in his fellow men. Thomas Moore wrote his biography, and Lord Byron said of him, "What a noble fellow was Lord Edward FitzGerald, and what a romantic and singular history his was! If it were not too near our times, it would make the finest subject in the world for an historical novel."

## THE REBELLION OF 1798

Meanwhile, in spite of Lord Edward's arrest, the rising began in Dublin on May 23, 1798, but it failed to become the grand war for which the leadership had hoped. FitzGerald's carefully laid out plans did not proceed as he designed. Although bloody, the Dublin rebellion was under control within a week, and plans of taking over Dublin Castle and pivotal government buildings did not materialize. An uprising in Antrim in Ulster, led by the Belfast Protestant leader Henry Joy McCracken, also ended in defeat. On July 17, 1798, McCracken was arrested and hanged as a rebel at Belfast market house.

Wexford was more difficult for the British to control, and there the rebel army enjoyed some success. Commanded by a number of keen and astute Catholic priests, the insurgents gained early victories. Under Father John Murphy they took control of the towns of Enniscorthy and Wexford, but when they tried to spread out to County Wicklow they were stopped. Father Murphy was arrested and later hanged. One of the heroes of the fight for Wicklow, Father Michael Murphy, carried a flag with a cross and the inscription

"Liberty or Death" as he moved forward with the final charge. He was hit by a canister and died instantly. On June 21 the rebels were finally defeated at Vinegar Hill.

## THE FRENCH TRY AGAIN

The French agreed to another attempt at invasion, and in August 1798 a French fleet of one thousand troops under the command of General Humbert landed at Killala Bay, County Mayo. It was too little and too late. They were met by the forces of the larger English army and forced to surrender. Still persistent, Tone's legendary charm and powers of persuasion did not desert him, and he managed to convince the French Directory to send yet another expedition to Ireland. They agreed and in September 1798 a larger French fleet of five thousand troops set sail for Ireland commanded by Admiral Bompard, with Tone as *chef de brigade*. The fleet was apprehended by the British navy in Lough Swilly on October 12, 1798, and Tone was captured. He was wearing a French military uniform and was immediately accused of treason.

Imprisoned first at Derry, Tone was then moved to prison in Dublin. He was found guilty and sentenced to death. The legal trials revealed the extent of the French connection with the Irish cause and stunned both the British public and the establishment, who apparently were not aware of the magnitude of the United Irishmen's efforts with the French. This was to be Tone's great legacy. When his request for a military execution was refused, he tried to commit suicide in prison. On November 19, 1798, he died of self-inflicted injuries. His widow was granted a pension by the French government.

In Irish history, the failed rising of 1798 was probably the most costly in terms of human life. Some thirty thousand people were killed. It had been an enormous feat with eighteen counties rising in rebellion. The memory of '98 served as a rallying call for future nationalist generations and heralded a new wave of political violence that continues to find expression today. The words and hopes of Wolfe Tone are to this day found on the walls of streets and pubs in Northern Ireland. Each year Sinn Féin marks the anniversary of his death with a memorial at his grave in Bodenstown.

Theobald Wolfe Tone became a symbol of
Irish nationalism for generations.
(*National Library of Ireland*)

## FIRST STIRRINGS OF CATHOLIC POWER

In spite of the Penal Laws, the Catholic church experienced a period
of development in Ireland in the eighteenth century. Perhaps because of Catholicism's role as a marginalized religion, the practice of
liturgy was not as formal as in more traditional Catholic countries. It
was also interspersed with older pagan customs. Belief in the healing
powers of holy wells, rag trees, and superstitions was rampant.
Church attendance and the use of the sacraments were irregular and
not confined to church buildings. Stations, or homes designated to
hold Mass, were common. The church was not a wealthy institution.
The use of Mass rocks, where Mass was said in the open, had more
to do with the poverty of the church than the penal code.

Yet the penal code highlighted an interesting situation—one
that was not wholly unfavorable to the survival of Catholicism. The

idea of an established church was to permit government jurisdiction over religious authorities, especially in the appointments of bishops. Ireland did not fit this picture. The majority religion was not the established state church but Catholicism. This essentially meant that the majority religion was outside the political control of government. Because the Catholic church in Ireland functioned outside the government's authority, it developed an informal but influential relationship with the people. In some ways it could be described as an alternative power. As official power was unpopular, the Catholic church became an unofficial authority willingly supported by a majority of average citizens. The autonomous influence of the church in Ireland paved the way for the more organized and authoritative church that would develop in the nineteenth century.

In the spirit of acknowledging this power and potential threat, the authorities wisely made attempts to build a government partnership with Catholicism. Among other gestures, they funded a new Catholic seminary in 1795, built in Maynooth, County Kildare. Until this time Irish Catholic priests were being trained mostly in France. Part of the reason for this decision to build the new seminary was to distance the Irish church from the more radical French. It was hoped that Maynooth would cultivate a more loyal priesthood and that an anglicized Catholic church would emerge in Ireland. This hope was never realized, however; the seminary at Maynooth would become the center of a distinctive Irish Catholicism.

As the century ended an ominous cloud was gathering over Ireland that would have grave ramifications. The population had begun to grow substantially toward the close of the eighteenth century. Why this occurred is not clear, but by 1770 it was increasing at the rate of 12 percent per decade. This rise would continue at a more rapid pace into the next century. Despite the scarcity of land, families were producing more children than ever before. In the mid-nineteenth century this, and political events, would eventually contribute to the humanitarian disaster of the Great Famine.

# [ 7 ]

# A Most Distressful
# Country:
# Union and Famine

❋

THE RISING OF 1798 was an alarm bell for the British prime minister William Pitt and members of the English establishment.
Theobald Wolfe Tone's seductive battle cry of a united Ireland for
Catholic, Protestant, and dissenter might prove to be a threat to
British interests. A strong, united, and independent Ireland would
not necessarily be willing to listen to Westminster. In addition, while
Britain was under pressure from the American colonies, in 1782 full
rights had been granted to the Irish parliament, permitting it to make
its own decisions independent of the British legislature, with only the
king's veto to control it. A united Ireland bent on further political independence would spell disaster for the growing British Empire.
Such a situation might lead to a French alliance with the Irish,
threatening British security. The Napoleonic Wars were not yet settled, and the French were considered a real threat to British aspirations. The growing consensus in Britain was that action was needed
to curb the Irish. The solution was advanced by Prime Minister
William Pitt—he announced plans to abolish the Irish parliament
and bring about a complete political union of Ireland with Britain.

In his address to the House of Commons on January 31, 1799, Pitt denounced the 1782 act that gave legislative freedom to Dublin, declaring it a "demolition of the system which before held the two countries together." Pitt wanted Ireland back under British legislative control, and the only way to accomplish this was through union. With Britain engaged in an ongoing war with France, Pitt feared the Irish parliament would not be loyal to Britain, placing its own interests first. That his words might offend many in Dublin did not apparently occur to him. In his thorough analysis of how he perceived the political situation in Ireland, Pitt also spoke of how his proposed change might affect the Irish economy. He understood that the fear of a greater tax burden on Ireland might give rise to anxiety, but, he assured doubters, "it is not from a pecuniary motive that we seek a union." He admitted that the loss of the Dublin legislature could mean that the number of absentee landlords in Ireland would increase because many of the Irish lords might move permanently to London to be near the British House of Lords. At this time many lords had homes in both England and Ireland. This possibility was dismissed as being of little impact. (In fact many Irish residences, especially in the beautiful Georgian Squares of Dublin, were subsequently abandoned.) The bill passed in the British parliament and was sent to Dublin for passage.

Union proved more difficult to accomplish than Pitt first thought. His bill met with angry opposition in the Dublin legislature. Commercial interests were also concerned and, ironically, the Orange Society in Ulster was opposed to union. When the Act of Union went to a vote in Dublin in 1799, it was defeated 111 to 106. Pitt was committed to union and was determined that the bill pass in Dublin, so he tried a different approach.

Fresh from the American war, Charles Cornwallis had been appointed lord lieutenant of Ireland in 1796; he was now charged with seeing the passage of the union. He was given one million pounds to hand out as enticements for a favorable vote. Some Irish landlords, happy with such a windfall, changed their vote and decided in support of union. Peerages were also on offer as enticements. The second debate in Dublin opened on January 15, 1800. One of the chief inducements was the promise of full Catholic participation in the Westminster parliament. Cornwallis was an honest negotiator and supported Catholic rights. He believed that peace would come to Ireland only with the abolition of the Irish parliament and the establishment of full Catholic rights. He convinced the Irish that Catholics would be given the right to sit in the newly expanded parliament at Westminster after union.

Those who championed Catholic rights believed this would happen and had good reason to trust that it would be so. Pitt, in his Commons speech, had explained that giving Catholics the right to sit in the British parliament would make their voice a more diluted one because they would not be a majority in the United Kingdom as they were in Ireland. In Ireland their majority was always a cause of fear for the Protestant ruling class. Nevertheless there continued to be many voices of dissent in Dublin against the union, with Grattan remaining implacable. Another voice of dissent in the Irish House of Commons was John Parnell. His great-grandson, Charles Stewart Parnell, was to be an even more important voice of dissent.

On May 21, 1800, the Act of Union was presented again to the Irish House of Commons and this time it passed. The Irish parliament was abolished. According to the act, the enlarged parliament at Westminster was now "to be styled, The Parliament of the United Kingdom of Great Britain and Ireland." In 1801 thirty-two Irish lords and one hundred Irish MPs took their seats in the new Parliament. A flag designed for this new Union, referred to as the "Union Jack," flew over Westminster in honor of this parliamentary fusion. The new flag symbolizing union incorporated the crosses of St. Patrick of Ireland, St. Andrew of Scotland, St. David of Wales, and St. George of England.

## ROBERT EMMET'S REBELLION

From the start it was a very uneasy Union. Within a short time the Irish expressed violent opposition, and a rebellion was planned by a younger brother of one of the United Irishmen. Robert Emmet was a teenager in 1798 when his brother Thomas Emmet had fought for Irish freedom. Robert was a student in Trinity College at the time and was secretary of one of the branches of the United Irishmen there in 1798. Now, shortly after the Act of Union, Robert Emmet planned an attack on Dublin Castle. His impassioned talk on the subject brought him a number of followers who believed in his suggestion that such a feat was possible.

There is little doubt that Emmet believed in his mission and that he was convinced of his success. He negotiated with the French but apparently was unable to come to decisive terms. The aim of his insurgency was to seize Dublin Castle and isolate the British army at the nearby barracks of Kilmainham. Emmet established a number of arms depots around the city. Forcing the army into an urban fight would have given the rebels the advantage. A problem arose when there was an unexpected explosion at one of the depots on July 16, 1803, and Emmet was forced to alter the date for his insurrection. When the rising was called for July 23, it proved to be fraught with bad luck. Only a small number of the expected force turned out, and French help did not materialize. The rebellion amounted to little more than street disturbances, though several government officials were killed. Emmet was arrested and then hanged on September 20. His speech from the dock remains his greatest legacy. It became so famous that it is still quoted today in political and literary circles in Ireland: "When my country has taken her place, among the nations of the earth, then, and not till then let my epitaph be written." No one has yet written Emmet's epitaph.

## THE EARLY DAYS OF UNION

The union with Britain marked the beginning of a long period of discontent for the Irish. For one thing, it did not lessen British control of the island. The king's chief representative in Ireland now became known as the viceroy, and the administration at Dublin Castle remained the same. The role of the chief secretary became more autocratic. The absence of an Irish parliament to check these English authority figures actually created more tension. The shift of parliamentary representation to London left the Irish feeling deserted by their own leaders and vulnerable to the authorities at the Castle. In Dublin it felt as though Ireland was more a colony than ever, with the only visible "government" being that of the English at Dublin Castle.

It soon became apparent that the Act of Union did not solve England's problems with Ireland. The Irish did not settle into the new relationship with vigor, and within a short time cracks began to appear. Most significantly, an important promise that was made in order to secure union—Catholic emancipation, or the right for

Catholics to sit in the Westminster parliament—was denied. This was the last of the Penal Laws, and with such a large Catholic population in Ireland the implication of the denial was great—a political disaster for those who had made the promise. It had been Pitt's intention that the Act of Union would include repeal of this law, but King George III vetoed the bill and forced the prime minister to postpone these plans.

Many in Ireland and England were enraged by the king's veto. Cornwallis resigned along with the other ministers in Pitt's ministry. Catholics in Ireland were incensed because some of them had voiced support for the Union in the belief that their right to sit in Parliament would be reestablished. If there had been no bitterness before the Union, this broken promise certainly created it. It is tempting to consider that had the British parliament granted this right, the Union might have developed more fruitfully. Instead, years of struggle to establish Catholic rights followed and left much animosity behind. In England, Catholics may have been disappointed at this turn of events; in Ireland that disappointment was channeled into political action. A refusal by the king was not about to be accepted. The Irish soon galvanized into a force willing to take direct constitutional action. Into the Irish arena stepped another great figure who would, by his determination, change the law and force the British parliament to become a more inclusive institution.

## DANIEL O'CONNELL—THE LIBERATOR

Politics in Ireland were changing. From the end of the eighteenth century and the relaxation of most of the Penal Laws, some Catholics had gained wealth and social position and were no longer willing to accept exile from political life. Young Catholic men had entered the legal profession and believed they were entitled to hold political positions and have a say in the running of the country. With a population that was now more than 75 percent Catholic, a number of elite Catholic families in Ireland were increasingly determined to take what they considered their rightful position in their own society. A young Catholic lawyer named Daniel O'Connell became the leading proponent of Catholic aspirations and, in the process, one of the icons of modern Irish history.

Daniel O'Connell had been born near Cahirsiveen in Kerry in August 1775. His family was an unusual one: they belonged to one of the few Catholic aristocratic families that had held on to its land and wealth. In addition to the new wealthy merchant Catholic families, there were an estimated fifty Catholic aristocratic families still living in Ireland holding their ancient lands. His wealthy childless uncle, Maurice "Hunting Cap" O'Connell, adopted Daniel at an early age and brought him up in his home at Derrynane, a large impressive estate of approximately forty thousand acres. For all the social advantages this brought him, young Daniel did not grow up isolated from the ordinary tenants who lived on the estate and worked the fields. He knew the Irish language and was interested in the traditional Gaelic culture that was still vibrant in the Kerry of his day. Throughout his life, Daniel O'Connell mixed well at all social levels and was astute in his handling of people and public affairs. Much of this had to do with the profile of Catholic families who had survived the centuries-long political chaos and land seizures. In spite of their position these were no pliable people. Their survival under frequently chaotic conditions made them strong and adroit. Aristocratic Catholic families who had endured against all odds had a reputation for being tough-willed and resilient. Sean O'Faolain, in his biography of O'Connell, described the landed Catholic survivors as "magnifying prudence, forethought, doggedness, tortuosity, a great deal of close-mindedness and a gift of silence." This silence was probably their greatest asset.

## THE YOUNG DANIEL PREPARES FOR THE BRITISH LION'S DEN

Like many wealthy Irish Roman Catholics, as a young boy Daniel was sent to France to be educated. French culture was quite familiar to Irish Catholic upper-class families who had maintained strong connections with France for hundreds of years. One of Daniel's uncles was a general in the Irish Brigade of the French army, so the boy would not have felt like a stranger there. His experience in France as a youth shaped many of his political attitudes in later life. He was educated there during the especially charged political time of the French Revolution and its aftermath, and his personal experience of this historical event was something he never forgot. By the time Daniel returned home to Ireland in 1794, he had witnessed much of the carnage of the French revolutionary period. This experience left him firmly preferring parliamentary methods to physical force.

On returning to Ireland Daniel studied the law and took advantage of the Relief Bill of 1792 allowing Catholics to enter the legal profession. In 1798 he was called to the bar. His studies went beyond the law, and he read widely of Voltaire, Rousseau, Godwin, Smith, and Bentham. These authors formed his political and economic thinking and influenced him toward Catholic liberalism. He established a legal practice in Munster and built it up. He was not well disposed to the rebellion of 1798 because he could not condone its violence. He became involved in politics when he appeared at a public meeting about the Act of Union and denounced it strongly. He wrote later that he heard with great sadness and anger the ringing of the bells of St. Patrick's Cathedral in Dublin when Union was announced.

O'Connell and others like him who had been against Union were further alienated when the Catholic franchise was not granted. The issue of Catholic rights, especially the right to sit in Parliament, became the focus of his political drive. His personal life was dominated by his happy marriage. He married his cousin, Mary O'Connell, in 1802, and they formed a true amity with each other. O'Faolain describes his courtship and love of her as "true eighteenth century style" in that it was forever filled with romance. In a letter to her before the birth of their first child, Daniel declared, "How sincerely will I express my affectation to the mother in the caress I bestow on the child, dearest sweetest wife." They had seven children who survived into adulthood.

Slowly politics drew him in, and he continued to keep a public profile. In a public speech in 1815 O'Connell attacked the Dublin Corporation (the City fathers) and denounced it as a "beggarly corporation." The choice of words was unfortunate because one of the members, Norcot D'Esterre, was almost bankrupt, and he took great personal offense. The aldermen and councillors were also infuriated. When it became obvious that O'Connell would not apologize, D'Esterre sent him a challenge to a duel. D'Esterre was a renownèd duelist, and the general expectation was that if O'Connell attempted to fight he would be killed. To the surprise of all,

O'Connell met D'Esterre and fatally shot him. Later he deeply regretted the exploit and gave the dead man's widow a lifelong pension. Dueling was not legally condoned but still held an air of romance and fascination, so this tragic adventure did not damage O'Connell's reputation. In some quarters it made him a quixotic hero and added an air of mystique to his personality.

## CATHOLIC RIGHTS ON THE AGENDA

Soon O'Connell was involved in a wide range of political activities involving Catholic rights. He was a member of the Catholic Committee and became the leader of a radical group within that society. In 1823 he formed the Catholic Association with the specific aim of using constitutional means to secure Catholic emancipation. Although other similar organizations existed at the time, the Catholic Association stood out. It ultimately had enormous success mostly because of the methods adopted by O'Connell. He made the decision to involve the great mass of rural tenants in the organization. These people were poor but, most important, were Catholic and identified with the Catholic cause. By gaining parish priests' and their parishioners' support O'Connell changed the way the political system in Ireland usually worked. It turned out to be a brilliant strategy.

O'Connell traveled throughout the country gaining support for the Association among ordinary tenants. Initially membership in the organization was open only to those who could afford the ten-pound annual membership fee, but O'Connell introduced an "associate" membership at only one penny a month. This had an enormous psychological effect on ordinary people who joined up in great numbers. The payment, which became known as "Catholic rent," was a way for ordinary individuals to take part in an important national organization which represented their interests.

By 1825 the Catholic Association had more than 300,000 members. Thanks to this large membership, the association amassed a large amount of money for its cause. Within nine months it collected £20,000 in funds. The Association charter is quite explicit in its intentions for the funds. It shows a wide concern for Catholic causes both within Ireland and abroad. In Ireland the Association directed funds toward "erecting schools, building Catholic churches, and erecting and furnishing dwelling-houses for the clergy in the poorer parishes."

O'Connell also declared his intention to help the fledgling Catholic church in the United States by donating £5,000 a year to the American church to train young men for the priesthood. This is an interesting aspiration because at this stage the American Catholic church would not have been greatly influenced by the Irish Catholic church, as it would be in the years following the Great Famine. Most important, the association also used its funds to assist parliamentary candidates who supported Catholic emancipation.

## CATHOLIC ACTION IN THE POLLING BOOTH

At the 1826 Parliamentary General Election the Catholic Association worked in counties where Catholic voters were in a majority and where they thought they might achieve some success. Because there was no secret ballot at the time, these candidates normally would not have been elected because the practice was for voters to say aloud whom they were voting for. Voting for a pro-Catholic candidate for Parliament might have resulted in repercussions for tenants, as this could mean going against their landlord's wishes. O'Connell traveled widely—as did other members of the Catholic Association—and spoke to crowds in each county. Tenants were asked to ignore their landlord's "advice" on voting and cast their choice for the Catholic-backed candidates. Priests were asked to give moral and physical support to their parishioners, and many priests went to the polling stations.

These efforts met with great success as the targeted counties returned pro-emancipation candidates. Liberal Protestant voters also contributed to the result. Supporters had great hope that with the election of these candidates the Catholic cause would gain ground. This did not happen. Conservatives in the British parliament resisted the pressure by simply ignoring it. A bill in Parliament to allow Catholics to sit failed to pass. All of this contributed to more resentment in Ireland and the determination to continue the long struggle.

## O'CONNELL THE CATHOLIC CANDIDATE

The Catholic Association decided that the answer to this deliberate rebuke was a direct confrontation. An opportunity presented itself when a parliamentary seat became vacant in County Clare. The circumstances were slightly convoluted because in those days a member of Parliament, or MP, who was made a cabinet minister had to return to his constituency for reelection. This is what occurred in Clare. Vesey Fitzgerald had been the member for Clare for more than ten years, and he needed to be reelected after his appointment to ministerial office. He was a local resident landlord and had a good reputation with his tenants; a popular candidate, his reelection was expected to be a mere formality. Instead the election made history. In the by-election—the term applies to any election held outside of a General Election—in June 1828, Daniel O'Connell decided to run in opposition to Fitzgerald. This was a bold step because if elected as a Catholic, he would not be eligible to take his seat. There was again no secret ballot, and because it was a by-election the voters had to travel to the county seat of Ennis and openly declare their choice.

The pre-election canvassing paid off with a large voter turnout, and O'Connell was elected. This presented the Conservative "Tory" party with a problem. They did not wish to admit a Catholic to Parliament, and many of them voiced strong opposition to doing so. But they knew that refusing O'Connell entry to Commons might result in a civil war in Ireland or, worse, the real possibility of more Catholic MPs winning elections and the Irish seceding from Westminster. This was no empty fear because it is precisely what Sinn Féin was to do a century later. By the 1820s many Catholics were members of the police and the Irish branch of the British army, so support for revolution could stretch across a broad spectrum. There might also be trouble in England from Catholics who were angry at being outside the political system. Reluctantly, the Duke of Wellington (of Waterloo fame), who was then prime minister, pushed through the Catholic Relief Act of 1829, which granted emancipation to Catholics and removed the ban on Catholics in the Westminster parliament. This act allowed O'Connell to enter Parliament. He was hailed in Ireland as "The Liberator."

## O'CONNELL IN PARLIAMENT

In February 1830 when Daniel O'Connell took his seat in the House of Commons he became the first Irish Catholic to hold legislative office since 1692. It had taken 140 years after the Boyne to achieve

A strong believer in constitutional methods, Daniel O'Connell won the right for Catholics to sit in the parliament in Westminster. (*National Gallery of Ireland*)

this. Catholics remained excluded from some offices; one in particular was that of lord lieutenant in Ireland. Likewise Dublin Castle would remain under English Protestant control. It would not be until the twentieth century that the position of lord lieutenant could legally be held by a Catholic. Of particular note is the reaction to Catholic emancipation in the northern part of Ireland, where the old worries about property and jobs arose again. In the 1820s the first Orange Lodges were formed as the Orange Society grew and prospered.

O'Connell is not without his critics. Some historians reproach him because most of the people who actually voted him into office lost the right to vote as the result of doing so. The Disenfranchisement Act passed at the same time as emancipation. The English Conservative party would grant Catholic emancipation only with this addendum. At this time qualification for voting depended on the value of a person's holdings. In Ireland this had stood at 40 shillings and above. Now it was raised to £10 and above, essentially quadrupling the wealth qualification for voting. As a result the Catholic Irish electorate was reduced from 216,000 to a mere 37,000 voters. O'Connell made a perfunctory objection but allowed the act to go through. Many Catholic activists were also not particularly upset. The main point was that emancipation was passed and Catholics had won the right to sit in Parliament. To these people the greater good had been served, and if blame should fall anywhere it should be on those in the British parliament who made the terms for Catholic emancipation so difficult.

## THE LIMITS OF CONSTITUTIONAL CHANGE

The fact that emancipation for Catholics, in spite of such enormous legislative effort, was approved so reluctantly was not lost on later generations of Irish nationalists, who felt that constitutional methods alone did not necessarily result in success. The disqualification for Irish voters was not rectified quickly. The Reform Act of 1832 gave the Irish the least amount of reform. This voter reform bill gave the vote to one person in five in England, to one in eight in Scotland, but to only one in twelve in Ireland.

Meanwhile O'Connell's career continued after his great triumph. His supporters expected further constitutional change, but new successes proved more difficult. O'Connell next threw his support behind an attempt to repeal the Act of Union. For the General Election of 1832 his motto was "Repeal, sink or swim." His reelection swam on the tide of a brighter future for Ireland. He was not seeking complete independence for Ireland but a restoration of the Irish parliament as it had been before the Union. In conjunction with this push for repeal and the general climate of populism to which emancipation had given rise, some Irish began to initiate more change. Some of those attempts were taking hold at the grassroots of Irish society.

## TITHE WAR

Beginning in the 1830s in Leinster but spreading around the country, a campaign was initiated against the payment of tithes to the established church. This became known as the Tithe War. Catholics were feeling their power and were reacting to laws they believed were unjust. The paying of a tax to the minority established church was one of their longstanding grievances. The older secret societies of the preceding century were again active in attacking tithe collectors; the refusal to pay tithes was a new element of this opposition. Although not a serious threat to order, these rebellious acts indicated the change in perspective of ordinary people. Irish tenants, previously so easily victimized or ignored, were now more confident that they could bring about change by their own actions.

By the late 1830s the government had stopped using police and the army to enforce tithe payment—one English official said, "It is costing a shilling to collect tuppence." The amount of the tithe was also reduced, which alleviated tensions. Further constitutional change, though, was not so easy to achieve. The British government was reluctant to give any quarter to the question of a devolved parliament for Ireland. The United Kingdom would not be broken up so easily; the prestige of the Empire depended on it.

## "WHAT GOOD DID THE UNION DO?"

Further reforms of local government followed in Ireland but not a repeal of the Union. When the reformed Municipal Corporations Act of 1840 went into effect, one of the first results was that Daniel O'Connell was elected lord mayor of Dublin. He was the first Catholic to hold this office in 150 years. As he hoped to repeal the Union, he organized large meetings known as "Monster Meetings." These large assemblies were held in some of the ancient historic sites which still held great meaning for the native Irish. He declared the year 1843 to be "Repeal Year." In a speech in the town of Mullingar in May 1843, O'Connell told the crowd, "My first object is to get Ireland for the Irish." To the cheers of the gathering he addressed the issue of the faltering Irish economy since Union when he said, "An Irish parliament would foster Irish Commerce, and protect Irish agriculture." He argued passionately on behalf of separation: "The present state of Ireland is nearly unendurable. . . . I would be glad to know what good did the Union do?"

Adhering to his philosophy of nonviolence and the use of constitutional methods, O'Connell declared that his object was to use everything in his power to return a parliament to Dublin. The repeal movement had enormous popular support, and the strong symbolism of the meeting places drew large crowds. In August 1843 more than a quarter-million people gathered at Tara, the ancient "capital" of a once-free Ireland, and listened to speeches on Irish self-government. Wearing green, now the symbolic color of nationalism, the crowd cheered on the idea presented of an Ireland free of the English yoke. A massive meeting was planned for October 1843 at Clontarf, where in 1014 the High King Brian Boru had defeated the invading Vikings. The British government banned the meeting the day before it was to be held and threatened military action should it go ahead. O'Connell feared an outbreak of violence. To the disappointment of many, he backed down and canceled the meeting. He was arrested and charged with sedition and sentenced to one year in prison. He served some months in jail where his health broke before the sentence was overturned by an appeal to the House of Lords.

## THE YOUNG IRELANDERS

Frustrated by the government's lack of response to O'Connell's position on repeal, a group of young men broke from O'Connell and formed a new organization with the express intent of using violence as a means of achieving their aims. They were discouraged by what they saw as the failure of O'Connell's constitutional methods and wanted more action. They called themselves the "Young Irelanders." This group of young rebels was comprised of Protestants and Catholics who had also grown concerned with what they perceived as the sectarian divisions facilitated by some of O'Connell's actions. He had antagonized some in Ireland by refusing to go along with a British proposal for a new university system in Ireland. The Queen's colleges, universities to be established in the major cities, were nondenominational. A Catholic archbishop, John McHale, had denounced the idea as "godless," and O'Connell agreed. Some young Catholics and Protestants felt that this kind of talk was causing a sectarian divide which ultimately would destroy the nationalist movement.

The Young Irelanders believed they were the voice of a new generation determined to unite the country and not allow sectarian division to impede a complete severance with Britain. In this way their objectives harked back to those of Wolfe Tone a century earlier. While O'Connell was looking for a break with the Union and a reestablishment of the old-style arrangement, the Young Irelanders had grander aspirations and wanted an Irish republic completely free of British interference. Thomas Davis, a Protestant, was the initial inspiration for this movement, but he died in 1845. His legacy remains enormous. Davis published a revolutionary newspaper called *The Nation*, which published many articles and poems on Irish nationalism. His poem, "A Nation Once Again," is one of the most popular songs in Irish repertoire and is still a rallying call for nationalists. The leadership in Young Ireland was taken over by another Protestant, William Smith O'Brien, who carried on Davis's legacy.

One significant member of Young Ireland was Thomas Meagher, who later became an important figure in the American Civil War. In July 1846, as a response to O'Connell and his followers' attempt to extract pledges from the repeal organization that no violence would be used in breaking the Union with Britain, Meagher gave a speech in Dublin. In an obvious departure from O'Connell he "dissented from these resolutions for I fear that by assenting to them I should have pledged myself to the unqualified repudiation of physical force in all countries, and at all times, and in every circumstance. This I could not do. . . . I do not abhor the use of arms in the vindication of national rights." The break with O'Connell's method could not be clearer. By the time Young Ireland had fully developed as an organization, O'Connell was a sick man. He gave his final speech in the House of Commons in February 1847, then left on a pilgrimage to Rome but died in Genoa in May.

## O'CONNELL'S LEGACY

O'Connell's contribution to the Catholic cause cannot easily be discounted. He became an honored figure not only in Ireland but also in Europe, where his fame had spread. French educated, he had absorbed the ideas of the liberal Catholic atmosphere in France and admired Thomas Paine's work. Roy Foster describes him as "a liberal Catholic moralist." His humanitarian interests reached beyond Ireland. He was a passionate anti-slaver and spoke out frequently in Parliament on behalf of Jewish emancipation in Britain.

Although he was of a privileged class, he had the common touch. In Ireland he was much more attuned to the ordinary people than the United Irishmen had been, and this was arguably the primary reason for his success. In his personal life in his role as a landlord he had a reputation for being indulgent and generous. His knowledge of the Irish language made it possible for him to identify closely with the common people and have intimate knowledge of how they lived. When the time came to take political action, it was to the people that he instinctively went. In making use of their support he won Catholic emancipation against tremendous odds. O'Connell's ultimate achievement was his use of mass participation to achieve a political goal, which was new and unique for the time. In addressing the Reform Club in London in 1997 on the issue of O'Connell's greatness, president of Ireland Mary Robinson compared O'Connell to Nelson Mandela and Martin Luther King.

After O'Connell's death the Young Ireland movement made a brief attempt at armed revolution in 1848, but it was feeble and did not attract the attention or the emotions of a wide following. By then far greater issues gripped Ireland: thousands of people were dying of starvation and disease. The years of the Great Famine had arrived, and Ireland was plunged into its greatest tragedy.

## THE GREAT FAMINE

The Great Famine of the 1840s is one of the most significant watersheds in Irish history. Although Ireland was no stranger to tragedy and loss, no event in Irish history comes close to the devastation and utter desolation that occurred during these years. It is without doubt the greatest social calamity in the history of the country, the ramifications of which are still felt. It was also one of the great silences in Irish history—a subject that few wished to address. In opening the Famine Museum in Strokestown, County Roscommon, in 1992, Irish president Mary Robinson referred to the "conspiracy of silence" that surrounded the subject and called for more openness in addressing its history. "A hungry and demoralized people becomes silent," President Robinson said. She also observed that while societies are willing to celebrate their triumphs, "they are less inclined to look at the dark events." For the Irish, the Famine is a dark event indeed.

The first significant study on the Famine did not appear until one hundred years after the tragedy, when Professor K. H. Connell published his analysis of population growth. Historians are divided over how the contemporary British government handled the Famine and over whether more could or should have been done to offset the tragedy. Few can deny the human suffering and the helplessness of innocent people caught up in a catastrophe beyond their control and not of their making. There was no silence or peace in the minds and hearts of the Irish people who lived through these years. Although the details of the Famine were seldom discussed, the long shadow of suffering was passed on to future generations.

## BACKGROUND TO THE TRAGEDY

The single crop that failed, the potato, was not native to Ireland. It was first introduced to the country in the late sixteenth century. It was said to have been brought to Ireland from North America by Walter Raleigh when he owned a large estate in Ireland in the Cork area. It soon proved itself an ideal crop as it grew well in the cool, damp Irish climate. Compared to other crops grown in Ireland, it had an enormous yield. One acre of land could yield six tons of potatoes annually. By the year 1800 it had become the standard crop of the Irish poor. By the 1840s more than one-third of the tilled land of Ireland was devoted to potato growing. The potato became the basic food for most of the country, surpassing bread as the main staple.

One of the reasons for its success is the extraordinary nutritious value of the potato, which is deficient only in Vitamin A. The Irish potato diet was usually supplemented with cabbage, carrots, milk, and fish. The poor could healthfully sustain themselves with potatoes and buttermilk alone. The Irish kept disease at bay with this nutritious diet, and scurvy, so common in Europe, was practically unknown in Ireland. Travelers to the country frequently remarked that in spite of poverty the people were remarkably well nourished. The Irish had a reputation for being physically robust and among the tallest people in Europe. It was nevertheless a precarious health. When the potato crop failed, it took millions of lives with it.

## SOCIAL AND ECONOMIC FACTORS

To try to understand how such a tragedy happened it is necessary to look at what was occurring in Ireland demographically, economically, and politically in the decades preceding the 1840s. Comparisons are made against the 1841 census, which was the last one taken before the Famine. The population had started to increase throughout the 1700s, but it accelerated markedly around the year 1800. Historians still do not understand why, but a number of facts are known. The population of Ireland according to the 1841 census stood at 8,175,124. From 1780 this reflects an increase of 175 percent. We know that the Irish marriage age was lower than the rest of Europe. The average age for women marrying in Europe at this period was 24–26. The 1841 census reveals that in Ireland the average age for marriage by women was 20–22. The census also shows a high birthrate of 40 per thousand of the Irish population. In conjunction with this high birthrate was a decline in infant mortality, so that more children survived infancy and lived into adulthood than had in the previous century. These patterns made Ireland one of the most densely populated countries in Europe, which strained land and resources. No large-scale industrialization existed to absorb this expanding population. The agrarian economy meant that more people were trying to live off the same amount of land.

In addition to the lack of resources there was a further drain on the economy. The social and economic life of the countryside had altered in the aftermath of the Act of Union, and numerous Irish landlords no longer lived at their homes in Ireland. Many Irish lords felt they had no reason to live in Ireland after the Irish House of Lords was abolished and they were placed in the Lords at Westminster. They simply used the rents they received from their Irish estates to live a fashionable life in London. Their estates were taken care of by middlemen or agents who saw to the rent collecting and land subletting. They were paid by the landlord if they successfully collected the rent; if not, they lost their jobs. Consequently the agents cared for little other than the collection of rents. Agents and landlords had reason to subdivide properties, as subdivision meant an increase in rents. It became a common practice as the population increased, resulting in more and more small farms. Economic circumstances offer an explanation, other than land scarcity, as to why the Irish subdivided so easily.

## THE BOOM BEFORE THE BUST

Tillage farming had become more prevalent in the eighteenth century because of the laws against exporting Irish cattle. In the late 1700s and early 1800s the Napoleonic Wars provided a ready market in the British army and navy for Irish farm crops. The result was a boom in farm prices. For some years the government demand for food to feed the expanded army kept prices high, and small farms could provide a tolerable standard of living. For a time this meant that subdivision did not necessarily mean substantially smaller income. Families could subdivide farms with a reasonable expectation of making a living. This circumstance altered greatly in the 1820s after the war with the French ended and farm crops declined drastically in price. According to the economic historian Louis Cullen, between 1818 and 1822 the price of grain declined by half. This dramatic downturn must have had an enormous effect on farm income. Smaller farms especially would have experienced a serious decline in income. Many Irish farmers, previously surviving comfortably, fell into poverty. Reliance on the potato became more pronounced as more people came to depend on it as their main food source. It was not grown as a commercial crop or an export food but almost exclusively as a domestic food source. It was also an important feed for animals. Approximately half the crop was used to feed pigs and farmyard fowl.

The 1841 census reports that more than 300,000 Irish families lived on farms of fewer than five acres. The cottiers, the landless laborers, had grown increasingly dependent on the potato crop as their sole food source. Many of these laborers were living close to starvation before the Famine hit. They worked for farmers, and their work went to pay the rent for the paltry huts in which they lived. They leased small plots of land where they grew food for their families. Most of these rented plots were less than an acre in size, and the potato was the exclusive crop. By 1841 more than 100,000 families lived in this manner. Small farms were common throughout the country, but they were most numerous in the west, in Connacht. The population in the west was very dense. According to figures in the 1841 census, it was almost three times what it is today. An alarming 70 percent of farms in this area were smaller than five acres. It is estimated that one-third of the Irish population depended entirely on the potato; in Mayo, traditionally the poorest county, the estimate was nine-tenths. A young laboring man might consume between five and ten pounds of potatoes per day as his only food. These startling statistics were not unknown to the authorities at the time. There were even more ominous warning signs of a possible catastrophe: between 1816 and 1841 a total of 14 crop failures had already occurred. In 1839, in a speech to the House of Commons, Daniel O'Connell tried to draw attention to the potential danger of a serious social disaster in Ireland when he warned that the Irish situation was a cause for great concern. He was right.

## POTATO BLIGHT ARRIVES

In 1845 a calamity struck the Irish countryside in the form of a potato blight, the fungus *Phytophthora infestans.* It arrived unexpectedly, spread with cruel rapidity, and within a short time had reduced much of the year's crop to rottenness. It is now believed that the fungus entered the country through the port at Dublin. It is thought to have originated in the United States but was carried to Europe. It may have arrived in Ireland via the southwest winds blowing in from the Continent and the south of England. The blight was first officially recorded on August 20, 1845, at the Dublin Botanical Gardens. A week later a total potato crop failure in County Fermanagh was reported. By October frightened reports came from the west of Ireland as farmers discovered that a large part of their crop had failed.

The blight is described in contemporary accounts as making the potatoes look like they had soot on them. The crop turned black, rotted completely, and emitted a distinctive putrid smell. Very shortly it was estimated that about half the 1845 crop would be lost. A relief committee was formed in October and a meeting held in Dublin at the Mansion House, the official residence of the lord mayor. Other committee meetings were held around the country. Calls were made for the government to send relief. The urgent request called for halting exports of native-grown corn and employing workers on public works.

By mid-October, British Prime Minister Robert Peel had privately admitted that Ireland appeared to be on the brink of disaster. Peel did not receive support from his own Conservative party for Irish relief because it would have meant repealing the protective laws known as the Corn Laws. These laws restricted the importation of grain into the United Kingdom in order to protect prices in the home market. In a controversial move Peel did manage to get the chancellor of the exchequer to agree on the importation of American corn or maize for Ireland. Approximately £100,000 was spent on an initial purchase.

The purchase of this product remains controversial. American corn was chosen because it was not typically sold in the country and therefore did not compete with the normal food supply. If corn is not properly cooked, serious bowel problems may result. In order to safeguard against this eventuality, pamphlets were sold describing the cooking process. But American corn gained such a bad reputation that it was given the nickname "Peel's brimstone." In addition to the cooking problem, the corn arrived in Ireland in an unmilled condition. It had to be commercially ground before it could be distributed. Thus it was almost two months before it was ready for consumption. It was not a free distribution. It was sold at market rates to the poor; as all food prices were rising in the face of scarcity, many of the poor did not have enough money to purchase corn.

## RELIEF WORKS

In all the British government spent more than £185,000 on American corn, including shipping and grinding, but the Irish treasury was expected to pay back most of this. In addition to the corn purchase, some public works were initiated so that poor people could work for wages. Public works were a standard way of dealing with distress in Ireland. The government would initiate a work plan to provide employment in a particular area. During the Famine some schemes involved drainage, navigation, and the linking of lakes. Considering that the social problem was starvation, labor was not always a successful way of getting relief to the needy. Starving or ill-nourished people often collapsed under the strain of this type of heavy manual work. Peel also ordered all the workhouses in the country to open and take in the destitute, but the total number of people helped this way was only about 100,000. It was estimated at the time that around three times that number were in abject need.

Consequently the workhouses quickly filled with the starving and distressed. Many workhouses had to be bolted shut at night to keep out the throngs of people trying to get in. In a poignant gesture The O'Connor Don, traditional head of the dispossessed O'Connors, wrote repeatedly to the local workhouses in his area of Roscommon asking that they accept more people.

## THE DEATH TOLL MOUNTS

Nevertheless Peel is regarded in Ireland as having responded sympathetically to the tragedy, in contrast to the later British government response, which was far less favorable. But Peel was dealing with a partial crop failure, one that had not yet reached the point of catastrophic disaster. The excessively high rise in food prices did not occur until the autumn of 1846, after Peel had left office. The situation deteriorated rapidly. In the spring of 1846 panic erupted as death from famine became increasingly commonplace. There was enough food in Ireland to feed the people, but the government would not release it. Large quantities of barley and oats were exported during this time. There is little doubt of the growing emergency and the desperate attempts of starving people to gain access to food. The news of this situation was not confined to Ireland. The British public was aware of the distress. In February 1846 Daniel O'Connell again spoke to the issue when he told the House of Commons, "It is your business to mitigate this calamity as well as you can. . . . Famine is coming, fever is coming and this House should place in the hands of the government power to stay the evil."

By mid-1846 disease became a problem; ultimately it was to become as great a killer as starvation. From sheer desperation some people were eating rotten potatoes and, coupled with the lack of nutrition, disease in the form of typhus and cholera broke out throughout the country. Dysentery, also a major killer, resulted from eating seaweed or insufficiently cooked American corn.

## "WE CANNOT FEED THE PEOPLE"

When Peel's government fell in the summer of 1846, he was succeeded as prime minister by the Liberal party leader John Russell. Addressing the growing catastrophe in Ireland, Russell issued a statement in October 1846 that shaped government strategy for the remainder of the tragedy: "It must be thoroughly understood that we cannot feed the people. It was a cruel delusion to pretend to do so." From this time on Ireland became an overflowing well of human misery as the Famine was allowed to take a natural course. Government policy at the time was wedded to laissez-faire economics, that is, no government interference in the economy. The Famine was a disaster on a grand scale for the Irish.

Sir Charles Trevelyan, permanent head of the treasury, came to represent the face of government policy toward the situation in Ireland. He assumed autocratic powers of life and death over the disaster and later issued a report, *The Irish Crisis*, in which he outlined his own attitude and his policies. It is an incredibly damning document and leaves little room for doubt that people starved because they did not receive the help they needed. Throughout the document Trevelyan does not disguise his disregard for the Irish. He speaks of Ireland as if it were an entirely separate entity and not part of the United Kingdom. He seems to think that the Irish economy exists beyond the control of the British government and ought to take care of itself. On the second page of his report Trevelyan openly exhibits his feelings when he poses the rhetorical question: "But what hope is there for a nation that lives on potatoes?" The head of the British treasury obviously felt no responsibility for the condition of Ireland's economy. Trevelyan was totally committed to laissez-faire economics. A chilling insight into the man's mind is the fact that one of his first responses to the Irish situation was to send a copy of Edmund Burke's book *Thoughts on Scarcity* to relief agencies in Ireland. This book warns of starving people becoming dependent on government for subsistence. Trevelyan seemed unable to treat the Irish situation as a disaster requiring a special response. "The great evil with which we have to contend is not the physical evil of famine but the moral evil of the selfish, perverse and turbulent character of the [Irish] people," Trevelyan wrote in his report.

The government's position was that trade and commerce were of greater importance than feeding the marginalized poor. That some of the starving people were trying to prevent the movement of food for export was viewed by Trevelyan as a crime, and he sent in police:

> . . . great exertions were made to protect the provision trade and the troops and constabulary were harassed by continual escort. . . . Convoys under military protection proceeded at stated intervals from place to place, without which nothing in the shape of food could be sent [out of the country] with safety.

In a dispassionate tone Trevelyan continues, "At Limerick, Galway and elsewhere mobs prevented articles of food from leaving the towns." The picture that emerges is one of people being denied access to what they needed to stay alive: "The plunder of baker's shops and bread carts and the shooting of horses and breaking up of roads to prevent the removal of provisions were matters of daily occurrence." What is most striking about Trevelyan's report is his total lack of compassion or empathy. He sees these acts of desperation as evidence of delinquency in the Irish character. The report confirms that authorities were well aware of the situation and that people were frantic in their attempt to survive this holocaust. Trevelyan offers cold details of the agony expressed by starving people as they tried to gain access to food and stay alive in the face of certain death.

## WHAT THE PAPERS SAID

Reports in newspapers of the period confirm these attempts by distressed people to gain access to food. The *Freeman's Journal* reported on April 15, 1846:

> There have been attacks on flour mills in Clonmel by people whose bones protruded through the skin which covered them—staring through hollow eyes as if they had just risen from their shrouds, crying out that they could no longer endure the extremity of their distress and that they must take food which they could not produce. . . . As we pass into sum-

One of the drawings by James Mahoney depicting the abysmal state of most of the Irish population during the years of the Great Famine. More than 1.5 million people died from starvation and disease. (*Illustrated London News*)

mer, we pass into suffering. . . . Every week develops the growing intensity of the national calamity.

One of the best original sources for information on how the average person fared during the Famine comes from James Mahoney, who wrote and sketched for the *Illustrated London News*. Mahoney, an illustrator who lived in Cork, was asked by the *News* to travel around the Cork region and send reports of what he saw. His sketches and firsthand observations are haunting. They are excellent historical resources on the effects of the tragedy on the lives of those who died under the most inhumane circumstances. A report by Mahoney published in the newspaper on February 13, 1847, related:

> [I] first proceeded to Bridgetown . . . and there I saw the dying, the living, and the dead, lying indiscriminately upon the same floor, without anything between them and the cold earth, save a few miserable rags upon them. To point to any particular house as a proof of this would be a waste of time, as all were in the same state; and not a single house out of 500 could boast of being free from death and fever, though several could be pointed out with the dead lying close to the living for the space of three or four, even six days, without any effort being made to remove the bodies to a last resting place.

## "NO FURTHER GOVERNMENT AID"

Government response to the suffering continued to be inadequate in the ensuing years of the Famine. Most accounts from the period indicate a slow starvation throughout the countryside and a helplessness that can only be described as wretched beyond human endurance. Christine Kinealy, in *This Great Calamity*, compares the reaction of other nineteenth-century governments to famine. During the period of the Irish Famine there were smaller famines in Belgium, Russia, and in the city-state of Alexandria. According to Kinealy, all these governments imported food for relief purposes and closed their ports to the export of food. The British government failed to do this for Ireland. From 1846 food prices soared, making it impossible for the destitute to feed themselves.

The crisis continued without abatement for a number of years. In the autumn of 1846 the potato crop totally failed, and prospects for the year ahead loomed ominously. The death toll mounted with each month. With the public attitude in Britain increasingly against further Irish assistance, the government felt no compulsion to act or make any further attempt to relieve the distress of the starving Irish. Within Parliament discussion turned against any relief effort for Ireland. In 1847 the government passed the Poor Law Extension Act, which eliminated public works altogether, and stated categorically that there was to be "no further government aid for any form of relief" in Ireland. In essence the British government washed its hands of the Irish situation. The burden for feeding the needy was shifted to local landlords, who were now solely responsible for the poor in their areas. As a consequence of this law, taxes for landlords rose by as much as 50 percent in some areas. In spite of the fact that many landowners had been unable to pay the old tax rate, they were now responsible for all of the destitute who could not enter the overcrowded workhouses. Ultimately this law meant bankruptcy for many Irish landlords, as they depended on rents that could not be paid.

Massive evictions followed for many who could not pay rent. As Irish-based landlords were going bankrupt, some were becoming desperate. On the other hand some absentee landlords sought to improve their economic situation by clearing their estates of poor tenants who could no longer pay. Many of these indifferent landlords did not reside in Ireland and had additional estates in England where they lived. In these cases it fell to local agents to evict tenants and see that the land was cleared. The Irish tenant was in a highly precarious position regarding rent payment during the Famine. The food grown for rent had to be surrendered to the landlord or eviction followed. In his report, Trevelyan acknowledged this pressure that the Irish felt to pay rent. He observed that the Irish rents "were generally well paid, being the first demand of all money, in order to secure that essential tenure."

Eviction was the sword of Damocles that hung over the tenant's head. The dilemma was whether to eat the crops usually grown for rent and stay alive—but face almost certain eviction; or to surrender the crops and avoid eviction but face possible starvation. It was a no-win situation. Outside the Ulster area, fixed tenure was practically unknown, and tenants had few property rights. The specter of eviction became another tragic and familiar part of the Famine scene. Newspapers from the period give us some fairly grim descriptions. *The Freeman's Journal* in October 1847 describes an eviction in County Galway:

> It was the most appalling sight I ever witnessed: women, young and old, running wildly to and fro with small portions of their property to save it from the wreck—the screaming of the children, and wild wailings of the mothers driven from home and shelter. . . . In the first instance the roofs and portions of the

wall only were thrown down. But that Friday night the wretched creatures pitched a few poles slant-wise against the walls covering them with thatch in order to procure shelter for the night. When this was perceived the next day the bailiffs were dispatched with orders to pull down all the walls and root up the foundations in order to prevent the poor people from daring to take shelter amid the ruins.

The Society of Friends stands out as a group that made heroic efforts to feed the starving masses, and it deserves much credit for its efforts. The Quakers were involved very early on in relief work throughout Ireland and showed an enormous degree of compassion and ability to organize in the face of such widespread disaster. Joseph Bewley and his family together with the Pim family were Dublin merchants who were chief among those who organized Quaker relief efforts that involved overseas aid from the United States. But their efforts could accomplish only so much. The Quakers declared in 1849 that charitable work was ultimately useless in the face of such enormous want and could achieve no permanent benefit. In a direct attack on British government policy, a Quaker circular of 1849 reads that "our permanent want is not money, it is the removal of those legal difficulties which prevent the capital of Ireland from being applied to the improved cultivation of its soil."

## THE CRISIS PASSES BUT THE CONTROVERSY LIVES ON

By the time the potato crop finally returned to health in 1850, more than 1.5 million Irish had died from starvation and disease. Another million had left to seek a home elsewhere. The controversy over who was responsible for this catastrophe or what should have been done to alleviate the suffering of so many people continues to this day. Historians disagree on the degree of culpability that should be directed at the British government of the period. In the 1970s and 1980s many historians tried to disperse blame or even avoid the issue of responsibility, but this position is now being challenged. Peter Gray, writing in *History Ireland* in 1995, declares that "the charge of culpable neglect [by the British Government] of the consequences of policies leading to mass starvation is indisputable. That a conscious choice to pursue moral or economic objectives at the expense of human life was made by several ministers can also be demonstrated." Christine Kinealy claims that "suffering, emotion, and the sense of catastrophe have been removed from revisionist interpretations of the Famine with clinical precision." Kinealy believes that "the British Government failed a large portion of the population in terms of humanitarian criteria."

The Famine was not such a brief event that it offered no opportunity to react. It lasted for four long arduous years, and help on a necessary scale was not forthcoming. Many Irish blamed public and private British indifference to the tragedy for the huge numbers that died. The British government knew of the extent of the disaster. Kinealy concurs that Irish feelings of resentment were "not without justification." It was a single crop failure; other food supplies were still intact and not redirected to the victims. The Irish believed that if the tragedy had occurred in England, government assistance would have been swift and decisive. Kinealy suggests a "hidden agenda" in government handling of the crisis—to clear Ireland of a large part of its population and reinvigorate the Irish economy in the cheapest way possible. She believes that a small number of very powerful people operating within the British government, "taking advantage of a passive establishment and public opinion . . . were able to manipulate a theory of free enterprise, thus allowing a massive social injustice to be perpetrated within a part of the United Kingdom."

There can be little doubt that anti-Irishness played a part in British hostility toward the Irish at this time. Although Ireland was a full member of the United Kingdom, it was generally treated as a foreign country whose problems should not impinge on British sensitivities. Irish stereotypes were common in the British press throughout the nineteenth century. *Punch* magazine frequently ran cartoons of the Irish as apelike, simian creatures below the level of human beings. English publications regularly depicted the Irish in caricature as dirty, unintelligent, given easily to emotional outbursts of rage, and violent by nature. The Irish culture was depicted as primitive, and distorted records of Irish history by British authors played into this stereotype. All levels of Irish society came under attack. One of the most surprising and prominent features of

Pejorative images of Irish people, often with simian
features, were rife in the British press in the
nineteenth and twentieth centuries. This illustration is
from *Punch*, May 1882.

these depictions of Ireland was the inclusion of Irish landlords in
the portrayal of the Irish as feckless and irresponsible.

## THE FAMINE LEFT "DEEP SCARS"

The scars left from the Famine period were deep and profound. It
would take years for the Irish to be able to talk about the tragedy or
even attempt to memorialize it. Since the 1990s this has changed
with the opening of the Famine Museum in Strokestown, the placing of a sculpture of famished figures along the dockside in Dublin,

and other similar memorials in Ireland and around the world. Because of the heightened publicity given the Famine in the 1990s, the British government finally addressed the issue of extensive neglect. In 1997 the British Prime Minster Tony Blair issued an apology to the Irish people for Britain's lack of response to the Famine. In the spirit of reconciliation, Blair said:

> It has left deep scars. That one million people should have died in what was then part of the richest and most powerful nation in the world is something that still causes pain as we reflect on it today. Those who governed in London at the time failed their people through standing by while a crop failure turned into a massive human tragedy. We must not forget such a dreadful event.

The most lamentable legacy of the Famine was the fact that it made emigration an Irish institution. It was as if an artery opened on the island and the young flowed out. After 1850 Ireland lost many of her people to emigration. Unique in Europe, as many young Irish women left as men. This pattern of large female emigration remained true into the twentieth century. The Irish born in the years following the Famine viewed Ireland as a land without resources, a country without a present or a future. In 1851 more than 300,000 people left. One of every two people born in Ireland between 1830 and 1930 left the island to make a permanent home elsewhere. It would take more than a hundred years for the country to begin to recover socially and economically. One significant outcome of the mass emigration from Ireland was the establishment of Irish communities in Australia, Canada, Britain, South America, and especially the United States. The Irish abroad did not forget the homeland and were regarded in Ireland as exiles. These diaspora communities would become the legacy of the Famine tragedy. Future generations of Irish born abroad would significantly impact the history of Ireland. A mute but keen awareness of what had happened when Ireland was vulnerable to the vagaries of British policy informed their participation in Irish politics from their new lands.

# [ 8 ]

# Struggling for Land Rights and Home Rule: Charles Stewart Parnell

THE FAMINE is the great dividing line in modern Irish history. Before it the Irish in the countryside married young and the population soared. In the years following the disaster, later marriage, and frequently no marriage, became the norm. The Irish language suffered dramatic changes too. Whereas before 1850 it was the language of the majority of the people, after the Famine it shrank as more and more people abandoned it and wanted their children to speak English. The economic advantages of the English language were paramount as emigration became more important. In addition, subdivision of farms stopped almost completely. Farmers began to will their holdings intact to one of their sons or sometimes one of their daughters. The average size of farms increased. In 1845 only 36 percent of farms were more than fifteen acres; by 1851 that figure had risen to 51 percent. Although this was an improvement, it still meant that many families were on holdings that could not generate a decent standard of living. The same 1851 census reports that 83 percent of the population still lived on the land. The most dramatic figure was the decline in total population. From 1841 the population fell by approximately 2.5 million.

Probably the most significant change was that after the Famine emigration became an established pattern as more and more rural people left Ireland in search of a better living abroad. Besides the obvious economic difficulty of living on a small farm, better shipping was bringing American beef and grain to the European markets and helping to drive down all farm prices in the latter part of the century. Coupled with this were the letters from relatives who had settled in America and were sending back reports of a better life, where jobs were plentiful and paid well. America became the great hope of many who could no longer make a living in Ireland. More than 80 percent of Irish emigration in the nineteenth century was to the United States.

## TENANTS FIGHT FOR LAND RIGHTS

As tenants found it increasingly difficult to meet their rent obligations, the fear of eviction rose. Landlords continued to press to collect their rents. The relationship between tenant and landlord, difficult before the Famine, became one of almost total distrust. The ongoing specter of easy eviction throughout the country had made tenants painfully aware of their precarious situation. They became determined to do something to protect themselves in the future. The Irish Tenant League was formed with the specific aim of establishing in law what was known as the three *F*s: fixity of tenure, fair rent, and freedom to sell interest in holdings. Although all three were considered of major importance, "fixity of tenure" would ensure that evictions would become more difficult for the landlords, as the tenants would be given a guaranteed lease. The first meeting of the new League was held in Dublin in 1850, attended by farmers from throughout Ireland. In their published manifesto they expressed the desire to protect the tenant and improve relations between tenant and landowner. They were committed to the constitutional methods established by O'Connell but were soon thwarted in their efforts.

In the election of 1852 the Tenant League was active in gaining support from candidates for their program. About forty of the Irish members elected to Westminster pledged support for tenant rights, but they failed to create any changes. Candidates were influenced more by the demands of the Catholic bishops and priests than by those who had actually voted for them. After election they quickly put aside the Tenant League that had helped to elect them and concentrated more on purely Catholic interests, such as Catholic education and the disestablishment of the Church of Ireland. The Irish, frustrated but never far from satire, labeled them "the Pope's brass band." As was to hold true for the future, when constitutional methods failed, other approaches became dominant.

## THE IRISH REPUBLICAN BROTHERHOOD AND THE AMERICAN IRISH

The Irish abroad were determined to remain involved in home politics and effect political change to avenge what they saw as appalling British governmental neglect during the Famine. For some the Famine crisis only increased the need for self-government in Ireland. The legacy of the failed 1848 rising would play a major role in channeling this emotional drive. James Stephens was a member of the Young Ireland movement who had fled to Paris after the attempted uprising. When in France he kept informed of events in Ireland and was more determined than ever to bring about an end to British dominance. In 1858 Stephens returned to Dublin and formed a new society, the Irish Republican Brotherhood, or IRB. This organization was based on the ideals of Wolfe Tone and the United Irishmen. It was militarily structured and was not intended to champion constitutional methods. Its members took military titles and were known as captains, sergeants, and colonels.

In New York the organization was established simultaneously with the same name and was also known there as the Fenian Brotherhood. The New York branch was formed by another Young Irelander, John O'Mahony. Like Stephens he too had fled to Paris but then proceeded to live in New York. O'Mahony became the leading figure among other Irish in the United States who sought to find answers to Ireland's political difficulties. IRB members were convinced that Britain would cede power only if forced to do so by military action. O'Mahony participated in the American Civil War on the Union side and had organized the Ninety-ninth New York National Guard, in which he served as a colonel. After he founded the IRB in New York, he became the main fundraiser for the organization.

The Fenian movement was extremely popular in America, and during the 1860s its membership grew enormously. One of those who joined the IRB was Thomas Meagher. Meagher had been arrested in Ireland and transported to Australia after 1848 but escaped and went to live in New York. He organized the Irish Brigade in the American Civil War and became a brigadier general in the Union army. Meagher and other Irish-American Civil War veterans joined the IRB with the intention of invading Ireland with an organized army and overthrowing British rule. At one stage O'Mahony boasted that he would send 200,000 troops to Ireland. With little support from Ireland this did not happen, but an alternative plan developed.

In 1866 things grew slightly bizarre when O'Mahony's group fractured. The split was led by New York merchant William Roberts over the issue of how best to attack the British. Roberts came up with a plan to attack Canada. If all went well and they managed to take over Canada, he argued, they could proceed to attack the island of Britain. O'Mahony would not go along with the scheme, but this did not deter the plan from going forward. With a great deal of hope in their hearts, in June 1866 a gallant Fenian army of eight hundred men crossed the Niagara River near Buffalo. They met with brief success, capturing the village of Fort Erie before Canadian forces drove them back. A series of other small raids on Canada followed, but none amounted to anything.

The Fenian movement contracted somewhat after the 1860s, but they were responsible for a number of bombings of key British government buildings, including the House of Commons, in London in the 1860s and 1870s. In one bombing of the Clerkenwell prison in London in 1867, twelve people who lived in nearby housing were killed. In Britain the term "Fenian" became a pejorative byword for Irish nationalists of every persuasion.

## CARDINAL PAUL CULLEN AND THE "DEVOTIONAL REVOLUTION"

Other important changes were stirring in Ireland at this time. The Catholic church, so long the religion of the poor and politically outcast, was about to come in from the cold and play a central role in the political life of the island. The strong Roman Catholic church that now developed in Ireland would become a powerful institution whose dominant position and influence would wane only in the 1990s. Previously an informal church with almost irregular practices, the Irish Catholic church was now being organized and structured as never before. Although Christianity had first arrived in Ireland in the fifth century, the Irish church had a long tradition of independence. Even the so-called twelfth-century reforms had not been entirely successful in organizing the Roman church in Ireland. It took until the nineteenth century for the Catholic church to establish itself there as a powerful and influential institution.

The person who is credited with developing this well-organized church structure and essentially developing the modern Irish Catholic church is Bishop—later Cardinal—Paul Cullen. Cullen was born in 1803 in Prospect, County Kildare. As a Catholic child he was in fact educated by Quakers at Ballitore and then attended Carlow College. He went to Rome in 1820 to attend the College of Propaganda Fidei and in 1829 was ordained a priest in Rome. In 1832 he was made rector of the Irish College there. These were the years of O'Connell's great parliamentary success when Catholics won the right to sit in the Westminster parliament. Ireland, for centuries Catholic in spirit if not regulation, was ripe for organization and ritual development. Cullen spent years in Rome before returning to Ireland in January 1850 as archbishop of Armagh. His Roman ideas included the belief that interference in political matters was a church obligation.

Cullen's first priority in Ireland was to organize a church council. The Synod of Thurles, held in August–September 1850, brought about dramatic changes in Irish worship. Dubbed the "devotional revolution," this period marked the foundation of the modern Irish Catholic church. Among the significant changes established by the Synod, "the sacraments were to be administered more often and only in church." Before this the Irish were not frequent practitioners of religion and were using homes to hold confession, Mass, and even marriage ceremonies. These and other "irregularities" were outlawed at the Synod, and bishops were told to encourage people to attend church for liturgies. The Synod established the Mass at the center of Irish religious practice. For Cullen, devotion to the Virgin Mary was also part of his spiritual plan for Ireland. The

Synod also voted to establish the Catholic University of Ireland, which first opened in 1854 in Dublin. A Catholic convert, John Henry Newman (later Cardinal), was the founding rector.

Although changes had been occurring in Irish church liturgy from the early part of the nineteenth century, and O'Connell had established funds for building up the church, there can be no doubt that this period was a major turning point for Catholicism in Ireland. Almost overnight the Irish became practicing Catholics. Emmet Larkin, in *The Historical Dimensions of Irish Catholicism*, explains why he believes this was so:

> The Devotional Revolution . . . provided the Irish with a substitute symbolic language and offered them a new cultural heritage with which they could identify and be identified and through which they could identify each other.

At this time Catholicism developed as a pervasive cultural statement of ethnic identity in Ireland. Larkin estimates that the pre-Famine figures for Mass attendance in Ireland stood at around 33 percent. Within fifty years that figure had risen to an impressive 90 percent. In June 1866 Paul Cullen was named the first Irish cardinal. With the disestablishment of the Church of Ireland as the official state religion in 1869, the road was paved for a strong Catholic church to enter Irish politics.

## GETTING BACK THE LAND

The situation in Ireland at the time can be seen through the eyes of many outsiders who visited. John Stuart Mill is one of the most famous commentators among those who wrote of the "desperate state" of the Irish people. He was a Liberal member of Parliament and spoke out often in favor of improving the lot of the Irish tenants. In the 1860s Mill called the English governing of Ireland a "disgrace to England and calamity to the whole Empire."

Poverty, with the added stress of eviction, was endemic. The issue of lease security had not been resolved, and landlords continued to drive out tenants and clear their estates of uncertain rents in order to give over the land to more profitable cattle-grazing. Farms in the west remained smaller and poorer than anywhere else and were always the most vulnerable to bad harvests. The year 1878 was particularly bad: many crops failed, and the threat and fear of famine gripped the country. As a result of crop failure there were large numbers of evictions that autumn and winter. County Mayo was particularly hard hit as many landlords sought to clear their lands of unprofitable tillage farmers. Mayo had long borne the brunt of bad economic times. From this poorest of counties came the springboard for a national movement that ultimately brought massive reform to Irish farming conditions.

In the face of another potential famine, some Mayo tenants who were threatened with eviction contacted James Daly, an editor of a Castlebar newspaper. Daly was a known sympathizer of the tenants' problems. In February 1879 Daly used his newspaper to help organize a rally of tenants in Irishtown. The Irishtown rally in April was the beginning of an effort to change the law on tenant rights. More than ten thousand people attended the meeting, many more than the organizers expected. Michael Davitt spoke to the crowd about its plight and became the main leader of this new drive.

Davitt was a Mayo native and a member of the IRB who had just been released from the English prison at Dartmore for his involvement in Fenian activities in England. His family had been Mayo tenants who were evicted from their holding during the Famine and had emigrated to England. Davitt's story has Dickensian overtones. From age nine the young Davitt worked in an English factory where he lost his right arm in an industrial accident. When he grew up, he returned to Ireland determined to do something about what he regarded as the abysmal land situation. Davitt was an intellectual who would later be known for his journalistic travels and support for causes beyond Ireland. He wrote *Within the Pale*, detailing the persecution of Jews in Russia, and wrote also in support of the Boers in Africa.

As more tenant meetings were organized, mass protests began to take place, with violence often erupting against local landlords and police. Residual anger from the Famine was finding an expression in public protest against the injustice of the land system. The focus of this protest took a more fortuitous turn when Charles Stewart Parnell, a young Irish nationalist MP, became interested in these public meetings and sought to channel this frustration into Home Rule for Ireland.

## CHARLES STEWART PARNELL,
## "THE UNCROWNED KING OF IRELAND"

By the time he met Michael Davitt, Charles Stewart Parnell had been a member of Parliament for three years. His political zeal was directed toward a repeal of the Act of Union and the establishment of a parliament in Dublin. Parnell was the most important figure to emerge in Irish politics in hundreds of years. He was born on June 27, 1846, in his family home of "Avondale" in County Wicklow. The Parnells, a Protestant, Church of Ireland family, were landowners in this picturesque area of Ireland, and their home is still standing. Tourists throng to visit the home and pay tribute to the famous leader who grew up there. The magnificent forest park setting is as beautiful now as it was in Parnell's boyhood when he played with his many siblings.

The Parnells were a large, close-knit family. Charles was the seventh of eleven children. The name Parnell had originally come to Ireland in the 1600s, and the Parnells had married into Irish families. Within a short time they were staunch Irish nationalists. Parnell's great-grandfather had voted against the Act of Union in 1800, and his grandfather had been an avid supporter and friend of Daniel O'Connell. His grandfather had also worked to have the Church of Ireland disestablished. His mother was born in Boston of Irish parents and was often described as being Anglophobic, a characteristic she is reputed to have passed on to her son.

Parnell was educated in English boarding schools and then attended university at Cambridge. He left Cambridge after three and a half unproductive years without a degree. The circumstances of his leaving are unclear; many stories circulated about the details. F. S. L. Lyons, in his biography of Parnell, recounts that he got into a fight in the street along with other undergraduates and was duly reprimanded by his college. He was sent home two weeks before the end of term with the expectation of returning in the autumn. Once he returned to Ireland he stayed. The reason for this is uncertain, but his brother later said that Avondale, which Charles had inherited on the death of their father, was so run-down that Charles decided not to waste any more time and money on Cambridge. What does seem certain is that his early experiences left him with

The leader of the Irish Home Rule
movement in the Westminster
parliament, Charles Stewart Parnell had
a fearless attitude to English
intransigence. (*Clare Library*)

an intense dislike and disrespect for the English, which stayed with
him all his life. He told his brother and later Michael Davitt that
the English were bullies and that "the way to treat an Englishman,
[is to] stand up to him." His total disregard for English convention
and lack of respect for English ways would make him a messianic
figure in Ireland.

## THE HOME RULE MOVEMENT

The Home Rule initiative to which Parnell was dedicated had its
beginnings in 1870 with an Irish representative at Westminster,
Isaac Butt. Butt formed a group within the Irish party to fight for a
repeal of the Union. Later this became known as the Home Rule

movement. Butt was a Protestant lawyer with great ambitions of establishing an Irish parliament in Dublin. His own political journey was an interesting one. Originally he had been against the violence of the Fenians, but as a lawyer he had represented them in court and was swayed by their political arguments. He did not adopt their methods. Butt regarded the Fenians' issues as parliamentary concerns and sought to achieve them by constitutional means.

An important development in election procedure occurred in 1872 when the secret ballot was introduced. It meant that tenants could vote as they wished and not as their landlords or priests wanted or directed them. In the general election of 1874 Butt's new Home Rule party won more than half of the Irish seats. Until this time the Irish party at Westminster had been very much under the influence of the Catholic bishops and had not been concerned with Home Rule or the reestablishment of a parliament in Dublin. Now the Irish party was taking a new direction. The young Charles Parnell was attracted by these new political aims, and in 1874 he joined the movement. In April 1875, at twenty-nine years of age, he was elected to Parliament at a by-election in Meath.

## PARNELL'S EARLY POLITICAL LIFE

In his first speech to the House of Commons, Parnell set the tone for his future career in politics when he asked: "Why should Ireland be treated as a geographical fragment of England, as I heard an ex-Chancellor of the Exchequer call it some time ago? Ireland is not a geographical fragment but a nation." Parnell's early politics aimed to win greater security for tenant holdings. Evictions continued to be the plague of the countryside, but passing laws to remedy this situation proved difficult. Noticing that bills pertaining to Ireland were not dealt with until late in parliamentary sessions, often too late to be heard, he perfected the practice that became known as "obstructionism" or filibustering. He organized other members of the Irish party to delay parliamentary proceedings by taking control of the discussion and not yielding the floor. On one occasion Parnell and six members of the Irish party together forced the House of Commons to sit for forty-five hours in continuous session. In Ireland Parnell's reputation rose on this arrogant approach, and soon he was a more popular figure than Isaac Butt. Butt was uncomfortable with the obstructionism and opposed Parnell's practice of it. Division within the Irish party might have proved difficult to resolve, but Butt fell ill, and in May 1879 he died of a heart attack. Parnell, at thirty-three, was shortly after elected leader of the Irish party.

Parnell's political stance incorporated a broad base. He first met Michael Davitt in Dublin in January 1878 just after Davitt had returned to Ireland from prison. Realizing that they both wanted the same for Ireland, and that each could help the other, they formed an alliance. Parnell instinctively knew that to win Home Rule he had to tap into the passion that was spilling out into what became known as the Land War.

## THE LAND WAR

In October 1879 the National Land League was organized by Michael Davitt. At the first meeting Parnell was elected its president. The League was established for the purpose of supporting tenants "and promoting organization among the tenant farmers . . . to bring about a reduction of rackrents . . . [and] to enable every tenant to become the owner of his holding." That one of the chief aims of the League was to obtain land ownership for those who actually worked it was an ambitious target for the time. The League also pledged its support to those tenants who suffered eviction. Fundraising was an immediate concern, and Parnell was sent to the United States to get financial help from "our exiled countrymen." Proper distribution of funds was one of the League's first concerns. The Land League rules stated that "none of the funds of this league shall be used for the purchase of any landlord's interest in the land or for furthering the interest of any parliamentary candidate."

In the following year branches of the Land League were set up in rural parishes throughout Ireland. Parnell's message to the tenant farmers was to "hold together" as a group in the face of landlord aggression, and to pay only that rent which was considered fair. His words resonated with the demoralized population. For the first time Irish tenants felt they had leadership and support.

Parnell's sister, Anna, organized the Ladies Land League, which proved itself as effective as its counterpart. Anna Parnell was as passionate about Irish rights as her brother. Her reason for put-

As tenacious as her brother, Fanny Parnell established the Ladies Land League in the United States to garner support among Irish Americans for tenant rights in Ireland.

ting forward the idea of a women's organization was so the women could continue supporting and running the League if the men were arrested. With "coercion" bills, laws that suspended civil rights, constantly enacted by the British, arbitrary arrest was an ongoing threat in Ireland. At first Parnell and the other men were against having a women's division in case they were accused of placing women in dangerous situations. But Anna Parnell was as tenacious and obdurate as her brother, and the women got their organization. In the United States Parnell's other sister Fanny started the American Ladies Land League. The American Irish remained very much connected to political events in Ireland, and their financial support and the publicity they got for Ireland was important.

## THE "BOYCOTTING" CAMPAIGN

Parnell's approach to solving Ireland's problems was nonviolent; he was unwilling to allow the League to engage in physical aggression. He was always careful to distance himself from the activities of the

Fenians. The question therefore arose as to how to deal with agents or landlords who evicted tenants and what appropriate group reaction should be adopted by the tenants. Parnell's solution was ingenious. At a public meeting in Ennis in County Clare in September 1880, a large crowd assembled to see the charismatic leader. Parnell's reputation and popularity had grown enormously, and he attracted huge crowds anywhere he went. His reputation within the Westminster parliament for what the Irish saw as standing up to English indifference to Ireland had given him iconic status. At the Ennis meeting Parnell addressed the crowd and told them of the need to stand together against evicting landlords and the equally malevolent "land grabbers," as they were called, who took over the farms of evicted tenants. He then set out his proposition for punishing any offender when he told the crowd:

> When a man takes a farm from which another had been evicted you must shun him on the roadside when you meet him, you must shun him in the streets of the town, you must shun him in the shop, you must shun him in the fairgreen and in the marketplace, and even in the place of worship, by leaving him alone, by putting him into a moral Coventry, by isolating him from the rest of his country as if he were the leper of old, you must show your detestation of the crime he has committed.

This plan held great attraction for the rural Irish who had a long and ancient tradition of community. We cannot determine whether Parnell knew it, but ostracism was also the traditional punishment meted out by the Druids to those who had offended the community in some way. Parnell chose to call it "a more Christian way" than violence for dealing with offenders.

One of the first victims of this policy was the English agent of a Mayo landlord, Captain Charles Boycott. Boycott evicted some tenants for nonpayment of rent and paid the consequences when he was outcast by the entire community. A newspaper report of the time described his treatment:

> Garrisoned at home and escorted abroad, Mr. Boycott and his family are now reduced to one female domestic. Farm laborers, workmen, herdsmen, stablemen, all went long ago, leaving the

corn standing in the field, the horses at stable, the sheep in the field, the turnips, carrots and potatoes all in the ground. The baker in Ballinrobe refuses to give them bread and the butcher refuses to send them meat.

"Boycotting" was born, and a new word entered the English language. While it was difficult to bring this action under the sanction of the law, the victims could not easily survive in a rural community isolated from all services. It was a brilliant way of retaliating, and its popularity grew. The huge campaign of boycotting and civil disobedience that soon spread throughout the country alarmed the British government, which responded by employing extra police in Ireland. The Ladies Land League assumed the care of evicted tenants and supervised various boycotting campaigns in many parts of the country. They proved to be so zealous that some of the women landed in jail. Dubbed the "plan of campaign," Irish landlords found themselves confronted with what amounted to a social revolt with very little that could be done to counter it.

## TENANTS WIN GUARANTEES

Parnell's method produced significant results. The land campaign had destabilized Ireland, and the British knew that something had to be done. In response, British Prime Minister William Gladstone introduced a land reform bill for Ireland. The Land Act of 1881 was a critical development in modern Irish society. For Irish farmers it meant that for the first time in hundreds of years their farmland became settled. The act guaranteed the three requests that had originally been made by the Tenant League in the 1850s: fixture of tenancy, fair rent (as determined by law), and the right to sell holdings. A system of land courts was created to establish rents, and both sides, tenant and landlord, were brought together to argue their case. Both were then obliged to abide by the decision of these courts.

Never before in the history of British rule in Ireland had mass protest produced such results. The act gave momentum to the Irish hope for complete independence from Britain. Parnell continued to organize large public meetings, and the Irish members of Parliament discussed plans to introduce a Home Rule bill. But the

British government believed this was a step too far. Prime Minster Gladstone was uncomfortable with what he heard from the Irish and gave no encouragement to this talk. Indeed the British press and public were against giving the Irish anything more than they had been granted in the Land Act. The English popular press ran cartoons of the Irish as gigantic pigs who could not be satisfied no matter how much they were given.

## THE ARREST OF PARNELL

Attempting to slow Parnell's momentum, the British then made a foolish move. In October 1881 the government arrested Parnell on bogus charges of Fenian membership and inciting public disorder. The news was greeted in England with celebration that the Irishman who was causing so much trouble was at last being brought to justice. In Ireland the reaction was equally as passionate but for a different reason. Far from isolating Parnell from his following, his status increased. Parnell was sent to Kilmainham Jail in Dublin where large crowds gathered outside each day to sustain their leader. Women knelt and prayed outside the prison walls, and the prison was inundated with gifts of knitted scarves and cardigans. By this time Parnell's stature was so enormous that he had been dubbed the "Uncrowned King of Ireland" by Tim Healy, a member of the Irish party and one of Parnell's most ardent supporters. This title attached itself to Parnell and remained his identity for generations after his death.

Prison did not suit his health. He fell ill, and a doctor diagnosed him with a heart condition. Now the government further enraged Irish public opinion by suppressing the Land League. Parnell's release from prison took some months while the cabinet and Gladstone communicated with him through a number of representatives. Some of Gladstone's advisers wanted Parnell to make a public declaration against the land agitation. In the final analysis the Kilmainham Treaty was agreed upon by a letter from Parnell outlining his position and restating his policies. This satisfied Gladstone, and Parnell was released from prison on May 2, 1882. Upon his release he was greeted by thousands of supporters. His standing as the Irish messiah was at a peak. Emotions were running high, and talk of a Home Rule bill was gaining even more momentum.

In spite of Parnell's influence, the ghost of violence was not completely banished. Within days of his release from prison an incident in Dublin almost derailed Irish hopes. Lord Frederick Cavendish, the recently appointed chief secretary of Ireland, and Thomas Burke, the undersecretary, were murdered in Dublin's Phoenix Park, close to the Viceregal Lodge. An underground group calling themselves the "Invincibles" was responsible. It was a devastating blow to the Home Rule party, and Parnell immediately offered to resign his parliamentary seat. Gladstone refused to accept his resignation, and the crisis passed. Some years later forged letters printed in the London *Times* attempted to link Parnell with the murders, but the forgery was exposed in court. It is worth noting that throughout his career Parnell proved such a threat to British dominance in Ireland that he was frequently under attack in the British press. This was just one of a series of attempts to discredit him.

## "KILLING HOME RULE WITH KINDNESS"

A defeat in Commons for Gladstone led to his resignation in June 1885 and gave parliamentary power to the Conservative party. The Conservatives were against any policy that would break up the United Kingdom, but they could not ignore Parnell's political strength. In order to "win" the Irish away from Home Rule they passed a number of measures calculated to placate them. Irish newspapers dubbed this "killing Home Rule with kindness." It was a gross misunderstanding of the dynamics that lay behind Irish political aspirations, but a number of concessions were granted, including funds for an extended railway system and, most significant, the Ashbourne Act of 1885, which provided for the purchase of large amounts of Irish farmland from impoverished landlords to be sold back to tenants. Long-term low-interest-rate loans were provided so that many Irish tenants could now buy their holdings. This was not as generous a gesture as it might seem, though, because the Irish treasury had to foot the bill for the cost. It was nevertheless an important moment in Irish history; for the first time in hundreds of years, land ownership was returned to Irish farmers. The Ashbourne Act was the forerunner for further laws allowing Irish tenants to purchase their own land.

As momentous a gesture as this was for the Conservatives, the Irish merely experienced it as justice for land taken by force centuries earlier. Having to pay for land they perceived to be theirs by ancient right did not impress. Memories in Ireland are long. This gesture was not seen as munificent by the Irish, nor would it in any way distract from their desire for an Irish parliament. The push for Home Rule could not be stopped, and Parnell continued to press for it.

## HOLDING IRELAND TOGETHER

Parnell's task of holding Ireland together was not an easy one. It is to his eternal credit that he was so successful. The Catholic church did not participate in the Home Rule drive and remained skeptical and concerned about its position in an independent Ireland. The new status of the church had brought it a position in Irish society that it was reluctant to lose. The bishops had become a powerful force in the country and did not wish to see power pass to politicians who might introduce nonsectarian schools. Catholic schools had been established under the British government, and the state promised financial support for the Catholic University. Conscious of their concerns, Parnell assured the bishops that in the event of independence he would guarantee them state Catholic schools. He also agreed that the party would consult with the bishops over which candidates would run for election. This important coalition was known as the Clerical Nationalist Alliance. Likewise, Parnell made the northern politicians feel comfortable with the idea of repeal so that a majority of the Ulster politicians pledged themselves to the idea of a Dublin parliament. It was a fragile union, but Parnell's personality and political savvy made it work.

The general election of November–December 1885 was a huge success for Parnell. His party won every seat in Ireland outside eastern Ulster and Dublin University. In Britain the Liberals won a plurality of seats but not an overall majority. To assume power they struck an alliance with the Irish party. Part of Gladstone's pact with Parnell and the Irish was a promise made in December 1885 to enter a Home Rule bill for Ireland in the upcoming parliamentary session—a major turning point in British policy toward Ireland. The British leader had long been considering how best to subdue

Ireland and bring peace to the island. Until this time "the Irish question," as it came to be called, was never seen by the British as "a British question." Under Parnell's influence this perception was about to change.

Gladstone could no longer ignore either Parnell's success within Ireland or the Irish desire, continually expressed, for their own parliament. Now they had voted overwhelmingly for Parnell and his political aspirations. It had also become obvious to Gladstone that the Act of Union had not been a success. For most of the nineteenth century Ireland had been in a state of agitation; additional police were constantly being deployed, coercion bills that limited civil rights were frequently enacted, and still no peace had been established. Gladstone argued, "These coercion bills are stiffly resisted by the members who represent Ireland." He concluded that Home Rule was the solution to Ireland's problems.

On April 8, 1886, the much-awaited Home Rule bill was introduced by Prime Minister Gladstone in the House of Commons. The Conservative party did not support it, and in spite of Gladstone's best efforts it did not have the support of the entire Liberal party. In initiating the discussion, Gladstone appealed to the House by explaining British policy toward Ireland and how that policy had failed: "In point of fact [British] law is discredited in Ireland, and discredited in Ireland upon this ground especially—that it comes to the people of that country with a foreign aspect, and in a foreign garb." Referring to the huge vote in favor of Home Rule within Ireland, Gladstone insisted that this was a factor in his own decision to support this measure because "I cannot conceal the conviction that the voice of Ireland, as a whole, is at this moment constitutionally spoken."

Unfortunately Gladstone's words fell on many deaf ears, and the bill failed to pass by a narrow margin of 341 to 311. Some of Gladstone's colleagues in the Liberal party voted with the Conservatives and against the bill. In all a total of 93 Liberal MPs voted with the Conservatives. Because of their failed parliamentary proposal, the Liberals were forced into a general election, in which Home Rule was an issue. There was little popular support in Britain for Irish Home Rule. Urged on by the British press and establishment talk of imperial entitlement, public opinion in Britain was very much opposed to the idea of the Irish seceding. The Liberals lost the election, and power passed to the Conservatives. Still the Irish remained hopeful, and Parnell was not greatly disappointed. He spent much time and energy traveling in Ireland and making public appeals to bolster confidence and maintain the belief that with another election another Home Rule bill could be introduced and possibly pass. Gladstone too remained committed to this effort.

## STORM CLOUDS GATHER OVER HOME RULE

Meanwhile in Rome, Pope Leo XIII was becoming uneasy about the possibility of Home Rule for Ireland. The pope had a number of reasons to be unhappy about the situation there. For some years he had been trying to establish diplomatic relations with Britain, broken since the Reformation. Correspondence between the papacy and British Conservatives demonstrates Rome's eagerness to begin a dialogue. The British, who were equally eager to eradicate support for Home Rule, made promises to Rome concerning Catholic education. This may have influenced the pope's attitude toward Irish nationalism. Emmet Larkin, in *The Roman Catholic Church in Ireland and the Fall of Parnell*, writes that the pope's diplomatic ambition clouded his judgment regarding the Irish situation. "In [Leo XIII's] dealings with the British Government over Ireland," Larkin writes, "his ability to distinguish between appearance and reality was seriously impaired by his diplomatic needs."

In June 1888—fearing that the Home Rule bill would pass next time—Leo XIII issued a decree condemning the nationalist movement and the boycotting campaign and forbidding Catholics in Ireland from partaking in these movements. His decree, called *Saepe Nos*, was addressed "To Our Venerable Brethren, the Bishops of Ireland." The words of the pope are autocratic in style: "We cannot disguise that tidings which have recently come to Us from Ireland have deeply pained and grieved Us." Leaving no doubt as to his condemnation, the pope proceeded: "These methods of warfare known as Boycotting and the plan of campaign . . . may not lawfully be used." The decree was sent to the primate of Ireland, who then ordered all bishops to tell the people they were in danger of excommunication if they took part in the nationalist movement.

The directive placed the Irish church in an extremely difficult position. The bishops, sensing the mood of the people, were afraid to broadcast the order. The pope was so angered by this reaction that at one point he refused to bless medals that were to be sent to Ireland. The church in Ireland was scarcely united on this issue, and many priests defied their bishops in supporting the nationalist campaign. Some bishops did read the decree, and newspapers reacted negatively to its contents. Irish Catholics remained faithful to their belief in Parnell and Home Rule, but not for long. Darker storm clouds were gathering over the Home Rule party, especially Parnell. His private life was about to become public, with revelations that would split the Home Rule party and Irish society for decades.

## PARNELL AND KATHERINE O'SHEA

Some years earlier Parnell had met and fallen in love with the estranged wife of Captain William (Willie) O'Shea, one of his colleagues in the Irish party. Katherine O'Shea became Parnell's lover in 1880. They lived as a couple from 1881 and had three children together. The public never knew of Parnell's private life. Indeed many of his closest political colleagues did not know either, though there is evidence to suggest that many probably turned a blind eye to the obvious. It is almost certain that William O'Shea knew. O'Shea had his own reasons for keeping quiet. He was always thought of as an inferior member of the Irish party, lacking in political knowledge and prowess. He constantly sought Parnell's help in retaining his parliamentary seat. Even a glimpse into his youth shows him in an unfavorable light. When he was a sixteen-year-old student at the Catholic University, Newman was troubled by him and wrote to a correspondent, "My youths, all through that O'Shea, or rather in the person of O'Shea, are giving me trouble—and I don't know how I possibly can stand another year. I think he must go at the end of the session." O'Shea lasted only half a year at the Catholic University.

It is evident that O'Shea knew of his wife's affair because he was aware of the births of the children, but he said nothing for years. He is reputed to have had as many as seventeen affairs himself during his marriage. When he decided to begin divorce proceedings against his wife in December 1889, the Parnell affair became dramatically public. It is not at all clear why O'Shea decided to act when he did. History has never revealed the motive for his actions. The reasons why he and his wife did not previously divorce are also uncertain. It is said that Katherine O'Shea did not wish to lose a legacy from her wealthy elderly aunt who disapproved of divorce, and that William O'Shea was to share in this inheritance. In any event, the aunt died in May 1889; O'Shea was left nothing.

In the divorce suit O'Shea named Parnell as co-respondent in his wife's adultery. Parnell did not defend the charge, perhaps out of fear that the evidence of O'Shea's collusion in the affair might result in a denial of the divorce. He had wanted for years to marry Katharine O'Shea, and the opportunity had now presented itself. Judging from his words and demeanor, Parnell did not appear to understand the possible implications of his situation. He told Michael Davitt that he expected to come out of the situation with his honor intact. Davitt took this to mean he was innocent, but Parnell probably meant that the affair was the business of the people involved and should not impinge on his professional life. He had a reputation for conducting his political career with detachment and a strong sense of the possible. Unfortunately in this aspect of his life he seemed to lack the objectivity and realism that were the hallmarks of his political career. He misjudged public opinion in thinking that his private life would have no effect on his political career. He was also sadly and tragically mistaken in not seeing the opportunity that this presented to his enemies.

## THE END OF THE DREAM

The months of November and December 1890 were fatal ones for Parnell. The divorce trial was widely publicized and the divorce granted on November 18, 1890, on the grounds of adultery committed by Mrs. O'Shea. The press covered the entire proceedings, and the British and Irish public devoured every detail. Parnell welcomed the verdict, as he and Katherine O'Shea planned to marry. Because Parliament was about to begin a new session, the question immediately arose regarding his suitability as leader of the Irish party. The party had to elect or reelect the parliamentary leader with whom the Liberal party would continue to negotiate for Home Rule. The Irish remained loyal to Parnell, and the Irish newspapers, the *Freeman's Journal* and the *Nation,* supported him. The

*Nation* declared that "it is the duty of every Irishman to rally and confirm the leadership of Mr. Parnell." But Michael Davitt was one of the first Irish to express doubts about Parnell's leadership. Davitt was devastated by the divorce verdict and privately expressed his disappointment concerning Parnell. Before long Parnell's political support was greatly divided.

The British press was generally hostile to the Irish leader. The *Pall Mall Gazette* viciously charged him with immorality. The *Times,* having previously tried to discredit Parnell by printing forged letters about him, was again vitriolic in its attack. One newspaper, the *Manchester Guardian,* mildly supported him. Gladstone was under heavy pressure from religious non-conformists, or fundamentalists who usually supported the Liberals but did not like the connection they had formed with the Irish party. On November 20, 1890, the *Methodist Times* ran an extraordinary editorial in which Parnell was attacked and the entire Irish nation implicated as reprobates should he be reelected as party chairman:

> We do not hesitate to say that if the Irish race deliberately select as their recognized representative an adulterer of Mr. Parnell's type they are as incapable of self-government as their bitterest enemies have asserted. So obscene a race as in those circumstances they would prove themselves to be would obviously be unfit for anything except a military despotism.

Gladstone expected Parnell to offer his resignation as he had done at the time of the Phoenix Park murders, but this did not happen. Parnell had no intention of giving in on this issue, which he continued to view as a purely private matter. Concerned that the Irish party would reinstate Parnell, Gladstone was in private communication with Irish MPs and expressed concern over Parnell's leadership. It is unclear whether the Irish were fully aware of the fragility of Liberal support, but at the party meeting in Dublin on November 25, the Irish party unanimously reelected Parnell as its leader. It was a strong statement under the circumstances, but was not without its warnings. Tim Healy gave Parnell ambiguous support by saying, "We have stood by Mr. Parnell. Mr. Parnell must stand by us." Healy would eventually turn bitterly against his leader.

Gladstone immediately responded to Parnell's reelection by issuing a letter of condemnation against the Irish leader, which was published in the British press the following day. Gladstone made the point that he and the Liberal party could not support Home Rule for Ireland as long as Parnell led the Irish party. While this was obviously declared with Gladstone's own constituents in mind, it was clearly not good news for the Irish. Worse was to follow.

## THE IRISH CATHOLIC CHURCH
## MOVES AGAINST PARNELL

In Ireland, the Catholic church authorities were not completely happy about the possibility of Home Rule, and the results of the O'Shea divorce trial added fuel to their objections. The pope had opposed the Clerical-Nationalist alliance and had already expressed his condemnation of the nationalist movement. When news came that Parnell had been unanimously reelected leader of the Irish party, the bishops were dismayed. "Is it not the duty of us Bishops to speak for our people and tell the *Freeman* [newspaper] and our MPs that God's commandments must be respected, and that He cannot be ignored?" argued the Bishop of Ardagh to a fellow bishop. Now, with the divorce details released, the bishops had an opportunity to split publicly with Parnell and denounce him as immoral and unfit to lead.

At first public statements from church leaders showed a degree of prudence. The archbishop of Dublin, William Walsh, wrote cautiously in the *Irish Catholic* on November 29, advising that any decision by the bishops should wait until after the next meeting of the Irish party. They clearly wanted Parnell to be dropped but did not wish to make a public move too soon. Private letters between the Irish bishops are filled with outrage but also express confidence that Parnell can be overthrown. One letter dated November 30, from Bishop Kirby, rector of the Irish College in Rome, to Bishop Walsh, asserts that "Parnell will never again be the leader of the Irish party. Bishops and priests will unanimously repudiate him." Parnell continued to fight the odds. In an attempt to reach out directly to the people he published his "Manifesto to the Irish People" in the *Freeman's Journal* on November 29, describing his plans for the next Home Rule bill and claiming that he alone could deliver it.

Parnell's direct appeal had the effect of further alienating the Irish bishops, who now felt compelled to act more decisively. Feelings against Home Rule were running high among some bishops. In a revealing comment, Archbishop John MacEvilly of Tuam wrote of the church's real fear of Home Rule led by men like Parnell who were not committed Catholics: "Home Rule with such men, what would it be but the crippling of the Irish Church, and relegating of the clergy to the sacristies?" This was likely the real issue. The church feared it would not have a political voice in Parnell's Ireland; at best its power would be diluted. Finally on December 3 the bishops' standing committee drew up conclusions regarding Parnell's lack of fitness for leadership and released the results to the press.

The church's public rejection marked the end for Parnell. In London a meeting of the Irish party began and dragged on for a number of days. Discussion centered on the question of which was more important, Parnell or Home Rule? It was widely believed at this time that Ireland could not have both, and the bishops' statement added credence to this. Some urged Parnell to step down voluntarily, even for a short time. Parnell refused to consider this. The party split into two factions, the Parnellites and the anti-Parnellites. In the end, on December 6 the vote went against Parnell, and he was forced to step down. Characteristically he refused to give up. He swore to fight and regain control of the party and bring about a Dublin parliament.

## DEATH OF THE "KING OF IRELAND"

Parnell now traveled to Ireland with the expressed intention of gaining support. The *Freeman's Journal* continued supporting him, and he knew that the people still loved him as their "chief." However, an organized effort led by the Catholic bishops soon began. From pulpits he was denounced as an adulterer, and his fight became hopeless. His name was linked with the very worst vices. The Bishop of Meath declared, "Parnellism like paganism, impedes, obstructs and cripples the efficiency and blights the fruitfulness of the preaching of the gospel." In June 1891 Parnell and Katherine O'Shea married in England as he continued trying to reestablish himself politically. He traveled to a number of by-elections supporting his candidates, but in each election the Parnellite was defeated. In a symbolic gesture that sent emotional shock waves through Ireland, quicklime was thrown in his face at Kilkenny.

Under this kind of pressure Parnell's health began to fail. He had had typhoid as a child, and this is thought to have contributed to the breakdown of his strength. On September 27 he contracted pneumonia in Ireland and returned to his wife in England. When he left Ireland on September 30 he said, "I shall be all right. I shall be back next Saturday week." He died on October 6, 1891, in Brighton. He was just forty-five years old. His body was returned to Ireland, and Dublin, which had remained faithful to him, gave him a massive funeral. A crowd of almost a quarter-million turned out for his last journey. Such was the mythic stature of the man that when his body was lowered into the grave observers, including the poet W. B. Yeats, reported seeing a star falling "in broad daylight."

Of all the tragedies that Ireland has suffered, Parnell's downfall ranks among the greatest. It deprived the Irish party of a man whose genius and drive were irreplaceable. Ultimately his inability to gain support from the British parliament to establish Home Rule resulted in a divided Ireland with rifts that remain unresolved. Irish writers took up Parnell's cause. W. B. Yeats stormed against "the bishops and the party" whom he jointly blamed for the tragedy. A very young James Joyce later made it the basis of his art. Joyce raged against a church too involved in politics and, as he saw it, a people too willing to follow their priests. The quicklime thrown in Parnell's face became for Joyce the high symbol of Irish self-destruction and what he called "the old sow who eats her young." That Parnell's downfall was at the behest of the combined forces of the English establishment and the Irish Catholic church was a bitter blow that many could not endure. Charles Stewart Parnell was buried on October 11, 1891, in Dublin's Glasnevin cemetery. Such was and remains his status as Ireland's "uncrowned king" that his gravestone contains just one word in capital letters: PARNELL.

# [ 9 ]

# *Murmuring Name Upon Name: From Literature to Armed Rebellion*

✴

THE EMOTIONAL STORM that followed the political fall and death of Parnell spilled into all areas of Irish life, but it particularly impacted the development of an Irish national consciousness, which was becoming increasingly intense during the late 1880s and early 1890s. There were valid sociological reasons for this need to establish a sense of nationhood in and legitimacy to Ireland. National pride had been severely damaged in the nineteenth century; the Act of Union had left Ireland without a parliament; the Famine of the 1840s had devastated Irish society and had left deep psychological scars on the Irish memory. One Irish historian has written: "The Famine was a crisis of the mind as well as the body."

Out of the ashes of this devastation sprang a need for rejuvenation. A fervent nationalism developed, and the search for an Irish cultural identity was born. A coupling of aspirations occurred: the political drive for national expression in an independent Ireland ran alongside the need to affirm a national cultural identity. This cultural regeneration was known as the Celtic Renaissance. Parnell's death, far from dampening the movement, gave life to it. Years later the poet Yeats was to credit the rejuvenation of national pride with the emotional complexity that grew from Parnell's political failure. In his address to the Swedish Academy in 1923 on accepting the Nobel Prize, Yeats observed, "The modern literature of Ireland, and indeed all that stir of thought which prepared for the Anglo-Irish War, began when Parnell fell from power in 1891."

Central to this cultural and literary drive was the belief that Ireland had lost contact with its own cultural and historical past, and consequently the Irish had lost their identity. It was felt that a durable Irish political expression could only emerge through a realization of a common cultural heritage. At the same time it was felt that if the country were to move forward politically and become a nation again, the foundation stone of a strong cultural identity would need to be established. It was believed that political unity could only come through cultural unity, thus pride and confidence in the culture were crucial. If necessary to aid in the establishment of a national sense of self, invention was employed.

## THE REVIVALISTS

The Celtic Renaissance attempted to restore Ireland to what had been lost through centuries of English occupation. The main revivalists were W. B. Yeats and Douglas Hyde, who began in the late nineteenth century to search out Ireland's ancient past. Their mission, as they saw it, was to establish or reestablish national confidence by seeking out the origins of Irish civilization and clearing away as much historical debris as possible. They held that confusion and a diminished national pride had been caused by the English presence because depreciatory English perceptions of the Irish were formed and broadcast to keep Ireland subservient. They sought to discover what Ireland and the Irish were like prior to the English invasion of the twelfth century and even before Christian influence.

First, the idea of a separate or "other" Irish identity had to be established. Hyde and Yeats believed the lines between English and Irish cultures were blurred. Hyde laid out the philosophy behind this in an address called "The Necessity of De-Anglicizing Ireland," which he gave in November 1892 to the Irish National Literary Society. "I wish to endeavor to show that this failure of the Irish people in recent times has been largely brought about by the race diverging during this century from the right path and ceasing to be Irish." Hyde urged a return to Gaelic roots as a way of achieving national political expression because "in anglicizing ourselves wholesale we have thrown away with a light heart the best claim which we have upon the world's recognition of us as a separate nationality."

Translations of the ancient Irish texts were central to this search. This work was carried out by scholars eager to rediscover what had been lost. Lady Augusta Gregory was one of the most talented of these translators. She brought English-language readers in Ireland stories of Fionn MacCumhaill, the Red Branch Knights, and the delight of the great Irish epic *An Táin Bó Cuailgne*. Some of these texts date to the sixth century. They were devoured by revivalists eager to learn about ancient Ireland, who saw these stories as containing the roots of Irish identity. They became a vital ingredient in establishing a valid picture of the origins of the Irish. At this time the idea of Ireland as a pure "Celtic" nation was developed. As one of the protagonists of this movement said, "Ireland is appealing to the past to escape the confusion of the present."

History was a central issue in the discussion of Irish identity. The historical writings of the Four Masters and Geoffrey Keating were translated into English and available for the first time to Irish scholars who no longer had knowledge of the Irish language. These historical texts were unknown and unread for centuries. Now they unlocked the past and revealed what was perceived to be the lost history of Ireland. An important component of deanglicization was to render English versions of Irish history illegitimate.

## TAKING ON THE "STAGE IRISH" IMAGE

The late nineteenth century was a time of great literary creativity in Ireland. At the close of the century the London stage was dominated by Irishmen. Before his tragic downfall, Oscar Wilde was the toast of the town, and George Bernard Shaw likewise enjoyed enormous success with his plays. The fact that both men were writing for an English audience did not detract from the frequently subversive nature of their work. Wilde assumed the role of Englishman in order to mock the English upper class and their questionable values. "Fortunately for us in England at least, education has had no effect whatever," he has a pompous Lady Bracknell proclaim in *The Importance of Being Earnest*. Ireland, in on the real joke, roared in agreement at this assessment. Shaw showed the fallacy of false cultural stereotypes in his *John Bull's Other Island*.

Irish writers of the period were also writing consciously against the image of the Irish in English literature. Although this was not a new position for them, now it took on greater importance. The stage Irishman, stupid and dim-witted, was a well-known English fictional representation and had been for centuries. While this pejorative image reveals more about English fears than Irish reality, it nevertheless had to be challenged. William Carlton had set the tone in the mid-nineteenth century when he addressed this problem in his writings. In his introduction to his collected works in 1860 he observed with a degree of bitterness that since the time of Shakespeare, "neither play nor farce has ever been presented to an Englishman in which, when an Irishman is introduced, he is not drawn as a broad grotesque blunderer."

This, then, was the job the revivalists set before them—to create an image of Ireland that rose above the dominant stereotype and gave to the Irish people a renewed sense of pride in their own culture. In the process an idealized counterimage had to be created. The poetry of Yeats achieved this beyond question. His lyrical images glorify the stories of Medb, Cú Chulainn, and ancient Ireland. Other writers took different approaches. James Joyce went into exile to create his own Irish "conscience." In so doing he mocked the attempts of the Celtic revivalists to establish what he considered a false idea of Ireland. Joyce was concerned that this new, narrow "Celtic" image of Irishness would give rise to a xenophobic country. But Joyce did not show the English much mercy. He coined the counterphrase "brutish empire" and beat the English with their own language. As the Joycean scholar David Norris points out, "Joyce smashed the language of the invader," and in so doing he got "his own revenge" on English dominance. He was no kinder to the new presence of the Catholic church on the island and remained bitter over its role in Parnell's downfall. In a diatribe in the spirit of a curse on both your houses, Joyce declared that the Irish were servants to two foreign masters, "an Englishman and an Italian."

## GAELIC ASSOCIATIONS

In reality a return to true Gaelic roots was impossible. Brehon Law could not be reinstated, and the dispossessed chieftains were long gone. But these permanent losses were less important than restoring a sense of cultural difference, of establishing Ireland as "other" to England. A number of organizations were established to pursue this aim. While the writers were appealing to an intellectual force within Irish society, many associations were established for a wider appeal. In 1885 the Gaelic Athletic Association (GAA) was formed to promote participation in native Irish sports. It was an enormously successful organization that brought life to many rural communities. The spirit of participation that was central to its plan dovetailed perfectly with the underlying culture. Gaelic football and hurling were developed at this time. Team games were organized using the county system to generate competition and strong identity with local teams. Within a short time the organized sports of the GAA became a key factor in developing a sense of Irishness throughout Ireland.

In 1893 the Gaelic League was established by Douglas Hyde and Eoin MacNeill, who were both linguistic scholars. By this time fewer than 15 percent of the population spoke Irish, and these Irish speakers were confined to the poorer western areas. The stated aim of the League was to preserve what remained of the Irish language and to restore it by encouraging others to learn it. It was an attempt to expand support for the Irish language and generate a broad interest in learning the language among those who lived in those areas of Ireland where the language was no longer spoken. Books in Irish were published. Trips to Irish-speaking areas were organized for middle- and upper-class people who mostly lived in Dublin and who previously may not even have known that such Gaelic areas still existed.

The League also attempted to develop and popularize Irish entertainments and encouraged the learning and reciting of Irish-language poetry. The need for a separate identity also included the requirement of a particular style of "Irish" dancing, which was developed out of the country dances of the period. The Munster style was preferred. League members organized the first *Céilí* in 1894 to have people socialize in a "Gaelic" setting where members hoped the Irish language would flourish. A degree of invention was often necessary because the need for national self-expression instinctively produced a reaction to any English position. Thus Gaelic football was developed as an answer to soccer, hurling was the answer to hockey or cricket, and kilts for men were championed as the better alternative to trousers.

In what might be seen as a bemusing contradiction, Yeats held up the Englishwoman Maud Gonne as the epitome of noble Irish womanhood, a role she willingly and brilliantly affected. Gonne was born in Hampshire, England, to a wealthy English family, and little evidence exists for her having a drop of Irish blood, though her father is said to have been of vague Irish descent. Her connection to Ireland came from spending eight years of her childhood in Dublin because her English father was a colonel in the British army stationed there. This ambiguous association did not prevent her from assuming the role of Irish radical, becoming Catholic, and proclaiming iconoclastically on Irish nationhood. Gonne may in fact have been rebelling against her own parents. Her unconventional private life, later revealed, was notorious for its sexual promiscuity. She had three illegitimate children, but no one seemed to notice. It was the age of masks. However sincere, Gonne's often public rants on behalf of Ireland's cause won her the nickname "Maud Gonne mad" among Dublin wags.

In its early days the revival movement crossed class and religious barriers. The founders were of mixed religious affiliation, both Protestant and Catholic. Hyde and Yeats were both Protestant members of the Church of Ireland. Hyde was the son of a Church of Ireland clergyman. Eoin MacNeill, an Ulster Catholic, was a renowned classics scholar and published extensively on ancient Ireland. Pointedly remaining outside of this Celtic Renaissance were the Ulster Presbyterians. This was not a religious issue; few Ulster Protestants felt any affinity with Ireland's Gaelic past and in no way identified with the Irish-speaking people of the west of Ireland. The imagery and romance of ancient Irish texts that so fascinated the Irish revivalists elicited little response from the Ulster Presbyterians. That the Ulster Presbyterians had never assimilated into Irish society became more apparent with the development of a national Gaelic identity. They were further alienated when the identification

of Catholicism with "true" Gaelic culture became more pronounced. This was much regretted by Hyde and others, but it was
inevitable as the power and influence of the Catholic church
spread to all aspects of Irish life. Hyde also grew disillusioned when
the Gaelic League became politicized. He eventually resigned over
this issue. As Ireland moved in this new direction, divisions that
had been sidelined or overlooked by the political achievements of
Parnell became greater.

## "ULSTER WILL FIGHT" HOME RULE

Ulster's political atmosphere had become more defined in the 1880s
as a result of the Home Rule bill and the pact the nationalists had
formed with the Catholic church. A strong Catholic church dictat-
ing parliamentary policy was seen as an unwelcome presence and a
threat to the Ulster Presbyterians. In 1886 the Unionist party
formed in Belfast with the intention of holding the Union together
and preventing the establishment of a Dublin parliament. The party
immediately found support in the English Conservative party,
which also wanted the United Kingdom of Ireland and Britain to
hold. Members of the Conservative party traveled to Ulster to garner support for preventing Home Rule and formed an alliance with
the Unionists. Lord Randolph Churchill's oft-repeated defiant cry
of "Ulster will fight and Ulster will be right" became the bravado
catchphrase of this determination.

Religious animosity, a feature of economic life in the northern
part of Ireland, now took on a more sinister dimension. With the
growing power of the Catholic church, the northern Presbyterians
believed their privileged economic position might be threatened.
Within the United Kingdom they knew they were part of a religious
majority with no tradition of listening to Catholic grievances. With a
Dublin government they would become a minority within a united
Ireland, now featuring a powerful Catholic church. The risk to their
economic position was one they did not care to take. Thus the
Unionist party grew in strength in the 1890s, with the espoused slo-
gan "Home Rule means Rome Rule." Candidates who ran against
Home Rule found favor among working-class Protestants.

For the Irish party the Home Rule dream continued after Parnell's death. A Home Rule bill was presented in 1893 in the House

of Commons and passed, but it failed in the House of Lords. The Irish party floundered for a number of years but recovered in 1900 when John Redmond assumed its leadership. Redmond and Parnell had many similarities. Redmond was a Protestant country squire from County Wicklow and an excellent orator, but he lacked the charisma of the former leader. Under Redmond, holding a variety of political aspirations together proved difficult. In light of the Celtic Renaissance and the enhanced feelings of national self-worth, many Irish were growing restless and impatient with the reality that Home Rule would not easily be granted by the British parliament. Soon other events would overtake the seemingly failed process.

## ARTHUR GRIFFITH AND SINN FÉIN

As the twentieth century opened, Arthur Griffith outlined a new political policy in Dublin in 1904, advocating abandonment of parliamentary action at Westminster and passive resistance to English rule in Ireland. At a convention in Dublin in 1905, Griffith explained this policy under the name "Sinn Féin." He also founded a newspaper and called it *Sinn Féin*. "Sinn Féin" is an Irish-language term that may be loosely translated as "we ourselves," indicating that Irish independence can be realized within Ireland and without the help of outsiders. Until this point the constitutional route could only succeed by a joint effort with the British Liberal party. Since this relationship had proved to be a precarious partnership for the Irish that so far yielded no result, the new approach advocated the abandonment of this policy. Griffith suggested that candidates run for election but instead of taking their seats in Westminster, the elected Irish members would simply form a parliament in Dublin. Griffith's method was to ignore Westminster.

Griffith was a Dubliner who had remained loyal to Parnell's principles and was not impressed by the direction in which the Irish party was heading. He saw his tactics as an extension of Parnell's obstructionism, ignoring the rules set down by the British to serve their own purposes but not necessarily those of Ireland. Griffith believed that the Act of Union of 1800 was illegal. He was not alone in this belief, but he took the idea further, holding that those Irish members who participated in the Westminster parliament were in fact assisting in the continuation of the crime. The only way to terminate this crime was to secede from London and form a Dublin government without waiting for "permission." Predictably the Sinn Féin scheme was not accepted by the Home Rule party, and for some time the proposal remained only a theory. The Sinn Féin political party was formed, and local elections were contested with mild success, but the party did not prove to be a serious threat to Redmond's.

In spite of not putting a dent in the Irish party vote, the Sinn Féin party found some sympathy among IRB members. The repeated disappointment and delay in obtaining Home Rule from the Westminster parliament was turning some toward the idea of more direct action. Many of those attracted to the proposed self-reliant notion were already IRB members. A loose alliance developed between the two organizations. Nationalist publications were thriving at this time, so the IRB started to publish its own newspaper, *Irish Freedom*. They took their inspiration from Wolfe Tone, and soon young intellectuals who had been schooled by the Gaelic League were attracted to their ranks. "To break the connection with England," Wolfe Tone's phrase, became a guiding motto for IRB members.

## PATRICK PEARSE—
## POET AND REVOLUTIONARY

Patrick Pearse was one of the most intense of those who joined the IRB. He talked and wrote about revolution of a glorious kind. Pearse was born in Dublin in 1879 to an Irish mother and an English father. He grew up during the years of the new national zeal for cultural identity and was deeply affected by it. Although he attended the Royal University and became a lawyer, he never practiced law. Instead he was attracted to the fervor of nationalism being expressed throughout the country in a variety of ways. A poet and a visionary, Pearse would become a sacred icon who symbolized quintessential Irish nationalism for most of the twentieth century.

In the late 1890s Pearse had been one of the earliest to join the Gaelic League. He became convinced that Ireland needed to rediscover its national character. He learned Irish and gave lectures on it to make more students aware of the richness of the ancient language. He agreed with Douglas Hyde on the need to build a sense of Irishness distinctive from all things English, and that the reestablishment of the Irish language was central to this. To this end he founded St. Enda's School for boys in 1908. His vision for St. Enda's was to make the Irish language a core part of the curriculum as an essential way of developing national consciousness in students. His dream for the school went beyond the development of a national identity; he hoped it would become a beacon for the whole of Irish education. A few years later he opened St. Ita's School for girls. Pearse was highly critical of the educational methods used in contemporary schools and referred to the system of education in Ireland at the time as "the murder machine" because he believed it killed the child's natural desire for knowledge.

Pearse's own intellectual interest in culture evolved into an equally intense interest in politics. His eulogy at the graveside of O'Donovan Rossa, a Fenian who died in 1915, was celebrated among Nationalists. Rossa was a native Irishman who had lived and died in New York and was central to the national movement in Irish-America. His body was brought home to be buried in Dublin, and his funeral turned into a huge Nationalist event. Ever astute to the occasion, Pearse seized the moment to speak for a broad spectrum of Nationalist feelings. His short speech at the graveside was fiery, prophetic, and poetic. It became the gospel for generations of Nationalists who found in Pearse the inspiration for their own actions. The oration is filled with Christological phrases and mingles Christian symbols and liturgy with the aspirations of a free Ireland. He declared that he was speaking "on behalf of a new generation that has been re-baptized in the Fenian faith, and that has accepted the responsibility of carrying out the Fenian program." With passion he urged those standing by the grave of the great Fenian to "let no man blaspheme the cause that the dead generations of Ireland served."

Pearse, for all the historical controversy that surrounds his subsequent actions, was no fool. He knew how to tap into Irish consciousness and how to reach into the hearts and minds of those listening, or even half-listening, to him. He linked the aspiration for Irish freedom to Tone and declared that Tone's definition of

The leader of the 1916 Rising, Pearse's words and actions inspired a generation of Irish to take up arms to secure Irish independence. (*National Library of Ireland*)

freedom was his too. He shot a broadside at the British authorities and their heavy-handedness in Ireland when he uttered his immortal and much quoted words, "The fools, the fools, the fools, they have left us our Fenian dead." This prophetic statement would reverberate after the events of 1916 when the legacy of the "Fenian dead" of that failed effort served to incite full revolution. His final statement spoke for many generations of Nationalists when he declared that "Ireland unfree shall never be at peace." Pearse wrote extensively in both the Irish and English languages, and his near obsession with blood sacrifice is obvious from his writings. He became convinced—and subsequent events would strengthen his view—that the British parliament would never concede Home Rule unless pressured to do so by physical force. Pearse allied the idea of blood sacrifice with the awakening of the Irish to their rightful destiny—the fight for Irish freedom.

## THE ELUSIVE DREAM OF HOME RULE

Meanwhile hope for Home Rule was resurrected in 1911 when the ancient authority of the House of Lords was greatly diminished. In a move toward greater democracy, the Parliament Act ended the veto power of this mostly hereditary legislative body. The House of Lords could now delay bills for only three sessions. The Liberal party had wanted to reduce the power of Lords for some time and finally succeeded with the help of the Irish party, which voted with them on the issue. In return for the help of the Irish, the Liberals once again promised to introduce a Home Rule bill for Ireland. With the power of the Lords now greatly reduced, Home Rule might finally become a reality. In April 1912 the long-awaited Home Rule bill was presented to Parliament and passed the House of Commons. The Lords were unable to prevent its passage but did delay it for two years. The bill was due to take effect in the autumn of 1914. Although the Irish were disappointed with the delay, they had hope for a new future.

The Home Rule law was not good news for the Ulster Union-ists. Not only the wealthy merchants feared a loss of economic stature; the Protestant working class also had much to lose. They enjoyed a status in the workforce that their Catholic neighbors did not. The great majority of higher-wage skilled workers in Belfast were Protestant. Conversely the Catholic population comprised about 30 percent of the Belfast population but held only 6 percent of the skilled jobs. The lower-paid jobs at the docks were usually held by Catholics, as were the low-paid jobs in the linen mills. Protestants feared that a Dublin legislature with a majority Catholic membership would seek to redress this situation. Further economic fears are described by Jonathan Bardon, in *A History of Ulster*, who cites evidence that the shipbuilders Harland and Wolff, the main employer in Northern Ireland, had tentative plans to relo-cate to England should Home Rule become a reality. The company feared overtaxation in the weak agrarian economy of Ireland. With such bleak prospects before them, Unionists mounted an aggres-sive campaign against the reality of an Irish parliament in Dublin.

## "THE PASS FOR THE EMPIRE"

A well-known Irish Protestant lawyer, Edward Carson, was approached by interested parties and offered the leadership of the Unionist party, which he accepted. Carson was known as a great orator, but he also proved himself to be a brilliant organizer. He soon galvanized support for the Unionist party throughout Ulster. The Unionists were determined to prevent the establishment of a Dublin assembly, and they had good reason to believe they could succeed. They were closely aided by British Conservatives, who continued to view a Dublin parliament as a breakup of the United Kingdom and a danger to the unity of the British Empire. In September 1912 members of the Conservative party, headed by the party leader Andrew Bonar Law, traveled to Belfast with the intention of ultimately preventing Home Rule. They pledged to oppose the Act of Parliament. Bonar Law told a large assembly in Belfast, "You hold the pass—the pass for the Empire."

The response was tremendous. In late September more than 400,000 men and women signed the "Ulster Solemn League and Covenant." The signatories pledged to "use all means which may be found necessary to prevent the establishment of an Irish Parliament in Dublin." There was no doubt this meant violence. In January 1913 a paramilitary group was formed and took the name Ulster Volunteer Force (UVF). Approximately 100,000 loyalists joined ostensibly for the "defense" of Ulster. Money flowed in from Ulster and from Britain. Within a short time more than a million pounds was collected for this cause. Arms were smuggled into Larne near Belfast from Germany, Austria, and Italy, amounting to 25,000 firearms and 3 million rounds of ammunition.

Concerned with the situation in Belfast, the British Liberal Prime Minister Herbert Asquith ordered the British army stationed in Ireland in the Curragh camp to disarm the paramilitary UVF. In an extraordinary event, the army refused. Some officers resigned their commissions rather than take action against Ulster. This was probably not a great surprise as the army officer class shared much of the Conservative sentiment. Officers tended to come from the same aristocratic background as Conservative party members and had a similar attitude to imperial possessions. The dissolution of the United Kingdom was to be prevented. The army's refusal is known as the "Curragh Mutiny." It was the first time since 1688 that the army had rejected instructions from Parliament. The prime minster was rendered helpless. The war office did not accept the officers' resignations, and plans to use the army against Ulster were abandoned. Meanwhile Unionists were already discussing the possibility of excluding the nine-county region of Ulster from the Home Rule bill. John Redmond was adamant that such a situation would not be acceptable, but the Liberal government insisted that such a policy would only be temporary. It was never explained how a resolution could guarantee a "temporary" solution.

## EOIN MACNEILL'S VOLUNTEERS

In response to the situation in Ulster, where members of the UVF were openly marching through streets in a show of strength, the Irish Volunteers were formed in November 1913 in the south. This group was organized by the Gaelic scholar Eoin MacNeill, and its intention was to promote Home Rule. Redmond was the supposed leader of this extra-parliamentary force, but its very formation was a sign that his power to control events in Ireland was slipping. The Irish Volunteers aimed to see that a parliament was established in Dublin as the Westminster parliament had decreed, and to resist any attempt to subvert this law.

A similar woman's military organization was also established, and in 1914 Cumann na mBan, the League of Women, was formed. Its recruits were from diverse backgrounds. Although the members were mainly professional women, the league also drew a significant number from the working class. As arms were being smuggled into Belfast, the same activity began in Dublin. The Volunteers received financial support from the Irish-American organization, Clan na Gael. The Howth gun-running near Dublin brought in 1,500 guns and 25,000 rounds of ammunition. The contrast with the much larger Ulster operation could not have been more obvious.

In addition to national political turbulence, Dublin was also experiencing labor unrest. The Irish Transport and General Workers Union (ITGWU) was ready to take action against the British authorities and had organized a small army known as the Citizen Army. James Connolly was the leader of this radical group, which con-

Molly Childers and Mary Spring-Rice bringing guns into Howth Harbour, Dublin, July 1914.

tained a number of women. The country was on the brink of civil war, but an event in Europe prevented any further action in Ireland. The Archduke Ferdinand was assassinated in June 1914, and by September all of Europe was plunged into war. It was the beginning of World War I. Initially it was believed that the war would be of short duration, that it would all "be over by Christmas" 1914. No one foresaw the considerably longer bloodbath that was to follow.

## HOME RULE POSTPONED

Prime Minster Asquith passed the final stage of the Government of Ireland Act establishing Home Rule in Dublin, but in a proviso he wrote that it would not take effect until after the war in Europe was resolved. The bill provided for a Dublin legislature with limited power. It would be closer to regional power than a true secession. Ireland would continue to send some representatives to the English parliament, and Irish taxes would still go to the British treasury. The bill stated that "the supreme power and authority of the parliament of the United Kingdom shall remain unaffected and undiminished over all persons, matters, and things in Ireland and every part thereof." In an additional stipulation, no religion was to be established by the Irish state:

> The Irish parliament shall not make a law so as either directly or indirectly to establish or endow any religion or prohibit or restrict the free exercise thereof, or give a preference, privilege or advantage or impose any disability or disadvantage, on account of religious belief or religious or ecclesiastical status.

Some read this as an assurance to Ulster that the Catholic church would not become too powerful in this new devolved and united Ireland. This provision might also have influenced the Catholic church in supporting the armed struggle for a cleaner break with the United Kingdom and the establishment of an Irish parliament not under the control of the United Kingdom.

## THE MAKING OF A REVOLUTION

The suspension of Home Rule until after the war was generally greeted in Ireland with frustration. To have come so close after a period of more than forty years and then, yet again, to be put off, this time for the duration of an unknown period, was too much for some Nationalists. John Redmond, leader of the Home Rule party at Westminster, asked his followers to enlist for the war and show the British that the Irish meant to stand behind them in their hour of need. Redmond believed that this would ensure Home Rule for Ireland when it was all over. There was no conscription in Ireland— signing up for the army was voluntary. Practically all the Ulster Unionists supported the war effort, but Redmond faced a different situation. Some were opposed to asking Irishmen to fight in a British war. Eventually a rift formed among the Volunteers, who by now were a sizable force. Many believed Redmond was being disrespectful to the spirit of Irish nationalism to expect Volunteers to fight in the war on the British side. On the other hand, many thought that the men were fighting for Ireland, and that their efforts would ultimately result in the granting of an Irish parliament. In all some 250,000 Irish men fought in the British army in this war. A total of 61,329 Irish soldiers and sailors were killed in World War I, including Redmond's brother Willie, who died in 1917 in Flanders Field.

The division that occurred in the Volunteers during the early years of WWI was led by Eoin MacNeill, who broke from Redmond on the issue of participation in the war effort. About 12,000 members, or 10 percent of the total, agreed with MacNeill. This breakaway group announced that their allegiance was first to Ireland and to Irish groups such as the Irish Republican Brotherhood, not to the British government. Redmond's stand on the war also had an effect on Patrick Pearse, who became more convinced that armed rebellion in Ireland was the only answer to what he saw as the constant refusal on Home Rule. Distrust of the British and the specter of the Conservative party's involvement in Ulster also turned many away from the constitutional route. Increasingly the idea of an armed struggle was forming in the minds of many Nationalists. Soon Pearse was developing a plan to attack the British stronghold in Dublin and had become leader of a small band of radical IRB volunteers. In January 1916 a military council was formed with the intention of staging an armed rebellion. The council members were Pearse and Connolly, along with Thomas Clarke, Eamon Ceannt, Sean MacDermott, Thomas MacDonagh, and Joseph Mary Plunkett—names destined for the most famous roll call of Irish patriots.

Easter Sunday (April 23) was selected as the date on which this rebellion would begin. It was not chosen arbitrarily: Pearse was obsessed with the idea of blood sacrifice, and the sacrifice of Christ on the cross, with His ensuing Resurrection, was symbolic of his plan for Ireland. Success was not seen in terms of a military win: he saw this planned rebellion as a sacrificial gesture. To Pearse this was a necessary way of stirring the country to his vision of a grand rebellion that would finally force the British out of Ireland. The final accord for the Rising brought together a number of groups, including the Citizen Army and Cumann na mBan, under a single banner.

At a meeting in Liberty Hall, Dublin, Connolly announced to the various Volunteer units that they no longer were merely the Irish Republican Brotherhood but the Irish Republican Army (IRA). He urged them as the IRA to be willing to strike for Irish freedom. Pearse was overall commandant-general, with Connolly in charge of the Dublin division. Notably absent from this ambitious plan was Eoin MacNeill. MacNeill had heard late in 1915 of Pearse's ideas and had condemned the notion of an armed rebellion. He argued that it could not succeed and therefore was not moral. He did not change his mind. In February 1916 MacNeill had again warned against the idea of such a plan and predicted that it would split the country and might lead to partition.

## THE 1916 EASTER RISING

As Pearse's plans began to unravel, in the week before the Rising it became clear that the rebellion could not possibly succeed. On Good Friday before the Rising, a German munitions ship arrived off the Kerry coast earlier than expected and was met by the British navy rather than the local IRB unit. The German captain promptly scuttled the ship, and all the arms went down with it. On the same day Sir Roger Casement, who was responsible for this German gun-running, was put ashore off a German submarine farther up the Kerry coast. He was promptly arrested. Casement was later hanged on August 3, 1916, in London. In spite of the loss of this vital arms support it was decided to press on. The rebellion was rescheduled for Easter Monday. When MacNeill heard that preparations were made to proceed, he became enraged, declaring that the Easter Rising was a "lunatic idea," and ordered the Volunteers not to take part in it.

On what was to become a momentous day in twentieth-century Irish history, Easter Monday, April 24, 1916, a small band of uniformed men and women Volunteers walked down the main street in Dublin and entered the General Post Office building, known locally as the GPO. They took control of the building and hung the Nationalist tricolor flag of green, white, and orange on the roof. Then Patrick Pearse came outside and read the Proclamation of Irish Freedom, written "From the Provisional Government of the Irish Republic to the people of Ireland." Approximately 2,500 copies of this document had been secretly printed in Liberty Hall and were now being distributed throughout the country. The proclamation was composed mostly by Pearse and Connolly and approved by the military council of the IRB. It called on all Irish men and women to seize the moment and strike for Irish freedom. People passing in the street on that Easter Monday had absolutely no idea that they were witnessing one of the defining moments in Irish history. Pearse stood by one of the large Doric columns and read the entire document, which began:

> Irishmen and Irishwomen: In the name of God and the dead generations from which she receives her old traditions of nationhood, Ireland, through us, summons her children to her flag and strikes for her freedom . . . supported by her exiled children in America and gallant allies in Europe. . . .

With these words Patrick Pearse essentially declared Ireland to be a republic and his fellow rebels the provisional government. Within minutes of this action, six rebel units seized positions throughout the city, including the Four Courts building. An attempt to take Dublin Castle almost succeeded, but the rebels withdrew. The British were taken completely by surprise by these actions. After seizing the German ship and arresting Casement off the coast of Kerry, they had assumed that the rebellion was aborted. Few could have fathomed Pearse's belief that this small band could incite the entire country in rebellion. Because of Mac-Neill's orders to his people not to participate, fewer than fifteen hundred men and women were on the streets in Dublin that day to take on the British Empire. The leaders were poets, writers, teachers—a woman, Constance Gore-Booth, commanded the forces at St. Stephen's Green. A futile gesture doomed to failure, the Easter Rising was nonetheless the stuff of high romance and caught the imagination of future generations like no other armed action in Irish history.

## BRITISH RESPONSE TO THE REBELLION

Although when originally planned the Rising was intended to be nationwide, in practice it scarcely spread beyond Dublin City. The British response was immediate. Martial law was declared, and a new British commander-in-chief arrived within days. He was General Sir John Maxwell, and under martial law he held full powers. His behavior would later draw criticism from both Irish and British sources. Nevertheless he was a soldier with much distinction within the British army and came to Ireland from Egypt where he had commanded the Anglo-Egyptian armies. He had no knowledge of the current political mood in Ireland, and like many other British army appointments, no knowledge of how deep the resentment against British rule ran. He had been told by Prime Minister Asquith to put down the rebellion as quickly as possible, and he did so regardless of the human or political consequences. His actions were later seen as committing more damage to the British presence in Ireland than the rebels could ever have done.

Troops were quickly sent in from England so that by mid-week there were 25,000 British soldiers on the Dublin streets. There was reportedly confusion among the British troops who arrived with such speed. Dublin folklore records that some of the soldiers thought that they were in France. A large British gunboat, the *Helga*, was brought up the River Liffey and shelled the headquarters of the Irish General Workers Union, Liberty Hall. The GPO was bombarded until it was no more than a hollow shell. Other buildings were likewise wrecked, and parts of the city were reduced to piles of rubble. Because they had been told that many of the insurgents were not wearing uniforms, the army often shot indiscriminately at civilian men. The rebels fought well. In one instance near the Four Courts it took 5,000 British soldiers, equipped with armored cars and artillery, 28 hours to advance about 150 yards against about 200 rebels.

## OUT OF THE ASHES OF FAILURE

But the rebels were hopelessly outnumbered, and within a week the uprising was crushed. The main contingent at the GPO was forced out of the building because it was about to collapse. The group made its way to another building around the corner on Moore Street. On Saturday morning, April 29, Pearse decided to surrender. He asked one of the Cumann women, Elizabeth O'Farrell, to act as a courier between him and the other rebel units holding positions throughout the city. She first went to the British command with a white flag of surrender. Under a negotiated protection from the British army she brought Pearse's surrender order to the insurgents still fighting. Pearse's statement begins:

> In order to prevent the further slaughter of Dublin citizens, and in the hope of saving the lives of our followers now surrounded and hopelessly outnumbered, the members of the Provisional Government . . . have agreed to an unconditional surrender.

It was over, and the other leaders surrendered. They were all immediately taken captive by the British.

The Volunteers marched from Moore Street and laid down their weapons at the five-year-old statue of Charles Stewart Parnell. Then they were told to lie in the grass of a nearby hospital. In a moment of bizarre cruelty not unlike many incidents in war, one of the British army officers, Lee Wilson, thought it amusing to strip Thomas Clarke naked and walk him around in front of the hospital windows. Clarke was almost sixty years old and a deeply religious man. It was a cruel thing to do and obviously meant to humiliate him. A young volunteer, Michael Collins, saw the humiliation and also saw to it five years later that the IRA took revenge on Wilson. He was shot in Gorey on Collins's orders. Most of the women had earlier been told by Pearse to leave the various positions around the city as the situation became hopeless. Those at the Four Courts decided not to leave. They stayed on, destroying incriminating papers and helping to evacuate the building. More than seventy women were arrested for participating in the Rising.

The leaders were quickly rounded up and taken to Kilmainham Jail. Connolly had been wounded in the fighting in the GPO and was taken to a hospital. Constance Gore-Booth was led out of her position and taken away. Her military uniform confused the British solders who arrested her; at first they apparently thought that she was a man. Like the other leaders, she was placed in solitary confinement. Among the leaders who were arrested was a man destined to play a major role in twentieth-century Irish history, Eamon de Valera. De Valera had commanded the forces at Boland's Mill on the south side of the city.

## "THE FOOLS, THE FOOLS, THE FOOLS . . ."

The British follow-up to the Rising was just as repressive as its immediate response. Orders came from the British cabinet to deal harshly with the rebellion, and British reprisals were brutal. General Maxwell showed no mercy in his handling of the situation. In the weeks following the Rising, arrests were widespread and went far beyond those who had participated. Extensive house searches throughout Dublin by the British army resulted in more than 3,500 arrests. The atrocities committed by the army against civilians were unspeakable by any measure.

Francis Sheehy-Skeffington was murdered by an army officer whom he had seen kill an unarmed child. The officer ordered Sheehy-Skeffington to be shot without a trial. Sheehy-Skeffington was a well-known figure in Ireland at the time, and his death provoked an uproar. His middle name was that of his wife, a well-known suffragette. He had campaigned on behalf of women's rights in University College, Dublin, and was also a vocal supporter of female suffrage. There was enormous public outrage at his cold murder and eventually the officer, J. C. Bowan-Colthurst, was put on trial and found guilty but insane and released. He spent the rest of his life as a bank manager. This incident alone had an enormous effect on public opinion.

The British seemed to be on an inexorable course of self-destruction. Pearse, Connolly, and the other rebel leaders were tried in Dublin by a secret military court, and the public was not informed. Each was convicted of treason. Connolly's trial was held in his hospital room while he lay wounded in his bed. Beginning on May 3 the leaders began to be executed. It was only after the execution of each that public statements were issued. By early June, fifteen rebels had been executed by the British. Each reported killing further incensed public opinion. There was an overwhelming belief that the executions were unfair, and that the men involved, at the very least, deserved a public trial.

Their handling of the Easter Rising was without doubt the greatest blunder the English made in seven hundred years of ruling Ireland. Fury greeted the news of each reported execution. Crowds gathered outside the prison walls and offered prayers. In a moment of what can only be described as sheer madness, James Connolly was taken out of his hospital bed, so badly wounded that he had to be tied and propped up in a chair, and executed. It was too much for even the most indifferent Dublin citizens. There was nothing short of massive revulsion at the way that Connolly had been shot. Public grieving became ubiquitous. Tales of the executed patriots took on mythic proportions. The story of the marriage of Joseph Mary Plunkett to his fianceé, Grace Gifford, on the night before his execution added to the intense romantic narrative that ensued. For decades after the Rising, Mrs. Joseph Mary Plunkett glided around Dublin in dark widow's clothes and was regarded as a living national shrine to the deceased rebels.

## ". . . THEY HAVE LEFT US OUR FENIAN DEAD"

The swift, violent response of the British did not win them much respect in Ireland. Pearse's foresight proved prophetic. Public outrage could hardly be contained; the rebels quickly became martyred heroes. Two rebel exceptions to the killings were Constance Gore-Booth and de Valera. Gore-Booth was sentenced to die but had her sentence commuted because she was a woman. On her release from prison she was greeted by cheering crowds. De Valera was released the following year; because of his American birth, the charge of treason was put on hold.

While much of the population had not initially supported the Rising and was reportedly somewhat annoyed at the destruction of property, the overwhelming response of the military might of the British Empire turned popular opinion fiercely behind the rebels. With their execution the main leaders were elevated to the status of sacred icons. Yet it is hard to imagine that such a strong and sustained response from the public did not reveal latent feelings of great hostility toward the British administration. The executions of the leaders alone could not have lit the fire that blazed throughout Ireland in the coming years. Support for the rebels' cause was enduring and could not be described as shallow in any way. It would last through years of destruction and casualties and would prove itself also in the political arena. Eoin MacNeill made the reflective comment that "Home Rule was a check that was constantly being post-dated." Although it is sometimes argued that had the rebellion not occurred the constitutional method might have yet yielded results, it is difficult to see how frustration over recurrent delays in granting Home Rule would not eventually have produced open rebellion.

The protests at civilian killings by the British army were ignored by the authorities, which added to the general feelings of resentment and distrust. In a series of incidents on King Street, the army shot dead thirteen unarmed civilians, including a father and young son who were taken from their home and shot in cold blood. It was only in 2001 that sealed documents released by the British government under Prime Minster Tony Blair showed that more than three hundred innocent civilian deaths, including those on King Street, allegedly caused by the British army in the days following the Rising, were covered up with no investigation. The sealed report revealed no evidence that any of these people was involved in the Rising. Sir Edward Troup of the Home Office had advised Prime Minister Asquith that "nothing but harm could come of any public inquiry." Hiding these incidents from the public was impossible, and stories of the killing of innocent civilians spread throughout Ireland. In describing the mistakes the British made in their handling of the Rising, one Irish historian remarked that "the British attempted to kill a fly with a cannonball and missed."

The sense of outrage against such heavy-handed response almost immediately found diverse visible expression. Protest marches were organized throughout the country by Cumann na mBan to draw attention to the atrocities. The marches drew large crowds as word spread to every corner of Ireland that a great injustice had been done by the British. In the center of Dublin a huge banner was hung from Liberty Hall which read "James Connolly murdered May 12th 1916." The Catholic church denounced British methods in Ireland, and priests made public statements about the "sacred" manner of the rebels' deaths. The British were increasingly finding themselves in a foreign country that was determined to see them leave.

Although at first Asquith defended British action in the House of Commons, when the public outcry persisted he changed his position and fired General Maxwell. Asquith would soon admit that "things are being done in Ireland which would disgrace the blackest annals of the lowest despotism in Europe." The poet Yeats crowned the moment of agony with his cry on behalf of the dead rebels: "a terrible beauty is born."

## HOME RULE NO LONGER ENOUGH— SINN FÉIN GOES TO THE POLLS

Within Ireland the big losers of the 1916 Rising were the Home Rule movement and John Redmond. Since 1914 Redmond had supported the British war effort and had encouraged young Irish men to join the British army as a gesture to show Irish support and to ensure that Home Rule would be granted after the war. Now that same British army had executed more than a dozen Irish republicans and imprisoned thousands more. The army's heavy-handed action turned Irish public opinion around. The constitutional path was abandoned. The IRA was expanding, and public sympathy was with them.

More important, the small political party of Sinn Féin began to have significant success at the polling booths. In early 1917, in the first by-election after the Rising, George Noble Plunkett ran as a Sinn Féin candidate. He was the former curator of the National Museum of Ireland and the father of the executed rebel leader Joseph Mary Plunkett. His candidacy in Roscommon challenged Redmond's Home Rule candidate. Plunkett won easily and immediately announced that he would refuse to take his seat at Westminster, as the Parliament did not represent the interests of Ireland. Although overshadowed by future events the election in Roscommon marked a major turning point in Irish political life. The electorate of north Roscommon pointed the way for future elections that would eventually herald an entire new chapter in Irish history. Later in the same year similar success for Sinn Féin came in by-elections in Longford, Clare, and Kilkenny. All of this spelled disaster for the Redmondites and the Home Rule movement. Seen as accomplices to the so-called Crimes of 1916, they stood by helplessly as public opinion turned bitterly against them.

Public resentment continued to fester against the British, and in February 1918 further fuel was added to the fire. With the massive loss of life in the European war and the number of military casualties showing no signs of abating, the British needed more men for their army. British Prime Minister David Lloyd George, who had replaced Asquith, announced the introduction of mandatory conscription for Ireland. The idea of sending Irish men to fight in the British army was met with almost total opposition in Ireland. The sense of disbelief among the Irish was matched only by fury. Catholic bishops now joined with the IRB leaders and the Home Rulers in open protest. They all united in an organization called the Irish Anti-Conscription League. In the face of such opposition, the British government withdrew its proposal.

But the tide of public opinion continued to flow in the direction of the militants, and the public was increasingly committed to a total break with Britain. Home Rule within the United Kingdom was no longer enough. Ireland had been declared a full republic by the 1916 rebels. The country seemed ready to fulfill that destiny.

## THE IRISH REPUBLICAN ARMY

The Irish Volunteers and their associate organizations, the IRB and the Citizen Army, were beneficiaries of the aftermath of 1916. They now collectively took the title of the Irish Republican Army, or IRA. They also continued to be known as the Irish Volunteers. Because of the public groundswell of resentment against the British army's tactics, support for the IRA grew. Its numbers increased, and its members could organize a more serious threat to the British authorities. The largest membership came from the west of Ireland and from Munster. In October 1917, at their first convention held after the Easter Rising, IRA members determined that their role was to pressure the British government to recognize the status of the Irish Republic as proclaimed by Pearse. With this purpose they decided to arm and train, publicly drilling in many parts of the country.

Michael Collins took over the leadership of the IRA and introduced guerrilla tactics because he maintained that traditional warfare, like the 1916 Rising, could not possibly succeed against superior military odds. Collins was a dynamic young man who had fought alongside Pearse in the GPO. He had been arrested but was later released. By 1918 he had gained a reputation as a brilliant military tactician who developed the IRA into an effective urban guerrilla force.

Michael Collins, IRA leader during the War of Independence. On signing the treaty he is said to have remarked, "I have signed my own death warrant." (*Clare Library*)

## SINN FÉIN IN THE VANGUARD

When World War I ended in November 1918 a general election was called and the date was set for December of that year. For the first time women over the age of thirty would have the right to vote. This factor and other reforms meant that the Irish electorate was almost three times larger than in the preceding election. Eamon de Valera was now the president of the Sinn Féin party, which decided to contest the upcoming general election. This meant of course that the party would run in opposition to Redmond's Home Rule party, but the Sinn Féiners set forth an unusual platform. If elected, Sinn Féin pledged to set up a parliament in Dublin and ignore the Westminster parliament. They explained that if they won seats they would refuse to sit in the London legislature but would instead form an Irish parliament. Given the heightened atmosphere in Ireland created by the new sense of nationalism and the anger against what many saw as the atrocities committed by the British government in dealing with the 1916 rebels, the Sinn Féin platform proved immensely popular.

Election results authenticated the revolution that had occurred in Irish life. Widespread public support for Sinn Féin and its policies was not in doubt. Outside of northeast Ulster, where the Unionists took their expected two dozen seats, the Sinn Féiners swept the country. Seventy-three Sinn Féiners won seats—Home Rule candidates took only six. Parnell's once-powerful political party was essentially destroyed as Sinn Féin stepped into the vanguard of Irish politics. Redmond had died in March 1918, so he was spared the degradation of seeing his party lose favor with the Irish electorate. This election featured some interesting results. Many of those elected were actually in prison, having been arrested by the British the preceding year on dubious charges of hatching a German plot. More important, Ireland had the distinction of electing the first woman to the British House of Commons—Constance Gore-Booth, known since her marriage as the Countess Markievicz. As a Sinn Féin member, she refused to take her seat, adhering to the promise made by Sinn Féin before the election.

## SINN FÉIN SECEDES AND FORMS A PARLIAMENT IN DUBLIN

All of the elected Sinn Féiners ignored the Westminster parliament and formed an Irish parliament in Dublin, declaring they had a mandate from the Irish people to do so. They met in the Mansion House (the lord mayor's official residence) in Dublin on January 21, 1919, and formally drew up the Irish Declaration of Independence. Part of this document reads:

> For seven hundred years the Irish people has never ceased to repudiate and has repeatedly protested in arms against foreign usurpation. . . . English rule in this country is, and always has been, based upon force and fraud and maintained by military occupation against the declared will of the people.

This new Irish government took the Irish title Dáil Éireann, or the Assembly of Ireland, and claimed to be the legitimate parliament of the entire country. The Dáil recognized the IRA as the official army of a now-declared independent and republican Irish state. The Democratic Programme, a document also drawn up by this new government, declared its intention to be a democratic body and allied itself to the actions of 1916:

> We declare in the words of the Irish republican proclamation the right of the people of Ireland, to the ownership of Ireland and to the unfettered control of Irish destinies to be indefeasible, and in the language of our first President, Pádraig Pearse, we declare that the nation's sovereignty extends not only to all men and women of the nation but to all its material possessions. . . . We declare that we desire our country to be ruled in accordance with the principles of liberty, equality and justice for all, which alone can secure permanence of government in the willing adhesion of the people. . . .

The Ulster Unionists were invited to participate in this now-declared Irish independent state, but they declined. The elected Unionists took their seats in Westminster. Many Unionists believed their position in Ireland was tenuous. They were a minority on the island and were outnumbered even in Ulster. They won a majority in only four of the nine Ulster counties—Sinn Féin won the rest. Sinn Féin maintained that they had won the consent of the Irish people to secede from Britain. A cabinet was formed and de Valera, who was one of those still in prison, was declared the first president of the Irish Republic. He was not the only elected member of Sinn Féin who was jailed, but imprisonment by the British actually enhanced the reputation of the rebels, affording them a certain status in the public eye.

## THE GREAT ESCAPE FROM LINCOLN JAIL

De Valera's escape from Lincoln Jail in England was seen as imperative to the new Dáil. In February 1919, Michael Collins engineered a plan to get de Valera out. In a daring move that is the stuff of drama, an imprint of a key was smuggled out of the prison. A key was then made and smuggled into the prison in a cake. Unfortunately the key did not work. Finally a working key was sent in another cake, and the scheme was on. On the night of February 3 Collins and Harry Boland went to Lincoln Jail and crouched outside in the grass. They gave a signal from a flashlight to de Valera, who was at his prison window. He replied with a lighted match. De Valera then made his way down to the front gate of the jail—the key also opened other doors on the way to the main gate. With a cliffhanger climax that involved Collins breaking his duplicate key in the lock from the outside and de Valera pushing out the broken key with his working one from the inside, the prisoner was finally outside.

The small group simply walked away from the prison, with de Valera disguised in women's clothing. He was then successfully smuggled back to Ireland where newspapers had reported his escape. It devastated and embarrassed the British authorities but delighted the Irish. De Valera was greeted openly by crowds of cheering Irish who now regarded "Dev," as he was called, as their "chief." He was the great survivor, the living icon of 1916. That magic would remain with him all his life.

# [ 10 ]

# A Terrible Beauty: The Irish War of Independence

✳

IN BRITAIN there was public outrage in the press at the instigation of a self-proclaimed government in Ireland. Formal retaliation came in the form of British governmental condemnation. In September 1919 Lloyd George declared Dáil Éireann illegal. The British army presence in Ireland was augmented. As the new Irish parliament tried to proceed with developing a national program, the British army attempted to arrest the leaders of this "illegal" government. Soldiers conducted house searches and arrested any of the rebel Sinn Féin members they could find. As members of the British army moved into all parts of the country searching for militants and making arrests, they found themselves confronted with the IRA. It was the beginning of the Irish War of Independence.

For two and a half years the British army and the IRA were engaged in Ireland's first urban guerrilla war. It was an almost impossible situation for the British. The IRA, though not as well armed and not as numerous, had two clear advantages: it had intimate knowledge of the countryside and, most important, the support of a large portion of the population who were willing to hide IRA members when they were on the run. Support for the Dáil and the IRA was widespread among the public. Sympathy for their position was evident in the reaction of many significant figures in Irish life. The chief rabbi of Ireland, Isaac Herzog, assisted and supported the fledgling government. He frequently hid Sinn Féin members, including de Valera, in his home. Rabbi Herzog later became the chief rabbi of the new Jewish state of Israel. His close friendship with de Valera would last until his death.

## PARTITION OF THE ISLAND OF IRELAND

Meanwhile in Parliament, the House of Commons sat without the Sinn Féin members from Ireland. Only six Home Rule candidates were present to represent Ireland's interests, and their influence had shrunk with their numbers. When the Home Rule bill came up for a vote it passed, but in a significantly modified form. It was named the Government of Ireland Act, 1920, and it called for two parliaments to be established in Ireland: one in Dublin and one in Belfast. It was a blow to the Nationalists but not one without warning. Within Westminster circles the idea of partition that had been floated since before the war now appeared to be the only way forward.

It was also less than Carson and the Unionists had wanted. They had wanted all nine counties of Ulster to be excluded from control of the Dublin government, but this was impossible. The Unionists held a majority in only four of the nine counties of Ulster. So a compromise was established whereby an area comprising six Ulster counties would have its own government. Two majority Catholic counties, Fermanagh and Tyrone, were brought together with four predominantly Protestant counties, Derry, Antrim, Down, and Armagh, to form a majority Protestant region. Although sometimes referred to as "Ulster"—it does not include the entire province—the legal term for this new state was Northern Ireland. The handful of old Irish party members in the House of Commons could not prevent passage of this "partition" bill. Partition of the island was established almost without a murmur.

## THE BLACK AND TANS

In Ireland the British army found itself in an impossible situation. With local support for the rebels so pervasive, the army could not fight a guerrilla war and win. After a year morale was exceedingly low, and army reports back to England suggest that many officers were feeling hopeless. Thus the idea of sending in auxiliary forces to back up the army and the police was suggested in January 1920. British Secretary of State for War Winston Churchill was the mastermind behind this decision, which marks another low point in relations between the English and the Irish.

The Auxiliaries were a mixed group of war veterans and criminals and were probably unprepared for the situation in Ireland. Whatever the reason, they soon gained a dubious reputation for their brutality and ruthless methods. Their distinctive uniforms earned them the nickname the "Black and Tans." They were given orders to restrain the rebellion and were invested with draconian powers to do so. With little to impede them, they soon rampaged out of control. Whole towns were burned to the ground as was a large part of Cork City. Civilians were shot at and murdered indiscriminately. Black and Tan actions entered Irish folklore.

The British government's instigation of its Black and Tan tactics destroyed the validity of their claim to be looking for a peaceful solution to the "troubles." These extreme methods brought reprisals, and the cycle of violence escalated. On November 21, 1920, the highly charged situation reached a tragic climax. Under orders from Michael Collins, the IRA killed twelve British officers in Dublin on information obtained through spies that the officers were intelligence operatives. Later that day Black and Tans and police went to Croke Park, a sports stadium in Dublin, where a crowd was attending a football match. They entered the stadium and fired into the crowd and at the players on the field. There remains a dispute about whether shots were fired from the crowd at the Auxiliaries—none was hit—but there is no dispute about the result. Fourteen unarmed civilians, including one of the football players, were killed, with more than one hundred people injured. The day was forever known as Bloody Sunday. A secret inquiry by the British was released more than eighty years later in 2003 but shed little light on the issue of responsibility and conflicted with eyewitness accounts.

Actions like this only made the population more hostile to the British and more willing to support and hide the IRA. By now the IRA controlled most of the rural countryside, and the army was unable to gain a foothold anywhere except in some towns. Meanwhile the Dáil was establishing itself as the legitimate government, and Sinn Féin was setting up a court system throughout the country. Money was being supplied from Irish-American groups. De Valera had traveled to the United States and spent eighteen months seeking the support of Irish Americans; by 1920 he had raised $5 million. Irish Americans were also sending guns; Thompson machine guns were arriving in Dublin by the caseload.

## THE NOTORIOUS CAPTAIN SWIFT, A.K.A. "A SMALL DUBLIN JEWISH MERCHANT"

Guns were also coming in from another, more significant source. In February 1920 Collins appointed IRA member Robert "Bob" Briscoe as his chief agent to go to Germany to buy arms covertly for shipment to Ireland. The most famous Jewish Irishman is Joyce's fictional Leopold Bloom, but real life produces equally valiant figures. Irish Nationalist Robert Briscoe is one of the most intrepid. Briscoe, who later became the first Jewish lord mayor of Dublin in the 1950s, was the main purveyor of guns and ammunition for the Irish War of Independence.

Born in Dublin in September 1894, Briscoe grew up above the family business in the heart of the city at Ormond Quay. His father, Abraham William Briscoe, had come to Ireland from Lithuania as a boy of fourteen. In his autobiography, *For the Life of Me*, Robert Briscoe recounts that "To Father, the soft green hills of Dublin harbor were the sheltering arms of justice." The elder Briscoe absorbed Irish history and culture, and the reality of how the Irish had struggled to survive became his reality. Although small in number, many of the Jews who came to Ireland in the nineteenth century would later say that there was such a similarity between the Irish and the Jewish experience that assimilation was instinctive. The Jewish population in Ireland never rose above six thousand, but the Jewish contribution to Irish life is enormous. Many were deeply involved in the independence movement. Sisters Molly and Fanny Goldberg, whose father had been a supporter of Parnell and Davitt, were active members of the women's Cumann na mBan. Michael Noyk was a committed Nationalist who worked closely with Michael Collins and was one of his most trusted advisers. Noyk was a lawyer who for years defended many IRA and Cumann

Chief of the IRA covert operation of obtaining and shipping arms into Ireland during the War of Independence, later in the 1950s Robert Briscoe became the first Jewish lord mayor of Dublin.

na mBan prisoners. He was arrested in 1919 in a curfew roundup but managed to dispose of incriminating evidence. He was also the primary agent in covertly acquiring premises for the underground Dáil's government departments. Noyk's own offices were raided by the Black and Tans, but he foiled their attempt to find anything of significance.

Robert Briscoe was the third of seven children, and one of his brothers was named Wolfe Tone after the great Irish patriot. Their father taught the children Hebrew and how to read the Torah but also inspired them with a strong sense of Irish nationalism. "All the time I was growing up, I was being steeped in the dark, storm-wracked, light-shot history of my country, of Ireland," Briscoe writes. A passionate supporter of Irish independence, Briscoe, like so many young Irish of his generation, was inspired by the events of

1916 to join in the fight for Irish freedom. He became involved with a number of Gaelic and Nationalist organizations. His ability to courier secret messages and small arms between rebel posts soon caught the attention of Michael Collins, who was organizing all aspects of the War of Independence.

Collins appointed Briscoe to the general headquarters of the IRA as chief in charge of the German gun-running operation. Briscoe traveled to Germany many times over a period of two years, where he covertly purchased large quantities of guns and ammunition. Operating under the dashing code name "Captain Swift"—Briscoe himself called it "swashbuckling"—he continually risked his life buying and shipping arms into Ireland under the very nose of the British blockade. Although it was illegal in Germany to sell arms, the German economy was in such bad shape that Briscoe found many willing sellers. He set up arms depositories in ports in Germany, Belgium, and Holland for shipment to Ireland. In his autobiography Briscoe tells how he used the cover of "a small Dublin Jewish merchant" to effect many daring exploits, including at one time hiding a secret dispatch from Collins in his baby daughter's diaper. His success in the gun-running operation was a major contribution to the outcome of the Irish war.

## THE BRITISH CAVE IN

As if this were not enough for the British to deal with, Michael Collins had successfully penetrated the spy system of Dublin Castle and essentially shut down British intelligence. The British were in a difficult position in a country where so much of the population supported the native side. As one example, Collins's cousin was given a key position in the Castle, and she immediately contacted Collins and became an important part of his intelligence network. Collins's response to this extraordinary tactical blunder by Castle authorities was his famous emblematic remark about the British: "How did these people ever get an empire?"

Eventually the situation became so hopeless that the British decided they could continue no longer. A dispatch from Ireland to the government in Westminster spoke of the "psychological distress" of the British army. Money was also an issue. Lloyd George had asked for an estimate of how much it would cost to win the war in Ireland and was stunned to be told that victory over the IRA would cost a further £100 million and 100,000 men. Obviously he could not pay that price. Unknown to him, Collins was concerned about how much longer the IRA could hold out. But Collins need not have worried; in a remarkable change of direction the British caved in first. In July 1921 the British called a truce and offered to talk to Sinn Féin about a treaty. The date for talks was set for the following October.

Almost at once de Valera announced that he would not be part of the Irish delegation. This came as a total surprise to all as he would not only have been expected to attend but it was assumed that he, as the declared president of the Dáil, would have headed the Irish group. Instead he insisted that Michael Collins go. History has never recorded the reason why de Valera chose not to go to London to participate in the Treaty discussion, or why he pushed so much for a reluctant Collins to do so. The event would mark a new relationship between the two that would eventually divide the country and provoke a civil war, the repercussions of which would last for generations. The Collins–de Valera split would overshadow Irish political life for decades.

## THE LONG FELLOW

Although they began as comrades in the fight for Irish freedom, Collins and de Valera were destined to stand opposite each other historically. In truth they were very different people. Born in New York in 1882 to an Irish mother and a Spanish father, Eamon de Valera had been sent home to Ireland at the age of two to be raised by his mother's family in County Limerick. His parents had separated, and his mother was reluctant to raise him alone. When she remarried within two years, she did not send for him. It was an odd decision for a mother to make. Rumors concerning this seemingly heartless act would surround de Valera all his life and beyond. The family in Ireland was poor, and he grew up in a laborer's cottage. He was a bright child and at age sixteen, when his local priest recommended him to the president of the school, he gained a scholarship at Blackrock College, the renowned secondary school in Dublin. This was to be the first of many fortuitous doors that opened, and Blackrock became an important emotional home for him. Tim Pat Coogan, in his biography of de Valera, sums up his life this way: "There is a kind of man to whom luck happens, de Valera was one of that kind." He never showed much interest in returning to the family that raised him, leading to speculation that he had no close bond there.

De Valera grew up in Ireland in a time when national expression was strong and national organizations were pushing the ideal of an Ireland free of English domination. He joined the Gaelic League in 1908 and was committed to the spread of the Irish language and the establishment of a national consciousness. In 1913 he joined the Volunteers, convinced that an armed struggle would be the only way to achieve Irish freedom. By then he was a teacher of mathematics at Maynooth College. He later said that in the long evenings during his periods in prison he would think of the mathematical problems that he loved to solve. Rumors about his family background haunted him from an early age, and the question of his legitimacy hung over him. In one of his letters to his wife in 1917 he noted that political enemies were claiming "that I am illegitimate." Illegitimacy was a social shame at the time in Catholic Ireland and would have been a source of humiliation for de Valera. His later ultra-conservatism regarding family life may have come from these uncertain origins.

The only surviving leader of the 1916 Easter Rising, he naturally became the principal figure of post-1916 Ireland. Known to his followers as the "Chief" and the "Long Fellow" (because of his height), the aura of the Rising drew people around him and gave him iconic status. In 1919 the Dáil voted him president of the declared Irish Republic. That he chose not to attend the Treaty talks with the British was a shock at the time and remains a historical mystery. The man he picked to go in his place, Michael Collins, though a man of action and leader of the IRA, was also a man of compromise. Perhaps de Valera knew this and decided that he did not wish to be responsible for compromises that he knew must be made.

## THE BIG FELLOW

For whatever reason, Michael Collins headed the delegation that went to London to negotiate the treaty. Different in temperament from de Valera, their differences could probably be best understood by their dissimilar family backgrounds. Eight years younger than de Valera, Collins had been born in Clonakilty in County Cork on October 16, 1890, to a warm, close-knit family. He was the youngest of eight children and the center of loving attention from his older siblings and his parents. The Collins family was part of the landed dispossessed. By the time of Michael's birth the family possessed only ninety acres of land, but the Collinses knew their history. His father was seventy-five when Michael was born and died six years later. The story told in the family reveals that on his deathbed Michael's father told the family to look out for the boy because "some day he will do great work for Ireland." His mother was a hardworking and intelligent woman who passed on to him stories of Irish survival through centuries of devastation.

As a young adult Collins joined the Gaelic League and believed in the reestablishment of the Irish language. He also believed in armed rebellion against British rule in Ireland. After the 1916 Rising he was arrested, and on his release from prison was determined to reshape the IRA into a formidable force. In the process Collins became the architect of the armed struggle and a popular and well-loved leader by the men in his command. He was affectionately called the "Big Fellow" because of his apparent total confidence in himself and his artless conviction that he was big enough to handle any situation. Michael Noyk once said of Collins that the word "cannot" was not part of his vocabulary. A man of action, Collins is also credited with an astute sense of practicality. This was the man who found himself reluctantly going to London to oversee treaty negotiations with the British. Accompanying him in a leadership role was Arthur Griffith, founder of Sinn Féin.

## NEGOTIATING THE TREATY

The Irish faced well-seasoned negotiators. Lloyd George, Austin Chamberlain, and Winston Churchill formed the British side. The negotiations lasted for a number of months, but the British wavered very little from their original stand. On December 6, 1921, the Treaty was agreed upon—though even the document's title is not in agreement. The Irish always refer to it as the Treaty whereas the

British call it the Articles of Agreement. Under the terms of this agreement Ireland, outside of the six-county divide, was to be given dominion status within the British Empire. This new state would be called the Irish Free State and would in many ways be far more independent of Britain than Northern Ireland would be.

For one thing, no representation at Westminster was required, and the Free State was to have its own armed forces. Full fiscal autonomy regarding taxation was granted to the Free State, a major reversal for Lloyd George who had been against granting this in the 1920 Ireland Act. On the down side for the Irish, each member of the Free State parliament was required to take an oath to the British monarch. This essentially meant that the link to the British monarch had to be maintained and that a total Irish Republic was not a possibility. Of more lasting consequence was the assertion that

> the powers of the parliament and the government of the Irish Free State shall not be exercisable as respects Northern Ireland and the provisions of the *Government of Ireland Act, 1920,* shall as regards as they relate to Northern Ireland, remain of full force and effect.

In other words, the Irish Free State would have no control over Northern Ireland. Yet the same document proposed that an all-Ireland council convene to discuss the subject of reuniting the now-divided country.

These were the terms that the Irish delegation signed and had to take back to Ireland for ratification. Without doubt it was a compromise document. To Collins the Treaty was not the final solution to the Irish question but a stepping-stone to further independence. He was willing to accept what was offered and believed that more would come later. Nevertheless he knew the task that lay before him in Ireland. On signing the Treaty Collins remarked, "I am signing my own death warrant." He was right. Nevertheless the Treaty was generally viewed as a victory for the IRA and Sinn Féin while Unionists were appalled by the terms. That such a large part of Ireland had succeeded in getting so much independence from Britain was shocking. The Unionist MP Henry Wilson, a major general in the British army, felt that it was a sell-out of British world power, and he declared that "the British Empire is doomed."

## DIVISION ON THE TREATY: CIVIL WAR

When the Irish delegation returned to Ireland the public was relieved that the Treaty was signed and that Collins had approved it. But there was also immediate opposition from de Valera and some others in the Dáil to what they saw as a betrayal of the 1916 ideals. De Valera's main problem with the Treaty was the oath of allegiance to the British monarch and the fact that the new state was not the Irish Republic as declared by Pearse but what he perceived as a lesser "Free State." The fact that the Treaty gave complete independence over domestic matters was not sufficient for de Valera. Ironically the establishment of Northern Ireland was not considered a major problem because the generally held opinion was that such a small region could not survive economically and would eventually be reincorporated into an all-Ireland government.

After a heated discussion in the Dáil, the Treaty was accepted on January 7, 1922, by a majority of 64 to 57. De Valera angrily walked out of the chamber, refusing to accept the ruling, and resigned as president. A number of delegates followed him, including Cathal Brugha, minister for defense, and Countess Markievicz, minister of labor. On the departure of these members Collins took command of a provisional government and immediately declared a general election. The IRA also split—some members joined the government of Collins and became the Free State army while others remained committed to the total fulfillment of Pearse's aspirations. Harry Boland and Robert Briscoe were among those who sided with de Valera. The result of this split was civil war.

Those of the IRA who refused to accept the Treaty seized the Four Courts building in Dublin in April 1922, and within weeks Collins moved against them with the Free State army. Here was the beginning of the Irish Civil War. The Catholic church, which had supported Sinn Féin and the establishment of the Dáil, condemned the anti-Treaty side and excommunicated its members. The casualty rate in the Civil War was light, but those involved fought with dedication and pain as former comrades found themselves confronting one another. In the midst of this chaos, in June 1922, the Irish general election was held, with the Treaty dominating political discussion. Michael Collins led the pro-Treaty position and de Valera the opposition. Both campaigned ardently for support. The results showed overwhelming public support for Collins and the Treaty. The pro-Treaty contingent won convincingly, taking fifty-eight seats to the opposition's thirty-six seats.

## DEATH OF MICHAEL COLLINS

Figures for the total number killed in the Civil War vary, but more lives were lost than in the War of Independence. There was one major tragedy. Michael Collins was killed in an ambush in Béal na mBláth in Cork on August 22, 1922, on his way to a meeting to negotiate a peace settlement. The shock was followed by bitter reprisals against de Valera, whom many blamed for the death. No one has established culpability, and Collins's death remains a mystery. The government initiated a policy of ruthless reprisal executions against the opposition. Eventually it became obvious to the anti-Treaty side that it could not win. Peace was eventually established and the Civil War ended in May 1923 when the IRA laid down arms and gave up the fight. The IRA did not recognize the Irish Free State as legitimate, however, and, likewise, those of Sinn Féin who left the Dáil with de Valera did not participate in the new Free State government. They continued to call themselves the Sinn Féin party whereas those in the new government formed new political parties. The party of Michael Collins took the name Fine Gael, and those who had been part of Connolly's Citizen Army formed the Irish Labour party. The first government of the Irish Free State was under the leadership of William Cosgrave.

## NORTHERN IRELAND IS BORN

The so-called Boundary Commission, the council of all-Ireland noted in the Government of Ireland Act, never really materialized, and political partition of the island became a reality. In the north of Ireland the act was met instantaneously with sectarian violence. The population of the new six-county state was around 1.25 million, of which approximately 37 percent was Catholic (by the 1990s this figure had risen to 46 percent). That they constituted such a large minority was perceived as a threat by the Protestant majority. As a harbinger of things to come, Catholics were immediately subjected to harassment of the worst kind. On July 21, 1920, Catholic workers were ordered out of the Belfast shipyard at Harland and Wolff and other places of employment. It is estimated that overnight 10,000 Catholic men and 1,000 Catholic women lost their jobs. These were ominous signs for the minority Catholic population in the new Unionist-dominated state.

In the south there was unified sympathy for the Catholic situation, and both sides in the Treaty conflict sent arms north to counteract Unionist arms shipping in from England. The IRA in Belfast tried to gain traction but because the security forces greatly outnumbered IRA members, they could put up little resistance. The Catholic population of Northern Ireland felt disillusioned and exhausted from the previous years of war. Without the rest of the country fully behind them, they felt abandoned. For some time they were left with neither arms nor hope. It would be left to future generations to take up the cause of Catholic civil rights increasingly denied to them in this new Northern Ireland state.

## "A PROTESTANT PARLIAMENT FOR A PROTESTANT PEOPLE"

A parliament was established in Belfast. By the early 1930s a large imposing building had been built at Stormont to accommodate this new legislature. For fifty years after the establishment of the Northern Ireland state the government in Belfast was dominated by the Unionist party, which viewed the Catholic nationalists as a threat to its position. Catholics found themselves in a state completely hostile to them, one determined to eliminate their political status. The first Northern Irish prime minister, William Craig, announced that the government had established "a Protestant parliament for a Protestant people." This seemingly paranoid behavior came from the Unionists' determination to maintain their link with Britain and not risk reunification of the island.

The Unionists believed that the only way to guarantee their position was essentially to disfranchise the Catholic population, which was accomplished with great effectiveness. Careful gerrymandering in the majority Catholic counties of Fermanagh and Tyrone rendered nationalist power impotent. The city of Derry, which was also majority Catholic, was run by Unionists because of the way the electoral districts were drawn. In addition an electoral qualification system was developed throughout the province which favored the better-off Protestant class. In county and urban council elections, only householders were allowed to vote. Since many Catholics were not owners of homes, they could not vote in these elections.

Economic discrimination was even more blatant and egregious. Most council jobs went to Protestants. In private industry Catholics were largely excluded from anything but the most menial jobs. The main employers, shipbuilders Harland and Wolff and Shorts Engineering, had workforces that were more than 90 percent Protestant. Most Catholic men were unemployed for most of their working years. Unemployment ran as high as 60 percent among Catholic men between the ages of sixteen and fifty-five in Belfast during most of the twentieth century.

The economic situation in Northern Ireland inevitably produced great tension between the communities, which festered beneath the surface for many years after the 1920s. The IRA continued as a small band of rebels but with low membership and little support from the Catholic population. For decades the Catholics of Northern Ireland could do little but try to survive economically and attempt to build their lives under dismal conditions.

# [ 11 ]

# North and South:
# The Two States of Ireland

❋

LIFE IN THE IRISH FREE STATE quickly settled down and a stable nation emerged. Two bodies now comprise the government, an upper house known as the Seanad, and a lower house called the Dáil. The leader of the Dáil is the taoiseach or prime minister. The president of Ireland is also an elected figure. In 1927 de Valera decided to return to the Dáil, and he ran for election and won. He abandoned his membership in Sinn Féin and formed a new political party, Fianna Fáil. Also winning election to the Dáil with de Valera were a number of people who supported him in founding this new political party. Chief among them were Sean Lemass who became taoiseach, Sean T. O'Kelly who became president of Ireland, and Robert Briscoe who served in the Dáil for more than thirty years and also became lord mayor of Dublin in the 1950s and early 1960s. Sinn Féin continued as a political party but refused to recognize the legitimacy of the Dublin government. Members insisted that the only legitimate government would be an all-Ireland one. As a way of expressing this stand they did not participate in Free State politics, becoming a marginalized entity. The country proceeded with the business of becoming a nation.

## CATHOLIC ETHOS IN THE FREE STATE

At partition the population of the Free State was approximately three million, with 95 percent of the people Catholic. A conservative Catholic ethos emerged in which the role of the Catholic church became central to government policy. Within a relatively short space of time the laws of the country reflected this Catholic culture. Although divorce had been available on a limited basis before independence, in 1926 a law forbidding divorce within the state was passed. This was not welcomed by all, and W. B. Yeats, who was a senator by this time, argued in vain against this bill, finally walking out of the Seanad discussion in disgust. In 1928, under pressure from the Catholic bishops, a censorship bill was passed and a censorship board established. This vigilant board would ultimately ban the works of many well-known authors, including F. Scott Fitzgerald, Sigmund Freud, Somerset Maugham, Graham Greene, and Voltaire. Most Irish authors were banned during the next fifty years. These included Sean O'Casey, George Bernard Shaw, Frank O'Connor, and Samuel Beckett (who won the Nobel Prize in 1969). This censorship of Irish authors resulted in an exodus from Ireland of native writers and intellectuals. In 1935 contraception was banned as was all information on the topic. What many saw as the long dark days of social repression had begun. In the north of Ireland these laws only confirmed the belief that Home Rule had indeed become "Rome Rule," as the Unionists had predicted. Both new states, north and south, were drifting farther apart.

In 1932 de Valera's party won a majority in the Dáil, and he became taoiseach. Over the following forty years de Valera would put his stamp on Ireland like no other twentieth-century politician. Almost immediately on taking office he abandoned the "land annuities" payments that were part of the Treaty. These payments had been required of Irish farmers as repayment to the British for the "purchase" of Irish land from the British. It was the job of the Irish Land Commission to collect these annuities from Irish farmers and pass them on to the British national debt collectors. De Valera's action was seen by many in Ireland as downright heroic and just. Farmers had been hard-pressed to meet these payments and in truth greatly resented paying for something they believed belonged to them originally. The British did not see the matter in quite this way and retaliated by imposing tariffs on Irish goods entering Britain. In a counteraction, de Valera levied tariffs on British goods entering Ireland. He could play hard. His continued stand against what the Irish thought of as the heavy-handedness of the British made him politically untouchable.

## THE IRISH CONSTITUTION

One of de Valera's first major political accomplishments was the writing of the Irish constitution in 1937. The first constitution, written in 1922, was known as the Free State constitution and was drawn up by a committee under Michael Collins. The new constitution was written by de Valera and is still in use today. It was put to a general vote by the electorate and passed by a large majority. It claimed sovereignty over the entire island of Ireland, which it referred to as "Eire." The Catholic hierarchy pressured de Valera to declare them the official church, but he stopped short of this in Article 44. This article recognized "the special position" of the Catholic church, but the church would not hold an exclusive place. Other Christian religions were also given constitutional status, as was the Jewish faith. Anecdotal evidence cited by Dermot Keogh suggests that de Valera and Rabbi Herzog consulted on this issue of Jewish rights and the wording in the constitution to protect them. The constitution also confirmed many of the laws that were already on the books. Although divorce had been outlawed by the anti-divorce bill of 1926, now it became a constitutional matter, with a formal ban written into the 1937 constitution. Any amendments to the Irish constitution can be made only by general plebiscite. The Dáil alone does not have the right to make changes.

## THE DE VALERA YEARS

In 1938 de Valera came to an agreement with the British prime minister for a onetime payment to Britain over the issue of land annuities. In addition, Irish ports would no longer be under the control of the British parliament. This was to have serious consequences for the British during World War II when they were anxious to gain access to these ports. The Free State did not participate in the war,

The only surviving leader of the 1916 Rising, Eamon de Valera—seen here in 1945—was the most influential political figure in twentieth-century Ireland. (*Irish Press Newspapers*)

mostly because of the centuries of bitterness against the British and the unresolved situation with the north of Ireland. At the start of World War II de Valera declared Ireland a neutral country, and he never altered his stand during the war years. At the end of the war Winston Churchill, who had never been a supporter of Irish independence, made a scathing attack on the Irish in the House of Commons, only to be answered by de Valera in a radio message sent out on the Irish national radio service. The Irish people had remained implacably against what they saw as helping the British, and de Valera's speech to Churchill was met with great public acclaim in Ireland. Copies of it were sold and distributed for decades. In December 1948 the Irish Free State declared that it was now to be known as the Republic of Ireland; it cut all remaining ties with the British monarch and the British Commonwealth. The fact that the north of Ireland was still an unresolved wound continued to shape Irish external concerns. Ireland did not join NATO.

Built by the FitzGeralds as a residence in the eighteenth century, Leinster House now is home to the Irish parliament. (*Carmel McCaffrey*)

For the almost thirty years between 1932 and 1960 that de Valera remained supreme in Irish politics, the country was economically stagnant. Under de Valera's leadership Ireland did not industrialize but remained a rural, agrarian-based economy. This was no accident; de Valera was against change or modernization of any kind. He held to the belief that it was for the good of all that Ireland remain a society of small farms. He had what only can be described as an idyllic view of Irish aspirations. He described the Irish in romantic terms as "a rural people, who value wealth only as a basis for right living . . . a people who are satisfied with frugal comfort and will devote their leisure to things of the spirit." A serious downside to this ideal was de Valera's inability to develop a viable economic program, which spelled poverty for most people. Consequently thousands of Irish were forced to emigrate during the de Valera years. More than 400,000 people left Ireland in the 1950s to seek work abroad, mostly in England and the United States. Ireland was stagnant both socially and economically. Social welfare was deplorable, and access to health care and education were the worst in Europe.

## THE NORTH OF IRELAND
## DRIFTS TOWARD DISASTER

However difficult the economics were in the Irish Republic, life in Northern Ireland for the minority Catholic population was even more dismal. They were viewed as Nationalists with a desire to reunite Ireland, and as such were considered enemies of the state. Employment and decent housing were denied to most of them as discrimination against Catholics became a way of life. This prejudice was accompanied by a yearly round of Orange Order marches which proclaimed the supremacy of the Unionist party and the stated determination never to reunite the country. Placards at these marches frequently attacked Catholicism and Irish nationalism. Signs of "No Popery" and "Hands off Ulster" were common, and lapel buttons with pernicious anti-Catholic statements were often distributed.

Nationalists made no public response to this situation; they remained a disfranchised, dispirited group. The minority attempted to secure help from the Westminster parliament, and appeals against the discrimination practiced by the Unionist party were sent to Westminster many times over a forty-year period from the 1920s to the 1960s. These requests were always met with the reply that problems within Northern Ireland were internal to that state and not the concern of Westminster. Accordingly, Catholic grievances received no hearing in London. It was a situation ripe for explosion. In 1966 the poet Seamus Heaney, born into the Catholic community in Northern Ireland, observed, "Life goes on here, yet people are reluctant to dismiss the possibility of an explosion. A kind of doublethink operates, something is rotten, but maybe if we wait it will fester to death."

## A NEW GENERATION OF CATHOLICS

Tension and frustration eventually gave way to an explosion that could not easily be quelled. During the 1960s a new generation of Catholics sought to change the situation in which they found themselves. One of the main contributing factors to this was access to education. While access to decent housing and jobs remained elusive, access to education was more difficult to deny. In 1947 free university education for the whole of the UK was introduced by the British Labour government. Now entry to university was based on academic merit and not according to ability to pay. It meant that even the lowest-income Catholics had access to education. They took advantage of this in large numbers, and by the 1960s Catholics were entering university at a rate never before seen. Catholics comprised 22 percent of the student body at Queens University Belfast in 1961; ten years later that figure had risen to 32 percent.

This new generation of educated Catholics was determined not to endure the kind of blatant discrimination routinely meted out by the Belfast government. Inspired also by the gallant civil rights marches in the United States by black Americans and especially by the words of Dr. Martin Luther King, Jr., similar marches began to be planned in Northern Ireland. This hope was further aided by the election to the position of prime minister of Northern Ireland of Terence O'Neill, a moderate Unionist who began to make attempts to find a dialogue with the Dublin government. Unfortunately he did not get much support for this initiative within his own government. O'Neill has been criticized for his lack of success in drawing in more of his colleagues to a conciliatory attitude to Catholic rights. His failure to gain support for his position resulted in his best intentions going nowhere, but within the context of the time his stand was nevertheless laudable.

## THE NORTHERN IRELAND CIVIL RIGHTS ASSOCIATION

Widespread frustration among Catholics about their situation prompted the formation in 1967 of the Northern Ireland Civil Rights Association. The founding of this association speaks to the failure of normal political channels in the province and the refusal of Westminster to pay attention to discrimination against Catholics. They were optimistic that media attention would at last be paid to the palpable inequality of their status within the United Kingdom. The Catholic community, Nationalist by political identity, continued to feel isolated from the main social and political life of the province.

Yet this very isolation gave them a sense of their communal injustice and a strong sense of group identity. Gerry Adams described the feeling of the minority community: "Although I was unaware of it at the time, there was a kind of collective Catholic thinking, which was conscious that, no matter what status the individual might achieve, Catholics in the north of Ireland were ghettoized, marginalized, treated as inferior." The civil rights movement gave them hope that they could alter their situation. After years of fruitless attempts at justice, Nationalists now believed they could gain outside attention for their plight. They also expected that much could be accomplished by nonviolent means.

On August 24, 1968, the first civil rights march was organized by Nationalists to protest against discrimination in housing. The Unionists felt immediately threatened by this new development and turned up at the march to protest and attempt to stop it. The Protestant paramilitary group, the Ulster Volunteer Force, had been reorganized in 1966 and posed a threat. The Orange Order was especially prominent in intimidating the marchers. In spite of this, the march went off without incident. The intimidation was repeated at other civil rights marches, with violence often erupting.

The initial response of both the British government and the Belfast government was to show little interest in meeting the demands of the marchers or even attempting to discuss the issues. Yet the Unionist Protestant population felt extremely threatened by the new visibility that the Nationalists seemed to be embracing and did not back off from their attacks on the marchers. The Protestant community believed that it was defending its economic position, which had become less stable over the years. The traditional industries in Northern Ireland, shipbuilding and linen, had begun to decline, and Protestants were either losing their jobs or suffering a drop in income. The threat of Catholics possibly entering the workforce further challenged their heretofore privileged position.

## CIVIL RIGHTS MARCHES BANNED

Because of the continuing violence these civil rights marches might provoke in Northern Ireland, the Belfast government responded by banning all civil rights marches or, as they stated, "all non traditional marches." In other words, Orange marches were permitted to proceed but not those demonstrating for civil rights. No concession was offered to the Nationalists. It was an incredibly narrow ruling and one that was sure to provoke resentment. This was a new era in northern politics, and the new generation of Nationalists was not about to be set aside so easily. Determined not to cower, the Nationalists decided to ignore the ban. A critical moment came on October 5 when the Derry Civil Rights branch decided to proceed with a march that had been banned. The march was peaceful, but the police—the Royal Ulster Constabulary, or RUC—moved in on the marchers with batons, with disastrous results.

Two days of rioting throughout Derry followed as rage gripped a Catholic community incensed against this police treatment. This 1968 incident is regarded as the start of the "Troubles" and the violence that would become an endemic part of northern Irish life for the next thirty years. In November the prime minister of Northern Ireland, Terence O'Neill, announced reforms for the gerrymandered districts and an end to housing discrimination, but this did not calm the waters. The Reverend Ian Paisley came out bitterly against reforms that might allow more constitutional status to Catholics. O'Neill's unpopularity within his own Unionist party forced his resignation in April 1969. The long-standing tension was about to come to the surface with a ferocious articulation that would send the province into a seemingly endless quagmire of violent conflict.

## THE BATTLE OF THE BOGSIDE

The situation quickly went downhill. Northern Ireland was becoming seriously destabilized, with anger on both sides finding violent expression. Catholic Nationalists felt they were unprotected from either the Orange Order or the civil authorities. The UVF was finding support from hard-liners within the Stormont government. The summer of 1969 saw the worst violence as clashes occurred between the communities during the so-called marching season. The Apprentice Boys march, a traditional Orange Order march, was legally permitted to proceed on August 12 despite warnings from many quarters, including business owners, that it could lead to a bloodbath. The long-standing problem with this march was that the route usually went into the city of Derry and through the Catholic areas. This had been de rigueur for decades, and Catholics ordinarily remained indoors and ignored the taunts of the marchers; but this year the situation was different. Buoyed by the civil rights movement and the strong belief that things must change, the Nationalist population was angry and frustrated that this march was allowed to continue while civil rights marches were banned.

Some fifteen thousand Unionists took part in the Apprentice Boys march of that summer. As they marched along the Derry city wall near the Catholic Bogside area, marchers and youths clashed. The situation was soon out of control. The RUC immediately intervened, attacking the Catholic youths with batons. The police then used gas grenades on Catholics. Within hours the situation had escalated into a full-scale riot, with Catholics using every means possible to prevent the marchers and the police from entering their homes. The "Battle of the Bogside" lasted for days. By contemporary reports the RUC appeared to be unrestrained, beating anyone they encountered. A reporter from the *Washington Post*, Robert Mott, was clubbed and kicked to the ground by police.

In defiance, Catholics erected barricades along the entrances to streets to prevent the police from gaining access to their neighborhoods. The police then used an armored car to break through the barricades, hurling more gas grenades at residents who had come out to see what was happening. Young children and the old were especially vulnerable to this gas, and many became ill. Anger mounted as the Catholics believed with some justification that they were without defense and at the mercy of the RUC. In all more than three thousand Catholics were driven from their homes by the police. Word was sent to Belfast to the civil rights organization there to protest events in Derry. Before long Belfast was in riot; other towns soon followed.

## REACTION IN THE REPUBLIC OF IRELAND

The unrest was blazed onto television screens throughout Ireland. In Dublin public outrage was palpable as Irish citizens saw what appeared to be abysmal police brutality against Catholics. Images of people beaten by police and sick from gas dominated the Irish television news, as did rumors of a deployment of British troops. The Irish taoiseach Jack Lynch, a quiet man who would not normally be described as militant, thought it necessary to take action in light of the appalling pictures coming out of Northern Ireland.

Lynch went on Irish television on August 14 to announce that the Irish army was being dispatched to the border to assist any Catholics who needed help should they wish to cross the border. Lynch explained his position and that of his government:

> The Irish Government can no longer stand by and see innocent people injured and perhaps worse. It is obvious that the RUC is no longer accepted as an impartial police force. Neither would the employment of British troops be acceptable nor would they be likely to restore peaceful conditions, certainly not in the long term.

Lynch announced that he was setting up field hospitals to aid those who had been beaten and poisoned by gas. He did not propose to send Irish troops *across* the border, but the fact that he sent Irish troops to stand *at* the border was an enormous gesture of support to northern Nationalists and a public condemnation of the failure of British police measures in Northern Ireland. Lynch also pointedly called for "the restoration of the historic unity of our country."

## THE BRITISH ARMY IN NORTHERN IRELAND

The British government was angered at Lynch's interference in what they considered their domain, and his further call for UN intervention was met with rejection. Within a day of this, on August 15, British Prime Minister Harold Wilson sent the British army to Northern Ireland, purportedly to assist the police. The Belfast government agreed with this decision. Controversy remains about the feeling of the Catholic community toward the action, and some Nationalists claim that "photo ops" were arranged for propaganda purposes to make it look like the army was welcomed as honest brokers by the Nationalists. There may indeed have been some relief among Catholics to see the army arrive. The police in Northern Ireland had been so discredited in the eyes of the Catholic community that their perception was that nothing could be worse than the Royal Ulster Constabulary. Any intervention must be an improvement. This was in fact a vain hope.

If the army received a warm reception, it was short-lived. It soon became obvious that soldiers were not there to act as peace negotiators, and the implied intention of a "limited operation" for a short period of time was not adhered to. The dark, tragic days of Northern Ireland's history had begun in earnest. The banning of the civil rights marches with the now-apparent backup of the British army only added to the resentment felt by the Nationalist community.

British politicians traveled to Belfast to view what to them was actually a foreign country. In attempting to cool the situation, government officials announced they would meet the requirements of the civil rights marchers. Stormont was told to develop better relations with the Nationalist Catholic minority, "one person one vote" was established, and the RUC was ordered to be disarmed. The Reverend Ian Paisley, one of the most outspoken proponents of unionism in Northern Ireland, was vocal in his opposition to giving Catholics further rights in the province. His stance caused misgivings and division within the civil rights organization as many felt that any concessions to Nationalists would be limited.

The Pandora's box was now open. Violence against the Catholic community by the authorities had prompted a resolve among many to reunite the country. Reunification was now viewed by many Nationalists as the preferred way forward. This aspiration was met with a non-negotiable resolve by the Unionists to prevent it from happening. The British army presence provoked antipathy on both sides of the Irish border. The perceived message was that the British would not negotiate further with the civil rights organizers, they would merely contain any possible violence that the marches provoked.

## IRA REDUX

Noticeably absent from these events was the IRA. As an organization the IRA had been fairly decimated in the Irish Republic mostly because of the tough stand taken against them by de Valera from the 1930s. Headquartered in Dublin, they were a small, marginalized group with little public support on either side of the border. The Belfast branch was an even weaker organization. By documents later released by Scotland Yard, it is estimated that when the army went into Northern Ireland in August 1969, total IRA membership in the province was probably around sixty-four. Such was the lack of participation by the IRA in the civil rights disturbances to this time that their acronym was scribbled in graffiti as "I ran away." This was about to change radically. A revamped IRA began to fill the vacuum felt by the Nationalists in Northern Ireland, who now perceived themselves to be at the mercy of all security forces in the province. With the rise in aggression against the civil rights marches, and the apparent threat to marchers from the UVF, police authorities, and the army, the IRA began to play a significant role in defending Catholics against what they perceived as state aggression.

In August 1969 the IRA in Belfast made contact with headquarters in Dublin asking for financial support in obtaining arms. But the movement was having internal problems of its own. Within the ranks of the IRA there was discussion about what role the organization should play in the Northern Ireland crisis. Based in Dublin, Cathal Goulding was the commander-in-chief of the IRA, and he had developed theories of nonviolent constitutional participation. Other IRA members disagreed with this philosophy. A division in the organization finally occurred at their convention, the Ard Fheis, in December 1969. The IRA split into two camps. The "Official IRA" under Goulding stayed away from the Northern Ireland troubles; the "Provisional IRA" took over the job of what they saw as defending Nationalists' rights. Money was being raised in the United States among Irish Americans who identified with the problems in Northern Ireland. With the aid of Irish-American funds and local support from Nationalists in Northern Ireland, the "Provisionals," or "Provos," quickly expanded to take on a major role in the province. Their expressed solution was the elimination of the border that they claimed had been drawn up illegally by the Government of Ireland Act of 1920. This they saw as the real basis of the problem.

The army policy of seeking out insurgents by random house-to-house searching and ransacking of Catholic homes did much to turn average people toward viewing the IRA as protectors. Tim Pat Coogan, a Dublin journalist with great experience of Northern Ireland's problems, makes the case for the attitude of the army and British officials toward Ireland and the Irish as the primary cause in the hardening of the situation. Coogan claims that "a hatred for the Irish" fed into the attitudes and treatment of the Irish by everyone involved on the British side. He maintains that "The British army called both the Protestants and Catholics 'paddys' and had little respect for either of them." The situation continued to degenerate with the IRA and UVF willing to explode bombs in public places, causing death and human misery on a grand scale.

## ANOTHER BLOODY SUNDAY

Further disaster was coming. In August 1971 the British government had introduced a policy of internment against the IRA. The measure provided that anyone suspected of being a member of the organization could be picked up and imprisoned without trial. Among the internees taken at this time was Gerry Adams, future leader of Sinn Féin. Resentment against this policy was predictably high in the Catholic areas, and rumors of many innocent people being arrested and held were common. Stories of torture were also widespread, and Britain was later condemned and found guilty of "inhuman and degrading treatment" by the European Court of Human Rights.

In this atmosphere the civil rights movement struggled on, its leaders continuing to believe they could find a resolution of the troubles. A civil rights march to protest the internment policy was organized for January 30, 1972. The march was banned by the authorities, but the ban was ignored by the marchers who felt that they had a right to a peaceful protest. Tensions were high, and the army was asked to monitor the marchers' route. The consequences of the march were catastrophic, even by Northern Ireland standards. Army paratroopers shot and killed fourteen unarmed civilians and wounded more than one hundred. Many of the victims were shot in the back. The tragedy is known as Bloody Sunday, the second one of the century.

The entire island was gripped by the disaster, and a few days later an angry crowd of approximately thirty thousand gathered outside the British embassy in Dublin and burned it down. Further innocent lives were saved as Irish police in Dublin alerted the embassy staff and all exited safely. The anger and bitterness caused by Bloody Sunday was overwhelming. In his recent publication *Armed Struggle*, Ulster historian Richard English writes that "the weight of evidence suggests that the killings of Bloody Sunday were utterly unjustified, and their consequences personally and politically, were dire. It is no surprise that this day has become the focus of lasting and public attention." The initial inquiry in 1972 exonerating the army caused a furor among the families of the victims. A British government inquiry into the killings by the army was reopened in 1998 and a full report is pending. In 2004 the current inquiry stated that all the victims were innocent, unarmed civilians.

## BELFAST GOVERNMENT ABOLISHED

After Bloody Sunday the gloves were off on all sides. IRA recruitment soared and the indiscriminate bombing of civilian areas became a way of life. The British government was forced to admit failure and make a decision on the future of its policy in Northern Ireland. In March 1972 the Belfast government was abolished and power was transferred to Westminster. The Sunningdale Agreement of 1973 tried to bring all parties together in an attempt at peace. It ultimately failed. Northern Ireland settled into a long, unfortunate cycle of violence, hostility, and seemingly endless carnage, as the army and the IRA engaged each other in one of the bloodiest guerrilla conflicts of the twentieth century.

Historical perspective is not possible for events since the 1970s; the future will determine how these years will be viewed and analyzed. Atrocities on all sides were committed. Many innocent Irish people were arrested by British authorities and wrongfully imprisoned. The best known are the "Birmingham six" and the "Guildford four," who had their prison sentences overturned and their innocence proclaimed in open court in the 1990s after twenty years of wrongful imprisonment in British jails. The UVF conducted bombings and killings against Catholics. When the IRA campaign of blanket violence lost the organization support in the United States, it turned to criminal activity for funds. Provisional IRA actions also drew much criticism from within Ireland. Even the *Irish Press*, the newspaper founded by de Valera, dissociated the Old IRA from the new campaign. On the seventy-fifth anniversary of the 1916 Rising in 1991, an editorial in that newspaper read:

> The Provisional IRA campaign of the past 20 years, with such horrific happenings as human bombs and no warning explosions in crowded streets would not, could not, be supported by the men and women of 1916. There is no justification today for the continuation of that campaign and it should stop now.

Sinn Féin leader Gerry Adams talking to reporters outside Leinster House, Dublin, summer 2005. (*Carmel McCaffrey*)

Hope came at last in the 1990s when peace talks were again started and the Good Friday Agreement of 1998 was signed by all parties to the conflict. Moving forward without looking back is the path to lasting peace.

## THE BOOMING ECONOMY OF THE IRISH REPUBLIC

While the north of Ireland continued to struggle with social issues in the twentieth century, within the Republic of Ireland sweeping changes occurred which would eventually alter the basis of the economy and bring about enormous social change. The area of education saw some of the first changes. A number of commissions reported to the government in the mid-1960s on the inadequacy of the Irish educational system. The result was that in September 1967 free secondary education was made available to every child and university education became free to all. It was the start of a new era for Ireland. A more modern curriculum was developed and new facilities were built for all school levels. Throughout the country small old school buildings were closed and replaced by larger, better-equipped facilities. University places were expanded and new universities built in areas where none had been before. The boom in education that began in the 1960s has carried on to the present day. Since the 1980s the number of students at university has increased five-fold. Ireland now has one of the most educated workforces in the world.

Economic changes accompanied these improvements in education. The Irish Republic joined the European Community in 1973, and for the next thirty years saw economic expansion at a rate never before experienced. One of the reasons for joining the EC was concern over the heavy reliance on the UK for Irish exports and a desire to expand markets. Substantial economic growth occurred in the 1990s. By lowering corporate taxes and opening the country to foreign investment, the economy underwent dramatic changes. Since the 1970s young people have been moving from rural areas to urban regions, and consequently the country is becoming much more urbanized. One of the most important transformations is the change from an agricultural economy to one of high-technology goods and services.

According to figures from the Irish Department of Finance, in 2004 only 7 percent of the workforce was employed in agriculture as opposed to 26 percent in 1973. The 1973 figure was twice that of the rest of Europe. The most significant job growth is now in the area of computer technology; by 2004 Ireland had become the world's largest exporter of software. The export market broadened from a dependence on the UK market, which in 1960 took 75 percent of Irish exports. By 2004 that figure had been reduced to 18 percent. As far as the average person is concerned the greatest achievement is in the area of total employment. Unemployment stood at a stubborn 15 percent in 1989 and by 2004 was reduced to 4.8 percent.

Women have entered the workforce in large numbers, accounting for approximately 42 percent of all workers in 2004 compared to 27 percent in 1973.

Alongside economic growth, some of the problems of other industrialized countries have also arrived. Congestion on roads and access to affordable housing are now pressing issues for the average family. Crime has risen in all areas of the country. One of the greatest social shifts has occurred in the area of religious attitudes. Laws that formally reflected a Catholic ethos were the first to be affected by these changes.

## IRISH CATHOLICISM—A NEW ERA

The power of the Catholic church began to wane in the 1960s when a new generation demanded changes to the strict Catholic ethos that had governed civil laws since independence. Change came gradually but steadily. In the late 1960s laws on censorship were relaxed. In a general plebiscite in the early 1970s, Article 44 of the Irish constitution, which granted a "special position" to the Catholic church, was removed. Limited access to contraception was allowed by law in 1979, followed later by more liberal laws. A series of clerical sexual-abuse scandals hastened a process already in motion. In 1995 the constitutional law forbidding divorce was overturned by the electorate. The law on abortion is still in limbo, with successive governments reluctant to address the issue. The result of this procrastination is that Irish citizens travel to Britain in large numbers for access to abortion. In 1992 the Irish electorate voted to allow citizens the right to abortion information and the right to travel for an abortion. These had been denied under an earlier law.

Are rumors of the death of Irish Catholicism greatly exaggerated? From its embryonic beginnings at the time of St. Patrick and the early missionaries in the fifth century, the Irish have always had a unique approach to Christianity. For centuries Christianity as practiced in Ireland was never mainstream and rarely orthodox. It was therefore frequently subjected to attempted "reforms," most noticeably in the twelfth century and again in the nineteenth century. But during all those intervening centuries it survived as an informal, unceremonial, unofficial but intense, deeply spiritual, passionate expression of a profound relationship with the Almighty.

For centuries the Irish have known that religion lies in spiritual expression and not at the altar of the law. The religion that was practiced by the people outside the harsh strictures of Roman authority survived around the hearths in the homes of the otherwise dispossessed. The heavy-handed dogmatic religion that Catholicism became in the late nineteenth century and the overly politicized institution that it evolved into in the twentieth are not surprising given the political background of the times. But Irish Catholicism had survived through its informality, not through its enforcement. There is an old joke about a country woman who was once asked if she believed in fairies. She responded, "I do not—but they're there anyway." The same response might be applied to the Catholic church in Ireland—the Irish may have moved away from orthodoxy, but the church is still there anyway.

# Chronology of

# Irish History

| | |
|---|---|
| c8000 B.C. | Arrival of first hunter-gatherers in the northern part of Ireland, gradually spreading across the country. |
| c4000 B.C. | First Neolithic farmers arrive in Ireland by boat. The beginnings of a settled agricultural economy. |
| c3500–2000 B.C. | Construction of Ireland's great Neolithic tombs. Larger tombs show knowledge of astronomy. |
| c800 B.C. | Gold archeological evidence suggests Ireland has become one of the wealthiest places in Europe. The height of the Bronze Age. |
| c700–300 B.C. | Traditionally believed to be the period when the Iron Age Celtic warriors arrived from Europe, although there is no archeological evidence for such an invasion. Iron technology gradually replaces bronze, and "Celtic"-style artifacts are made in Ireland. |
| A.D. 43 | Roman conquest of Britain. Ireland never becomes part of the Roman Empire. |
| c150 | Ptolemy's map shows Ireland to be a Celtic-speaking country. The Celtic culture and language come, but there remains no material evidence of a shift in population or a Celtic invasion of any kind. |
| c432 | Christianity comes to Ireland around this time. Although there were other missionaries to the Irish, Patrick becomes the patron saint because of later politics. Writing comes to Ireland, and the first written history begins to be recorded. |

| | |
|---|---|
| c550–650 | The flowering of early monasticism in Ireland. Because the Irish had no political center and no towns or cities, Christianity took on a rural monastic form. But Irish monasteries were not isolated from the rest of the population. |
| 600–750 | The writing down of Irish laws and vernacular literature begins. The written vernacular language is Gaelic. |
| c700–1150 | The Irish monasteries of this period become great centers of wealth and affluence. They are large centers of population and secular life. They produce great works of art, the illuminated manuscripts, the beautiful chalices, and large stone crosses. |
| 795 | First Viking attacks against the centers of wealth, the monasteries. |
| c800 | The pinnacle of Irish scholarship. Over the next centuries Irish scholars, like the philosopher Scotus, travel to the Continent to be courtiers and advisers in the Carolingian and Frankish empires. |
| 841 | Vikings "winter" in Dublin and eventually form a settlement there. The start of Dublin as a center of economic power. |
| 976 | Brian Boru becomes king of Munster and begins his attempt for the high-kingship. He must take on the Uí Néill dynasty and have them recognize him as high king. |
| 1002 | The Uí Néill submit to Brian, recognizing his claim to the high-kingship. Most of the country is united under his control, by consensus, not tyranny. |
| 1013 | In Dublin Vikings do not like the idea of a powerful high king. Likewise, the Irish king of Leinster refuses to recognize Boru as high king. The Vikings assemble an army to threaten King Brian. |
| 1014 | The Battle of Clontarf, the first major conflict on Irish soil. Brian's forces are victorious over the Vikings and their invading armies, but Brian is killed at the end of the battle. A powerful high-kingship has been established but there is no one to succeed Brian. Political chaos ensues within Ireland as regional kings battle over the high-kingship. |

Dublin becomes the economic center and capital of this new Ireland.

c1100    "Reform" of the Irish church begins. Propaganda against Irish Christianity is rife on the Continent, where Gregorian reforms are turning the Christian church into a Rome-controlled model.

1155    Pope Adrian IV (the only Englishman to hold the title) issues a papal bull, *Laudabiliter*, giving Henry II of England permission to invade Ireland so that the Roman reforms are properly implemented. Henry is too preoccupied with a French war to act. But he will use this later.

1160s    Dermot MacMurrough is ambitious to be high king. Rory O'Connor has the same ambition, and the two become enemies. When O'Connor becomes high king, his ally, Ua Ruairc, seeks revenge for his wife's abduction and has MacMurrough removed from his kingship in Leinster.

1167    MacMurrough goes to England to seek the help of King Henry II in regaining the Leinster kingship. Henry agrees to send an army to help. The Anglo-Normans arrive, and the invitation becomes an excuse for an invasion of Ireland.

1172    Synod of Cashel. The diocesan model of Christianity is brought to Ireland. Monasteries can no longer be family owned.

1175    Treaty of Windsor is drawn up as a truce between Henry II and High King Rory O'Connor dividing Ireland. The treaty is broken by the English who continue to seize fresh territory.

1177    Henry II declares his son John, Lord of Ireland. The pope agrees to this. When John becomes King of England the title is incorporated into the English monarchy.

1297    First significant meeting of Irish parliament to deal with the issue of lawlessness as native Irish fight for their land on the borders of the now-occupied territories.

1315    Edward Bruce, the brother of Robert King of Scotland, arrives in Ireland at the invitation of the O'Neills

|       |                                                                                                                                                                                                                 |
|-------|-----------------------------------------------------------------------------------------------------------------------------------------------------------------------------------------------------------------|
|       | to fight the English incursions. He is unsuccessful and is killed in 1318.                                                                                                                                      |
| 1366  | Statutes of Kilkenny attempt to segregate the colony and keep the Irish and Norman settlers apart, but they are unsuccessful as assimilation on a grand scale has already taken place.                           |
| 1394  | Richard II visits Ireland to bolster his prestige. A futile gesture, in a second trip to Ireland in 1399 he loses the kingship of England.                                                                       |
| 1400s | As the English battle over the English throne in the Wars of the Roses Ireland goes its own way.                                                                                                                |
| 1460  | The Irish parliament asserts its independence from England with the Declaration of the Independence of the Irish Parliament.                                                                                     |
| 1478  | Garret Mór FitzGerald becomes the 8th Earl of Kildare and head of the FitzGerald family.                                                                                                                          |
| 1485  | Henry VII, the first Tudor king, takes the throne of England.                                                                                                                                                    |
| 1487  | Lambert Simnel crowned King of England in Christ Church Cathedral Dublin by the FitzGeralds in concert with the Irish parliament and Irish prelates. Henry VII is outraged.                                      |
| 1494  | Henry VII sends Edward Poynings to Ireland to curtail the power of the Irish parliament and the FitzGeralds. Irish parliament ceases to have any independent power. Known as Poynings' Law.                       |
| 1509  | Henry VIII ascends the throne of England on the death of his father. The FitzGeralds are still a problem for the Tudors as they run the administration in Dublin and ignore the king.                            |
| 1513  | Garret Mór dies and is succeeded by his son Garret Óg FitzGerald.                                                                                                                                                |
| 1533  | Henry VIII breaks with the papacy on the issue of his annulment from his wife. He marries Anne Boleyn. After years of unsuccessfully trying to control FitzGerald power, Henry VIII summons Garret Óg to London to investigate charges of disloyalty. |

| | |
|---|---|
| 1534 | Garret goes to London in February and leaves his lordship in the hands of his twenty-seven-year-old son, Lord "Silken" Thomas FitzGerald. The young lord leads a failed revolt against the king. The FitzGerald leaders are rounded up and executed. Garret Óg dies in the Tower of London. |
| 1536 | The Irish parliament recognizes Henry VIII as head of the Irish church. This Anglican church will eventually take the name Church of Ireland. |
| 1541 | Henry VIII orders the Irish parliament to declare him King of Ireland. The title will be carried on by his successors. |
| 1570–1590 | Elizabeth I, daughter of Henry VIII, continues to have the problems that her father had in Ireland. In response to Irish resistance she sends in vast armies to Ireland to remove native Irish landowners from their properties. Only Ulster remains to be conquered. |
| 1595 | In defiance of English law and as a public declaration of the O'Neill leadership, the Great Hugh O'Neill, who holds the English title Earl of Tyrone, has himself inaugurated "The O'Neill" in Tullaghoge at the O'Neill ancestral site. |
| 1598 | An alliance between Hugh O'Neill and Red Hugh O'Donnell, the O'Donnell chieftain, results in a victory for the Irish at the Yellow Ford, and the Elizabethan army is forced to retreat. |
| 1599 | Elizabeth sends an army of twenty thousand men to Ireland under the command of the Earl of Essex. The Elizabethan army is badly defeated and scattered. The earl leaves Ireland in disgrace. |
| 1601 | Determined to take over Ulster and rid the country of the powerful O'Neills and their allies, the O'Donnells, Elizabeth sends in another army under the command of Mountjoy. The Irish get Spanish help but to no avail. At the Battle of Kinsale the Irish are defeated. Almost immediately the English army marches on Ulster and brings it under its control. |

| 1607 | Accompanied by the aristocrats of Ulster the Great Hugh O'Neill leaves Ireland, never to return. This is known as "The Flight of the Earls." |
| 1609 | The plantation of Ulster begins. In order to secure loyalty to the Crown, Protestant families from Scotland and the north of England are brought into Ulster. Native Irish are removed from their lands in order to accommodate this change. |
| 1641 | Rebellion by the native Irish begins in Ulster and spreads to other parts of the county. Thousands of Protestant settlers are killed in the space of three days. |
| 1649 | Oliver Cromwell, having taken over the English parliament, travels to Ireland to subdue the native population now in open rebellion against the English presence. Among Cromwell's atrocities is the general massacre of the entire town of Drogheda. |
| 1660 | Charles II is brought back from exile, and the monarchy is restored. |
| 1690 | James II is dethroned and decides to battle King William of Orange who has been given the English throne by Parliament. The Irish gather behind King James II with the hope that he will restore Catholic land ownership. The two armies meet at the Battle of the Boyne, and James and the Irish are defeated. The Irish hope of land restoration is now dead. The Irish leaders leave for continental Europe. They are remembered as "The Wild Geese." |
| 1700 | The Penal Laws are introduced in order to secure Protestant land ownership and prevent Catholics from sitting in the Irish or British parliament. |
| 1775 | Henry Grattan elected to the Irish parliament. He initiates reforms to make it more independent. His supporters in parliament bring in some reforms, but they are not completely successful and others want more direct action. |
| 1776 | The revolutionary war in America impacts Ireland. The British army is withdrawn from Ireland to fight in America. Volunteer units are formed in Ireland for |

the "defense" of the country. These Protestant volunteer units quickly become nationalist in sentiment and pose a threat to the authorities. They find leaders in Theobald Wolfe Tone and Lord Edward FitzGerald.

1782    Under pressure from the threat of an Irish rebellion the British government overturns the centuries-old Poynings' Law and the Irish parliament is given power to make its own laws.

1791    United Irishmen established under Theobald Wolfe Tone with the expressed aim of a violent revolution to break the link with England completely.

1798    The United Irishmen with French help stage a failed rising. FitzGerald is captured and dies in captivity. Wolfe Tone attempts suicide after his capture and later dies of his wounds.

1800    The Irish parliament is dissolved and Ireland is brought politically under the control of the Westminster parliament in the "United Kingdom of Great Britain and Ireland."

1823    Daniel O'Connell forms the Catholic Association to use constitutional means to secure Catholic emancipation—the right of Catholics to sit in the Westminster parliament.

1826    Four pro-emancipation candidates are elected to Westminster but they are ignored, and their attempt to secure Catholic rights goes nowhere.

1829    Daniel O'Connell, a Catholic, is elected to Parliament as a member for County Clare. His election forces Parliament to change its rules and allow Catholics to enter the British parliament. It is a landmark achievement for Irish Catholics and O'Connell vows to dissolve the union and bring a parliament back to Dublin.

1846    Breaking the union with Britain proves difficult and a split occurs in O'Connell's support. The breakaway group, known as the Young Irelanders, rejects the constitutional means of O'Connell and pledges to use force. The group's subsequent rising is a failure.

| | |
|---|---|
| 1845–1850 | Ireland is gripped with the greatest disaster to befall the country. The failure of the potato crop results in the Great Famine. A million and a half people die from starvation and disease. Another million leave the country to seek a better life abroad. Those who leave carry a bitterness with them that will manifest itself in support among the "exiles" for Home Rule for Ireland. |
| 1850 | Synod of Thurles brings about enormous organizational change to the Catholic church in Ireland. This is considered to be the foundation of the modern Irish Catholic church. Irish Tenant League formed to fight for tenant land rights. |
| 1858 | The Irish Republican Brotherhood, IRB, established in New York and Dublin. They pledge to bring a parliament to Dublin using any means necessary. |
| 1875 | Charles Stewart Parnell elected to Parliament. He forms an alliance with Michael Davitt who is concerned with tenant rights. |
| 1879 | Formation of the National Land League by Michael Davitt. Parnell is voted president. Shortly after the Ladies Land League is founded by Parnell's sisters. This is the beginning of the "Land War." |
| 1881 | Land Act gives Irish tenants three rights: fixture of tenancy, fair rent (as determined by law), and the right to sell holdings. |
| 1885 | Clerical Nationalist Alliance brings together nationalist and Catholic aspirations. The Catholic church had not previously been behind the Home Rule movement. |
| 1886 | Home Rule bill introduced in House of Commons by Liberal Prime Minister Gladstone. It fails to pass, but the narrow loss gives hope that next time it will pass. |
| 1888 | Pope Leo XIII condemns the Nationalist movement in Ireland and orders Irish bishops to tell their people to desist in their support. |
| 1889 | Willie O'Shea starts divorce proceedings against his wife on the grounds of adultery with Parnell. |

| | |
|---|---|
| 1890 | Under condemnation from the English Liberal party and the Catholic bishops in Ireland Parnell is denounced as "immoral" and loses the leadership of the Irish party. |
| 1891 | On October 6 Charles Stewart Parnell dies and with him the hope of his generation for Home Rule. |
| 1890s | This is the period of the Celtic Renaissance in literature and an intense interest in establishing a sense of "Irishness" on both a social and a political level. |
| 1893 | Foundation of the Gaelic League. |
| 1904 | Arthur Griffith introduces his idea of Sinn Féin or going it alone politically. He starts a newspaper with the title *Sinn Féin*. The small new political party with the same name sees itself in opposition to the Home Rule party. |
| 1912 | Home Rule bill succeeds in the House of Commons in April but is predictably delayed by the House of Lords for two years, due to become effective in 1914. In September 1912 members of the English Conservative party travel to Ulster to encourage the Unionists to break the Home Rule bill. The Ulster Volunteer Force, a paramilitary group, is formed and arms. |
| 1913 | Owen MacNeil organizes the Irish Volunteers in reaction to the arming in Ulster. |
| 1914 | Prime Minister Asquith directs the British army in Ireland to march on Ulster and disarm the Unionists. The army refuses to obey the order. This is known as the "Curragh Mutiny." Cumann na mBan, the women's organization, is founded. In June 1914 WWI commences, and Home Rule for Ireland is postponed. |
| 1916 | In January Irish Volunteers split and a military council is formed with the idea of staging an armed rebellion against British rule. On Easter Monday, April 24, under the leadership of Patrick Pearse and James Connolly an armed Rising in Dublin occurs. The leaders are rounded up and executed by the British. |

| | |
|---|---|
| 1918 | Public outrage at the handling of the Rising and frustration over the Home Rule issue result in a Sinn Féin victory in the General Election. They secede and form a "rebel" parliament in Dublin. |
| 1919 | British prime minister Lloyd George declares Dáil Éireann, the Dublin government, to be illegal. |
| 1920 | The Government of Ireland Act passes in the House of Commons and calls for two parliaments to be established in Ireland, one in Dublin and one in Belfast. Catholics in Belfast are subjected to violence and many are forced to leave their employment. Auxiliaries, known as "Black and Tans," are sent to Ireland to suppress the IRA rebellion. |
| 1921 | In July the British declare a truce and offer to talk to Sinn Féin. The Treaty is agreed upon on December 6. |
| 1922 | Dáil Éireann ratifies the Treaty in January but de Valera refuses to accept it. Civil war ensues. On August 22 Michael Collins is killed in Béal na mBlátha. |
| 1926 | De Valera breaks with Sinn Féin and forms a new party, Fianna Fáil. He reenters the Dáil the following year. |
| 1937 | Irish Constitution—the one in use today—passed by a general referendum. |
| 1947 | The British Education Act introduces free university education for the entire UK, including Northern Ireland. Catholics in Northern Ireland begin enrolling in university in large numbers. |
| 1948 | The Irish Free State becomes a republic and breaks all ties with Britain. |
| 1967 | Free secondary and university education introduced in the Irish Republic. In Northern Ireland the Civil Rights Association is formed. Almost immediately its marches are banned by the authorities. |
| 1968 | In August clashes between police and civil rights marchers end in rioting. |
| 1969 | The Apprentice Boys march through Catholic areas in Derry results in the worst violence seen in Northern Ireland. Decision made in Westminster to send |

in the British Army. In December the IRA splits over how to respond to the violence, and the Provisional IRA or "Provos" is formed.

1972    Civil rights march protesting the policy of internment organized for January is banned. It goes ahead. British paratroopers shoot at marchers and kill fourteen civilians and wound more than one hundred. The tragedy is known as Bloody Sunday. In March the Belfast government is abolished, and power is transferred to Westminster.

1979    Catholic ethos which informed civil law in the Irish Republic begins to wane. Laws on contraception are relaxed.

1990s   Irish Republic overturns ban on divorce and enters a new secular period. The economy booms, and the country enters a new era of prosperity. In Northern Ireland, the Good Friday Agreement signed in 1998.

# Bibliography

Gerry Adams. *The Politics of Irish Freedom*. Kerry, Ireland, 1986.

Jonathan Bardon. *A History of Ulster*. Belfast, 1992.

Marc Bloch.Translated from the French by L. A. Manyon. *Feudal Society*. London, 1961.

Robert Briscoe with Alden Hatch. *For the Life of Me*. Boston, 1958.

Thomas Carlyle, ed. *The Letters and Speeches of Oliver Cromwell*. London, 1904.

Michael Collins. *The Path to Freedom*. Dublin, 1996.

Tim Pat Coogan. *De Valera*. London, 1993.

———. *The IRA*. London, 1987.

———. *Michael Collins*. London, 1990.

L. M. Cullen. *An Economic History of Ireland Since 1660*. London, 1972.

Edmund Curtis and R. B. McDowell, eds. *Irish Historical Documents 1172–1922*. London, 1943.

L. Perry Curtis, Jr. *Apes and Angels: The Irishman in Victorian Caricature*. Washington, D.C., 1997.

Mary E. Daly. *The Famine in Ireland*. Dublin, 1986.

Eamon Duffy. *Saints and Sinners. A History of the Popes*. New Haven, Conn., 2002

Seán Duffy. *Ireland in the Middle Ages*. New York, 1997.

Mairead Dunlevy. *Dress in Ireland*. Cork, 1989.

Steven G. Ellis. *Tudor Ireland*. Essex, England, 1985.

Richard English. *Armed Struggle: The History of the IRA*. New York, 2003.

A. Martin Freeman, ed. *Annals of Connacht*. Dublin, 1944.

Gerald of Wales (Giraldus Cambrensis). *History and Topography of Ireland*. Wiltshire, 1982.

———. *Expugnatio Hibernica: The Conquest of Ireland*. Dublin, 1978.

G. A. Hayes-McCoy. *Irish Battles: A Military History of Ireland*. Belfast, 1990.

Geoffrey Keating. *A History of Ireland*. Electronic text. www.ucc.ie/celt/

Dermot Keogh. *Jews in Twentieth Century Ireland*. Cork, 1998.

Christine Kinealy. *This Great Calamity: The Irish Famine*. Dublin, 1994.

Emmet Larkin. *The Historical Dimensions of Irish Catholicism*. Dublin, 1976.

———. *The Roman Catholic Church in Ireland and the Fall of Parnell, 1888–1891*. Chapel Hill, N.C., 1979.

F. S. L. Lyons. *Charles Stewart Parnell*. London, 1977.

Mary Ann Lyons. *Gearóid Óg FitzGerald*. Dundalk, Ireland, 1998.

Seán Mac Airt, ed. *The Annals of Inisfallen*. Dublin, 1944.

Seán Mac Airt and Gearóid Mac Niocaill, eds. *The Annals of Ulster*. Dublin, 1983.

Laurence McCorristine. *The Revolt of Silken Thomas*. Dublin, 1987.

Tom McNeill. *Castles in Ireland: Feudal Power in a Gaelic World*. London, 1997.

Hiram Morgan. *Tyrone's Rebellion*. London, 1993.

Denis Murphy, ed. *The Annals of Clonmacnoise*. Dublin, 1896.

Máirín Ní Dhonnchadha and Theo Dorgan, eds. *Revising the Rising*. Derry, 1991.

K. W. Nicholls. *Gaelic and Gaelicized Ireland in the Middle Ages*. Dublin, 2003.

Lughaidh Ó Clérigh. *Aodh Rua Uí Domhnaill*. Dublin, 1948.

E. E. O'Donnell, ed. *Annals of Dublin*. Dublin, 1987.

John O'Donovan, ed. *The Annals of the Kingdom of Ireland by the Four Masters*. Dublin, 1990.

Sean O'Faolain. *The Great O'Neill*. London, 1942.

———. *King of the Beggars: A Life of Daniel O'Connell*. Dublin, 1980.

H. G. Richardson and G. O. Sayles. *Parliament in Medieval Ireland*. Dublin, 1964.

Ruth Taillon. *The Women of 1916*. Belfast, 1996.

Stella Tillyard. *Citizen Lord*. London, 1997.

Charles Trevelyan. *The Irish Crisis*. London, 1848.

# Index

# A NOTE ON THE AUTHOR

Carmel McCaffrey is a native of Dublin, Ireland, and lectures on Irish history, literature, culture, and language at Johns Hopkins University and the Smithsonian Institution. Active in literary and historical societies in both Ireland and the United States, Ms. McCaffrey founded *Wild About Wilde*, the acclaimed literary review she published and edited between 1986 and 1996. Along with her popular university courses on Irish history and Celtic studies, Ms. McCaffrey also lectures on major Irish writers. She is a Gaelic speaker and frequently travels to Ireland. Her earlier book, *In Search of Ancient Ireland*, written with Leo Eaton, was a companion to the PBS/RTE series, for which she was the historical consultant. She lives in Mount Airy, Maryland.